disha
Publication Inc

HAND BOOK of Mathematics

Complete NCERT in One Liner Format

for JEE/ CBSE Class 11 & 12

In the interest of student community

www.dishapublication.com
Books & ebooks for School & Competitive Exams

www.mylearninggraph.com
Etests for Competitive Exams

Write to us at **feedback_disha@aiets.co.in**

Contents

Sets

Sets and their Representations

- **Set** is a well-defined collection of objects in the sense that we can definitely decide whether a given particular object belongs to a given collection or not.
- Objects, elements and members of a set are synonymous terms.
- Sets are usually denoted by capital letters A, B, C, X, Y, Z, etc.
- The elements of a set are represented by small letters a, b, c, x, y, z, etc.
- If a is an element of a set A, we say that $a \in A$ or "a belongs to A".
- Some examples of sets used particularly in mathematics

  N : the set of all natural numbers;

  Z : the set of all integers;

  Q : the set of all rational numbers ;

  R : the set of real numbers;

  Z^+ : the set of positive integers ;

  Q^+ : the set of positive rational numbers

  R^+ : the set of positive real numbers

Representations of Sets

Roster or tabular form :

- In roster form, all the elements of a set are listed, the elements are being separated by commas and are enclosed within braces { }.
- In roster form, the order in which the elements are listed is immaterial.
- It may be noted that while writing the set in roster form an element is not generally repeated.

Set-builder form:

- In set-builder form, all the elements of a set possess a single common property.
- We describe the element of the set by using a symbol x (any other symbol like the letters y, z, etc. could be used) which is followed by a colon " : ". After the sign of colon, we write the characteristic property possessed by the elements of the set and then enclose the whole description within braces.

The Empty Set

- A set which does not contain any element is called the **empty set** or the **null set** or the **void set**.
- The empty set is denoted by the symbol ϕ or { }.

Finite and Infinite Sets

- A set which is empty or consists of a definite number of elements is called **finite** otherwise, the set is called **infinite**. e.g. The set of the days of the week is finite and the set of points on a line is infinite.
- The number of distinct elements of the finite set A is denoted by n (A).
- It is not possible to write all the elements of an infinite set within braces { } because the numbers of elements of such a set is not finite.
- If a set A has only one element, we call it a singleton set.
- All infinite sets cannot be described in the roster form. For example, the set of real numbers cannot be described in this form, because the elements of this set do not follow any particular pattern.

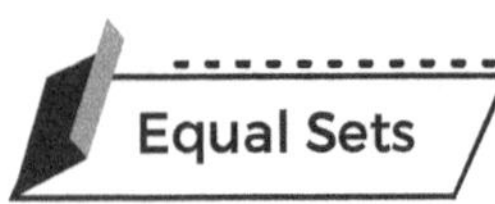

Equal Sets

- Two sets A and B are said to be **equal** if they have exactly the same elements and we write A = B. Otherwise, the sets are said to be unequal and we write $A \neq B$.
- It two sets A and B have equal number of elements then A and B are called equivalent sets.
- A set does not change if one or more elements of the set are repeated. For example, the sets A = {1, 2, 3} and B = {2, 2, 1, 3, 3} are equal, since each element of A is in B and vice-versa. That is why we generally do not repeat any element in describing a set.
- Equal sets are always equivalent but equivalent sets may or may not be equal.

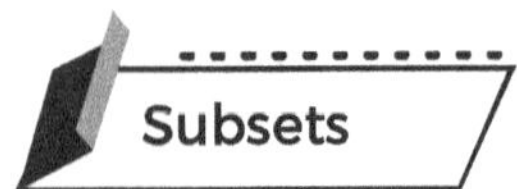

Subsets

- A set A is said to be a subset of a set B if every element of A is also an element of B. It is denoted by $A \subset B$.
- In other words $A \subset B$ if $a \in A \Rightarrow a \in B$. We read the above statement as "A is a subset of B if a is an element of A implies that a is also an element of B". If A is not a subset of B, we write $A \not\subset B$.
- If every element of set A is in set B and every element of set B is also in set A. In this case, A and B are the same sets so that we have $A \subset B$ and $B \subset A \Leftrightarrow A = B$, where "$\Leftrightarrow$" is a symbol for two way implications, and is usually read as if and only if (briefly written as "iff").
- Every set A is a subset of itself, i.e., $A \subset A$.
- Since the empty set ϕ has no elements, we agree to say that ϕ is a subset of every set.

♦ Let A and B be two sets. If $A \subset B$ and $A \neq B$, then A is called a **proper subset** of B and B is called **superset** of A.

♦ Total number of subsets of set having n element is 2^n.

Subsets of set of real numbers :

There are many important subsets of R.

♦ The set of natural numbers $N = \{1, 2, 3, 4, 5, \ldots\}$

♦ The set of integers $Z = \{\ldots, -3, -2, -1, 0, 1, 2, 3, \ldots\}$

♦ The set of rational numbers $Q = \{ x : x = \dfrac{p}{q}, p, q \in Z \text{ and } q \neq 0\}$

♦ The set of irrational numbers, denoted by T, is composed of all other real numbers. Thus $T = \{x : x \in R \text{ and } x \notin Q\}$

♦ Some of the obvious relations among these subsets are:

$N \subset Z \subset Q, Q \subset R, T \subset R, N \not\subset T.$

Intervals as subsets of R :

♦ **Open Interval :** Let a, $b \in R$ and $a < b$. Then the set of real numbers $\{ y : a < y < b\}$ is called an **open interval** and is denoted by (a, b). All the points between a and b belong to the open interval (a, b) but a, b themselves do not belong to this interval.

$$(a, b)$$
$$a \quad\quad b$$

♦ **Closed Interval :** The interval which contains the end points also is called **closed interval** and is denoted by [a, b]. Thus $[a, b] = \{x : a \leq x \leq b$

$$[a, b]$$
$$a \quad\quad b$$

♦ **Semi-open or Semi-closed Interval :** We can also have intervals closed at one end and open at the other, i.e., $[a, b) = \{x : a \leq x < b\}$ is an open interval from a to b, including a but excluding b.

$$[a, b)$$
$$a \quad\quad b$$

$(a, b] = \{ x : a < x \leq b \}$ is an open interval from a to b including b but excluding a.

$$(a, b]$$
$$a \quad\quad b$$

♦ The set $[0, \infty)$ defines the set of non-negative real numbers, while set $(-\infty, 0)$ defines the set of negative real numbers. The set $(-\infty, \infty)$ describes the set of real numbers in relation to a line extending from $-\infty$ to ∞.

♦ An interval contains infinitely many points.

♦ The number (b – a) is called the length of any of the intervals (a, b), [a, b], [a, b) or (a, b].

Power Set

♦ The collection of all subsets of a set A is called the power set of A. It is denoted by P(A). In P(A), every element is a set.

♦ If A = { 1, 2}, then subset of A are ϕ,{1}, {2}, {1, 2} and P(A) = {ϕ,{1}, {2}, {1, 2}}.

♦ If A is a set with n(A) = m, then n [P(A)] = 2^m.

Universal Set

♦ Usually, in a particular context, we have to deal with the elements and subsets of a basic set which is relevant to that particular context. This basic set is called the "Universal Set". The universal set is usually denoted by U, and all its subsets by the letters A, B, C, etc.

♦ Universal set is a set which includes all the elements of the sets under consideration.

♦ Every set is a subsets of universal sets.

♦ e.g. The universal set consists of all the people in the world.

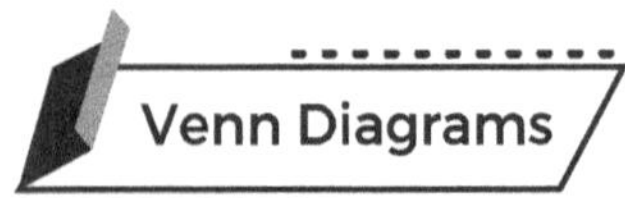
Venn Diagrams

♦ Most of the relationships between sets can be represented by means of diagrams which are known as Venn diagrams.

♦ The universal set is represented usually by a rectangle and its subsets by circles.

♦ In Venn diagrams, the elements of the sets are written in their respective circles.

e.g. U={1,2,3,4,5,6,7,8,9,10}, A= {2,4,6,8,10}

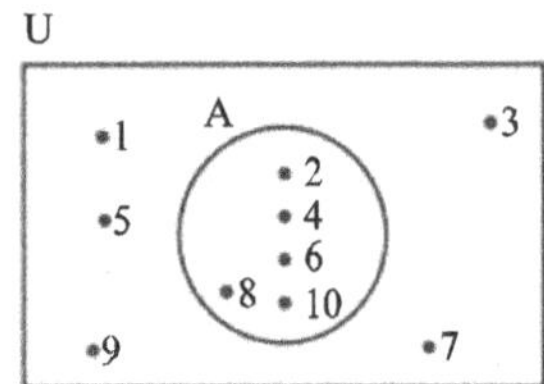

Operations on Sets

♦ There are some operations which when performed on two sets give rise to another set.

Union of sets :

♦ The union of two sets A and B is the set C which consists of all those elements which are either in A or in B (including those which are in both).

♦ the common elements being taken only once.

♦ The symbol '∪' is used to denote the union. Symbolically, we write A ∪ B = {x : x ∈ A or x ∈ B} and usually read as 'A union B'.

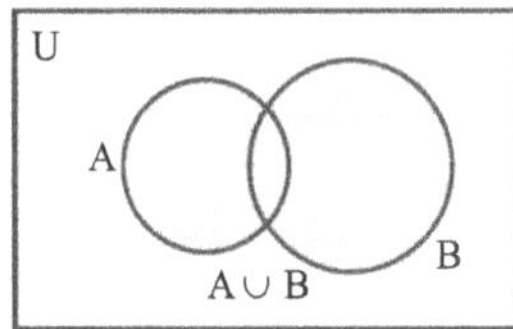

♦ **Some Properties of Operation of Union :**

  ❖ A ∪ B = B ∪ A   (Commutative law)

  ❖ (A ∪ B) ∪ C = A ∪ (B ∪ C)   (Associative law)

  ❖ A ∪ ϕ = A (Law of identity element, ϕ is the identity of ∪)

  ❖ A ∪ A = A   (Idempotent law)

  ❖ U ∪ A = U   (Law of U)

Intersection of sets :

♦ The intersection of sets A and B is the set of all elements which are common to both A and B. The symbol '∩' is used to denote the intersection.

♦ The intersection of two sets A and B is the set of all those elements which belong to both A and B. Symbolically, we write A ∩ B = {x : x ∈ A and x ∈ B}.

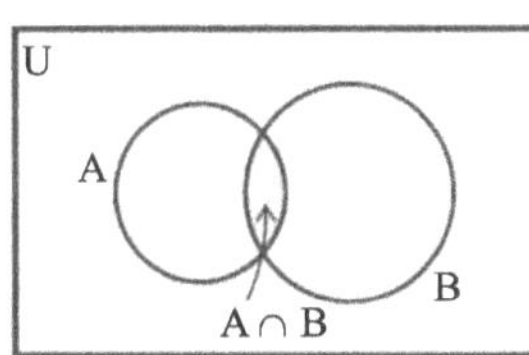

♦ If A and B are two sets such that A ∩ B = ϕ , i.e. there are no elements which are common to A and B then A and B are called **disjoint** sets.

♦ **Some Properties of Operation of Intersection :**

  ❖ A ∩ B = B ∩ A   (Commutative law)

  ❖ (A ∩ B) ∩ C = A ∩ (B ∩ C)   (Associative law)

  ❖ ϕ ∩ A = ϕ, U ∩ A = A   (Law of ϕ and U)

  ❖ A ∩ A = A   (Idempotent law)

  ❖ A ∩ (B ∪ C) = (A ∩ B) ∪ (A ∩ C)

                    (Distributive law, i.e., ∩ distributes over ∪.)

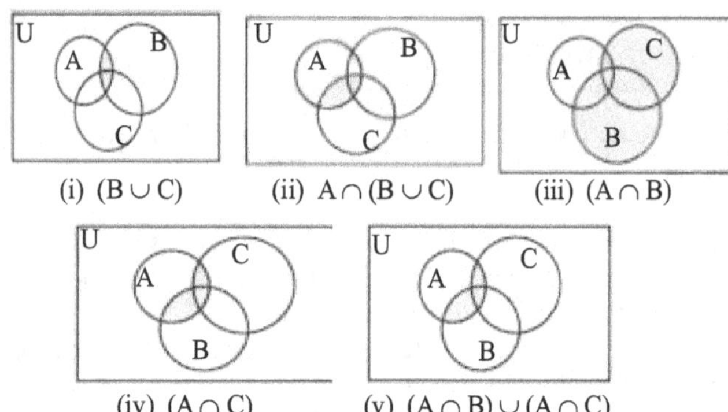

(i) $(B \cup C)$ (ii) $A \cap (B \cup C)$ (iii) $(A \cap B)$

(iv) $(A \cap C)$ (v) $(A \cap B) \cup (A \cap C)$

Difference of sets :

♦ The **difference** of the sets A and B in this order is the set of elements which belong to A but not to B. Symbolically, we write $A - B = \{x : x \in A \text{ and } x \notin B\}$ and read as "A minus B". Similarly, $B - A = \{x : x \in B \text{ and } x \notin A\}$

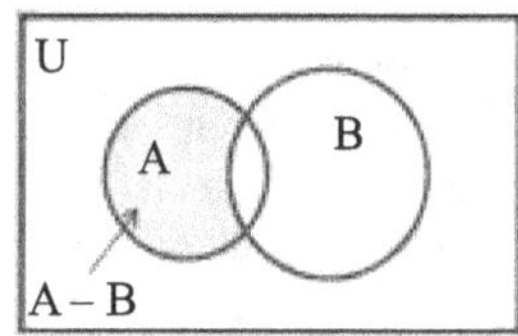

♦ The sets $A - B$, $A \cap B$ and $B - A$ are mutually disjoint sets, i.e., the intersection of any of these two sets is the null set.

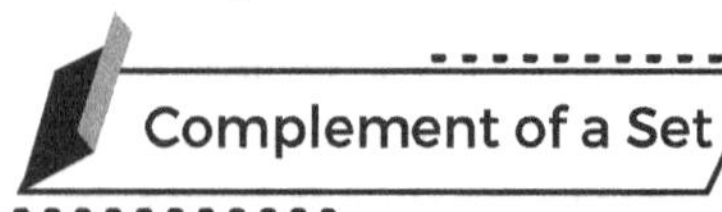

Complement of a Set

♦ Let U be the universal set and A a subset of U. Then the complement of A is the set of all elements of U which are not the elements of A. Symbolically, we write A' or A^c to denote the complement of A with respect to U. Thus, $A = \{x : x \in U \text{ and } x \in A\}$. Obviously $A' = U - A$.

♦ If A is a subset of the universal set U, then its complement A' is also a subset of U.

♦ **Some Properties of Complement Sets :**

❖ Complement laws : (i) $A \cup A' = U$ (ii) $A \cap A' = \phi$

❖ Law of double complementation : $(A')' = A$

❖ Laws of empty set and universal set $\phi' = U$ and $U' = \phi$

De Morgan's laws :

♦ The complement of the union of two sets is the intersection of their complements and the complement of the intersection of two sets is the union of their complements. These are called De Morgan's laws.i.e.

(i) $(A \cup B)' = A' \cap B'$ (ii) $(A \cap B)' = A' \cup B'$

Practical Problems on Union and Intersection of Two Sets

♦ The following formulae are used to solved some practical problems related to our daily life.

Let A and B be befinite sets. If $A \cap B = \phi$, then

❖ (i) $n(A \cup B) = n(A) + n(B)$

In general, if A and B are finite sets, then

(ii) $n(A \cup B) = n(A) + n(B) - n(A \cap B)$

❖ $n(A \cup B) = n(A - B) + n(A \cap B) + n(B - A)$

❖ (iii) If A, B and C are finite sets, then

$n(A \cup B \cup C) = n(A) + n(B) + n(C) - n(A \cap B)$
$- n(B \cap C) - n(A \cap C) + n(A \cap B \cap C)$

Past Years ONE-LINERS
JEE Main/Board

♦ The difference of the sets B from A in the set whose elements belong to A but not to B.

i.e., $A - B = \{x : x \in A \text{ and } x \notin B\}$.

♦ If A and B are finite sets and $A \cap B \neq \phi$ then
$n(A \cup B) = n(A) + n(B) - n(A \cap B)$

♦ If A and B are finite sets and $A \not\subset B$ then
only $A = n(A) - n(A \cap B)$
only $B = n(B) - n(A \cap B)$
If A and B are finite sets and $A \subset B$ then
only $A = \phi$
only $B = n(B) - n(A)$

Tips/Tricks/Techniques ONE-LINERS
(Exam Special)

♦ Cardinal number of a set is the number of the elements in that set. If $X = \{1, 2, 3, 4\}$, then cardinal number of $X = n(X) = 4$.

♦ A set 'X' is said to be a proper subset of a set 'Y' if every element of 'X' is in element of 'Y' and 'Y' has atleast one element which is not an element of 'X' is denoted by $X \subset Y$.

- An improper subset is a subset containing every element of the original set.
- For any set A, ϕ and A are improper subsets and all other subsets of A are called proper subsets.
- **Symmetric Difference of Two Sets :** It is denoted by $A\Delta B$.
  $A\Delta B = (A - B) \cup (B - A). = (A \cup B) - (A \cap B)$.
  Also, $A \cap (B \Delta C) = (A \cap B) \Delta (A \cap C)$.
- Number of elements of the set whose elements exactly belong to two of the sets A, B, C $= n(A \cap B) + n(B \cap C) + n(C \cap A) - 3n(A \cap B \cap C)$.
- Number of elements of the set whose elements exactly belong to one of the sets A, B, C $= n(A) + n(B) + n(C) - 2n(A \cap B) - 2n(B \cap C) - 2n(A \cap C) + 3n(A \cap B \cap C)$
- Number of elements belongs to only A for two non-empty sets A and $B = n(A) - n(A \cap B)$
- Number of elements belongs to only A for three non-empty sets
  $= n(A) - n(A \cap B) - n(A \cap C) + n(A \cap B \cap C)$.
- $n(A' \cap B') = n(A \cup B)' = n(U) - n(A \cup B)$.
- $A - B = A \cap B'$
- $A \cup (A \cap X) = A = A \cap (A \cup X)$.
- $P(A) \cup P(B) \subseteq P(A \cup B)$, where P(A) is the power set of A.
- $n(A\Delta B) = n(A) + n(B) - 2n(A \cap B)$.
- Let $n(A) = p$ and $n(B) = q$. Then,
  (a)   min. $\{n(A \cup B)\} = $ max. $\{p, q\}$, (b) max. $\{n(A \cup B)\} = p + q$,
  (c)   min. $\{n(A \cap B)\} = 0$,   (d) max. $\{n(A \cap B)\} = $ min. $\{p, q\}$.
- If $A_1, A_2, \text{-------}, A_m$ are disjoint sets, then
  $n(A_1 \cup A_2 \cup \text{----------} \cup A_m) = n(A_1) + n(A_2) + \text{--------} + n(A_m)$.
- Number of proper subsets of a set having 'n' elements $= 2^n - 1$.
- $\{(A - B) \cup (B - C) \cup (C - A)\}' = A \cap B \cap C$, for any three sets A, B & C.

2 | Relations and Functions-1

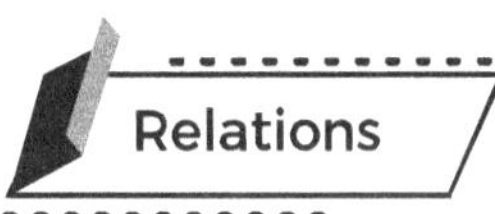

Cartesian Products of Sets

- Let two non-empty sets P and Q. The cartesian product $P \times Q$ is the set of all ordered pairs of elements from P and Q, i.e., $P \times Q = \{ (p, q) : p \in P, q \in Q \}$. Which represents the coordinates of all the points in two-dimensional space.
- If either P or Q is the null set, then $P \times Q$ will also be empty set, i.e., $P \times Q = \phi$.
- Note that the order in which these elements are paired is crucial. (Order of elements in the pair is important, i.e., (1, 2) and (2, 1) both pairs have the same elements but they are distinct ordered pair)
- Two ordered pairs are equal, if and only if the corresponding first elements are equal and the second elements are also equal.
- If there are p elements in A and q elements in B, then there will be pq elements in $A \times B$, i.e., if $n(A) = p$ and $n(B) = q$, then $n(A \times B) = pq$.
- If A and B are non-empty sets and either A or B is an infinite set, then so is $A \times B$.
- $A \times A \times A = \{(a, b, c) : a, b, c \in A\}$. Here (a, b, c) is called an ordered triplet. Which represents the coordinates of all points in three-dimensional space.

Relations

- A **relation** R from a non-empty set A to a non-empty set B is a subset of the cartesian product $A \times B$. The subset is derived by describing a relationship between the first element and the second element of the ordered pairs in $A \times B$. The second element is called the **image** of the first element.
- **Domain:** The set of all first elements of the ordered pairs in a relation R from a set A to a set B is called the **domain** of the relation R.
- **Range:** The set of all second elements in a relation R from a set A to a set B is called the **range** of the relation R.
- **Codomain:** The whole set B is called the **codomain** of the relation R. Note that range $\subset$ codomain.

♦ Consider the two sets $P = \{a, b, c\}$ and $Q = \{$Ali, Bhanu, Binoy, Chandra, Divya$\}$.

Here, Subset of $P \times Q$ is known as Relation.

The diagram which represents the relation is called an Arrow Diagram.

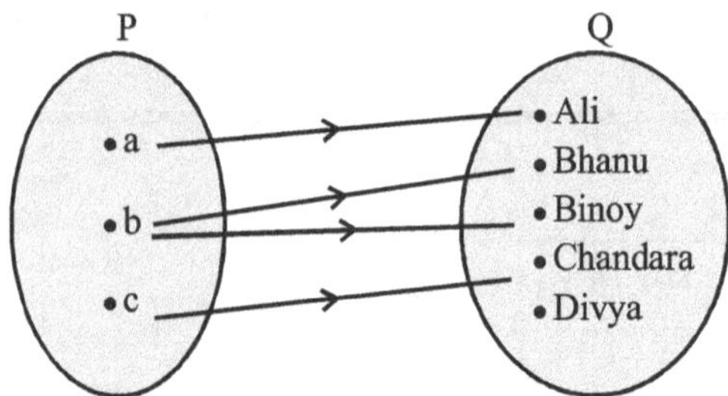

♦ The total number of relations that can be defined from a set A to a set B is the number of possible subsets of $A \times B$. If $n(A) = p$ and $n(B) = q$, then $n(A \times B) = pq$ and the total number of relations is $\mathbf{2^{pq}}$.

♦ A relation may be represented algebraically either by the Roster method or by the Set-builder method.

♦ A relation R from A to A is also stated as a relation on A.

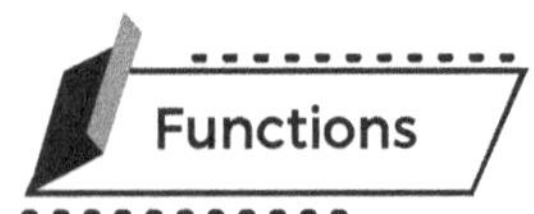

Functions

♦ In this section, we study a special type of relation called function. It is one of the most important concepts in mathematics.

♦ We can, visualise a function as a rule, which produces new elements out of some given elements. There are many terms such as 'map' or 'mapping' used to denote a function.

♦ A relation f from a set A to a set B is said to be a **function** if every element of set A has one and only one image in set B.

♦ In other words, a function f is a relation from a non-empty set A to a non-empty set B such that the domain of f is A and no two distinct ordered pairs in f have the same first element.

♦ If f is a function from A to B and $(a, b) \in f$, then $f(a) = b$, where b is called the image of a under f and a is called the **pre-image** of b under f.

♦ The function f from A to B is denoted by $f : A \to B$.

♦ A function which has either R or one of its subsets as its range is called a **real valued function.** Further, if its domain is also either R or a subset of R, it is called a real function.

♦ The function f defined by $f(x) = mx + c$, $x \in R$, is called linear function, where m and c are constants.

Some Functions and Their Graphs

(i) **Identity function:** Let R be the set of real numbers. Define the real valued function $f : R \to R$ by $y = f(x) = x$ for each $x \in R$. Such a function is called the **identity function.**

♦ Here the domain and range of f are R.

♦ The graph is a straight line as shown in figure below. It passes through the origin.

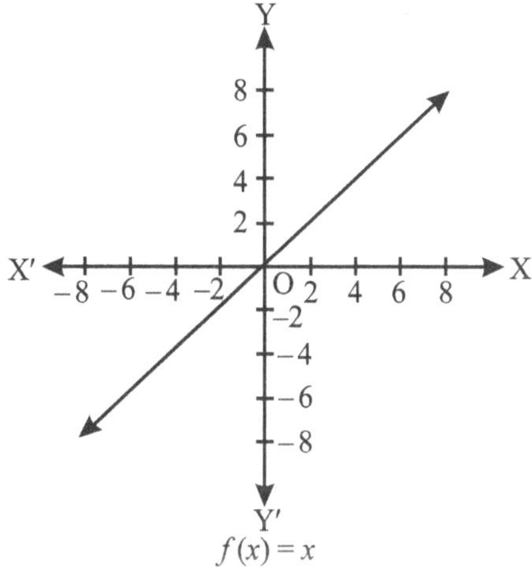

$$f(x) = x$$

(ii) **Constant function :** Define the function $f : R \to R$ by $y = f(x) = c, x \in R$ where c is a constant and each $x \in R$.

♦ Here domain of f is R and its range is $\{c\}$.

♦ The graph is a line parallel to x-axis. For example, if $f(x) = 3$ for each $x \in R$, then its graph will be a line as shown in the figure below.

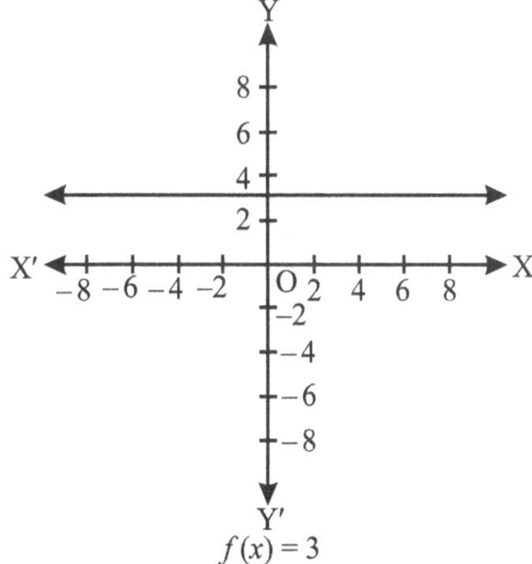

$$f(x) = 3$$

(iii) Polynomial function: A function $f : R \rightarrow R$ is said to be polynomial function if for each x in R,

$$y = f(x) = a_0 + a_1 x + a_2 x^2 + ... + a_n x^n,$$

where n is a non-negative integer and $a_0, a_1, a_2, ..., a_n \in R$

♦ The functions defined by

$$f(x) = x^3 - x^2 + 2 \quad \text{and} \quad g(x) = x^4 + \sqrt{2}x$$

are some examples of polynomial functions, whereas the function h defined

by $h(x) = x^{\frac{2}{3}} + 2x$ is not a polynomial function (because n is non-integer).

(iv) Rational function : These are functions of the type of $\dfrac{f(x)}{g(x)}$, where $f(x)$ and

$g(x)$ are polynomial functions of x defined in a domain, where $g(x) \neq 0$.

(v) Modulus function : The function $f : R \rightarrow R$ defined by $f(x) = |x|$ for each $x \in R$ is called **modulus function.**

♦ For each non-negative value of x, $f(x)$ is equal to x. But for negative values of x, the value of $f(x)$ is the negative of the value of x, i.e.

$$f(x) = \begin{cases} x, & x \geq 0 \\ -x, & x < 0 \end{cases}$$

♦ The graph of modulus function is shown the figure below :

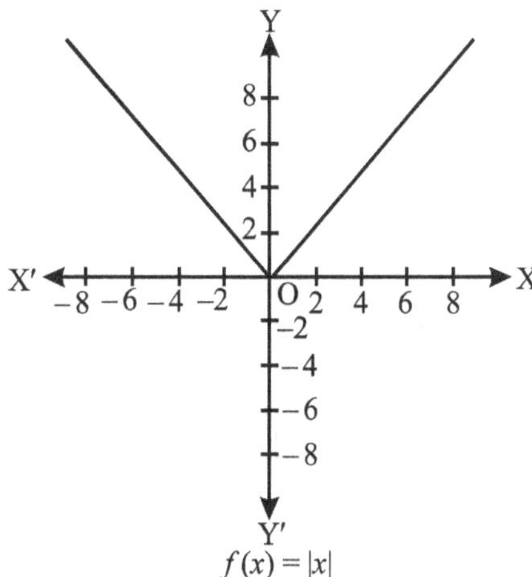

$$f(x) = |x|$$

♦ Here, domain is the set of all real numbers and range is the set of all non-negative numbers.

(vi) **Signum function :** The function $f : R \rightarrow R$ defined by

$$f(x) = \begin{cases} \dfrac{|x|}{x}, & x \neq 0 \\ 0, & x = 0 \end{cases} = \begin{cases} 1, & \text{if } x > 0 \\ 0, & \text{if } x = 0 \\ -1, & \text{if } x < 0 \end{cases}$$

is called the **signum function.**

♦ The domain of the signum function is R and the range is the set $\{-1, 0, 1\}$.

♦ The graph of the signum function is shown in the figure below.

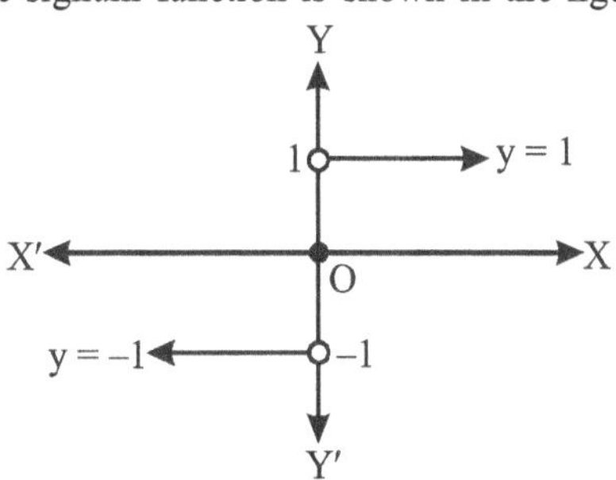

(vii) **Greatest integer function :** The function $f : R \rightarrow R$ defined by $f(x) = [x]$, $x \in R$ assumes the value of the greatest integer, less than or equal to x. Such a function is called the **greatest integer function.**

♦ From the definition of $[x]$, we can see that

$[x] = -1$ for $-1 \leq x < 0$

$[x] = 0$ for $0 \leq x < 1$

$[x] = 1$ for $1 \leq x < 2$

$[x] = 2$ for $2 \leq x < 3$ and

so on.

♦ The graph of greatest integer function is shown in the figure below :

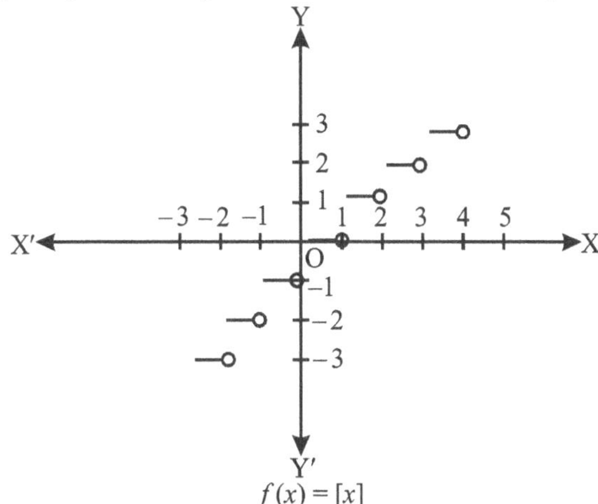

$$f(x) = [x]$$

♦   Here domain of a function is set of all real numbers and range of function is set of all integers.

Algebra of Real Functions

(i) Addition of two real functions :

♦   Let $f : X \to R$ and $g : X \to R$ be any two real functions, where $X \subset R$. Then, we define $(f + g) : X \to R$ by $(f + g)(x) = f(x) + g(x)$, for all $x \in X$

(ii) Subtraction of a real function from another

♦   Let $f : X \to R$ and $g : X \to R$ be any two real functions, where $X \subset R$. Then, we define $(f - g) : X \to R$ by $(f - g)(x) = f(x) - g(x)$, for all $x \in X$.

(iii) Multiplication by a scalar :

♦   Let $f : X \to R$ be a real valued function and α be a scalar.

Then the product αf is a function from X to R defined by $(\alpha f)(x) = \alpha f(x), x \in X$.

(iv) Multiplication of two real functions :

♦   The product (or multiplication) of two real functions $f : X \to R$ and $g : X \to R$ is a function

$fg : X \to R$ defined by

$(fg)(x) = f(x) g(x)$, for all $x \in X$.

This is also called pointwise multiplication.

(v) Quotient of two real functions :

♦   Let f and g be two real functions defined from $X \to R$, where $X \subset R$. The quotient of f by g denoted by f/g is a function defined by,

$$\left(\frac{f}{g}\right)(x) = \frac{f(x)}{g(x)}, \text{ provided } g(x) \neq 0, x \in X$$

Past Years ONE-LINERS
JEE Main/Board

♦   If $\dfrac{f(x)}{g(x)} \geq 0$. Then

   (i) $f(x) \geq 0$ and $g(x) > 0$

   (ii) $f(x) \leq 0$ and $g(x) < 0$

♦   (i)   When $|x| < a$, then

        $x < a$ and $x > -a$

(ii) When $|x - b| \geq a$, then

$$x - b \geq a, \quad x - b \leq -a$$

$$x \geq a + b, \quad x \leq b - a$$

♦ For finding the range of function

Let $f(x) = y$, then make $x = g(y)$

and find the domain of $g(y)$

♦ If $f(x) = |x - a|$, then

(i) $f(x) = x - a,\ x \geq a$

(ii) $f(x) = -(x - a),\ x < a$

♦ If $a\, f(x) + b\, f\left(\dfrac{1}{x}\right) = cx$ ...(i)

Replace x by $\dfrac{1}{x}$, $a\, f\left(\dfrac{1}{x}\right) + b\, f(x) = \dfrac{c}{x}$ ....(ii)

∴ $f(x)$ can be determined by eqs. (i) and (ii).

Tips/Tricks/Techniques ONE-LINERS
(Exam Special)

♦ **Results on Cartesian Product:**

(a) $A \times (B \cup C) = (A \times B) \cup (A \times C)$.

(b) $A \times (B \cap C) = (A \times B) \cap (A \times C)$.

(c) $A \times (B - C) = (A \times B) - (A \times C)$.

(d) $(A \times B) \cup (C \times D) \subseteq (A \cup C) \times (B \cup D)$.

(e) $(A \times B) \cap (C \times D) = (A \cap C) \times (B \cap D)$.

(f) $(A \times B) \cap (B \times A) = (A \cap B) \times (B \cap A)$.

(g) Let A and B be two non-empty sets having 'n' elements in common, then $A \times B$ and $B \times A$ have n^2 elements in common.

♦ **Even and Odd Functions:** A real function $f(x)$ is an even function if $f(-x) = f(x)$ or $f(x) - f(-x) = 0$.

E.g.; x^2, cos x, (x) are examples of even function.

A real function $f(x)$ is an odd function if $f(-x) = -f(x)$ or $f(-x) + f(x) = 0$.

E.g.; $x^3 - 4x$, sin x, are examples of odd functions.

- **Explicit and Implicit Functions:** A function is said to be explicit, if it can be expressed directly in terms of independent variable. E.g.; $f(x) = x^2 \log x$; $f(x) = e^x + \log x$.

  A function is said to be implicit, if it cannot be expressed directly in terms of the independent variable.

  E.g.; $x^3 + y^3 + 3axy + c = 0$; $x^y + y^x = a^b$.

- **Periodic Function:** A function $f(x)$ is said to be periodic function if, there exist a positive real number T, such that $f(x + T) = f(x)\ \forall\ x \in$ Domain.

  Also; $f(x) = f(x + T) = f(x + 2T) = f(x + 3T) = \ldots\ldots$

  Properties: If $f(x)$ is periodic with period T, then

  (a) $c.f(x)$ is periodic with period T.

  (b) $f(x + c)$ is periodic with period T.

  (c) $f(x) \pm c$ is periodic with period T, where c is any constant.

- **Equal Functions:** Two Functions $f : A \to B$ and $g : C \to D$ are called equal functions if and only if

  (a) domain of f = domain of g,

  (b) co-domain of f = co-domain of g &

  (c) $f(x) = g(x)\ \forall\ x \in$ domain.

- **Fractional Part Function:** It is defined as:

  $y = \{x\} = x - [x]$, where $[\ ]$ is greatest integer function.

- **Rules for Solving Problems on Domain of a Function:**

  (a) $(x-a)(x-b) > 0 \Rightarrow x < a$ or $x > b$, for $a < b$.

  (b) $(x-a)(x-b) < 0 \Rightarrow a < x < b$, for $a < b$.

  (c) $|x| < a \Rightarrow -a < x < a$.

  (d) $|x| > a \Rightarrow x < -a$ or $x > a$.

  (e) $\log_b a > k \Rightarrow \begin{cases} a > b^k, \text{if } b > 1. \\ a < b^k, \text{if } b < 1. \end{cases}$

3 — Trigonometric Functions

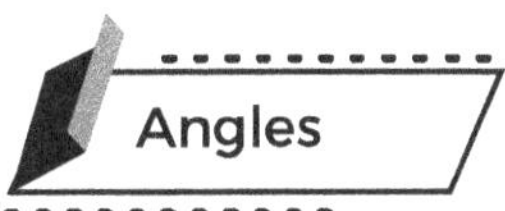

Angles

- An angle is a measure of rotation of a given ray about its initial point. Here OA is initial position and OB is the final position of the given ray.

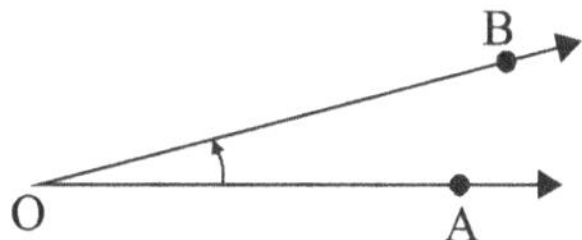

- The original ray is called the initial side and the final position of the ray after rotation is called the terminal side of the angle.
- The point of rotation is called the vertex.
- If the direction of rotation is anticlockwise, the angle is said to be positive and if the direction of rotation is clockwise, then the angle is negative.

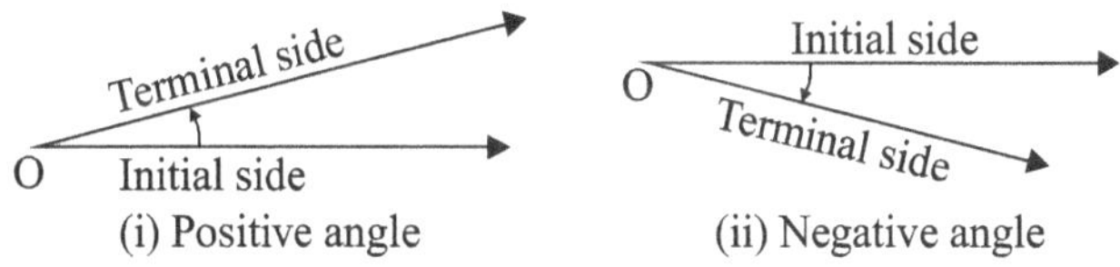

(i) Positive angle   (ii) Negative angle

Angle Measurement

A. Degree measure

- If a rotation from the initial side to terminal side is $(1/360)^{th}$ of a revolution, the angle is said to have a measure of one degree, written as $1°$.
- A degree is divided into 60 minutes, written as $1'$, i.e. $1° = 60'$.
- A minute is divided into 60 seconds, written as $1'$, i.e. $1' = 60''$.

B. Radian measure

- Angle subtended at the centre by an arc of length 1 unit in a unit circle (circle of radius 1 unit) is said to have a measure of 1 radian.
- The figures show the angles whose measures are 1 radian, −1 radian

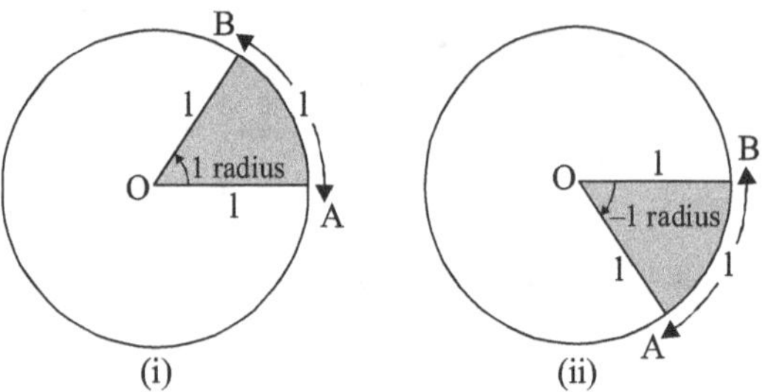

♦ One complete revolution of the initial side subtends an angle of 2π radian.

♦ A circle of radius r, an arc of length r subtends an angle whose measure is 1 radian, an arc of length l will subtend an angle θ radian whose measure is

$$\theta = l/r \text{ radian, or } \boxed{\text{Angle} = \dfrac{\text{Arc}}{\text{Radius}}}$$

C. Relation between radian and real numbers

♦ From the figure. If we rope the line AP along the circle in the anticlock wise direction, we find

♦ Every real number will correspond to a radian measure and conversely. Thus, radian measures and real numbers can be considered as one and the same.

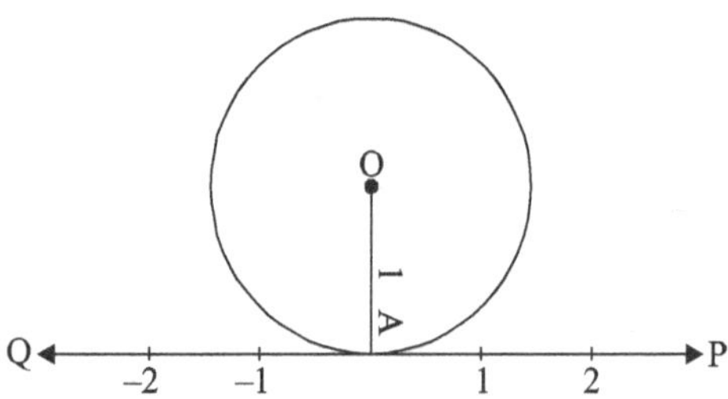

D. Relation between degree and radian

♦ A circle subtends at the centre an angle whose radian measure is 2π and its degree measure is 360°.

Hence, 2π radian = 360° or π radian = 180°

♦ Using approximate value of π as 22/7, we have

1 radian = 180/π ° = 57° 16′ approximately. Also 1° = π/180 radian = 0.01746 radian approximately.

The relation between degree measures and radian measure of some common angles are-

Degree	30°	45°	60°	90°	180°	270°	360°
Radian	$\dfrac{\pi}{6}$	$\dfrac{\pi}{4}$	$\dfrac{\pi}{3}$	$\dfrac{\pi}{2}$	x	$\dfrac{3\pi}{6}$	$2x$

E. Notational Convention

♦ In this convention, we generally omit the word 'radian', when we expressed an angle in radians.

e.g. $45° = \dfrac{\pi}{4}$, $180° = \pi$

Note: Radian measure $= \dfrac{\pi}{180} \times$ Degree measure

$\qquad$ Degree measure $= \dfrac{180}{\pi} \times$ Radian measure

Trigonometric Functions

♦ The extension of the definition of trigonometric ratios to any angle in terms of radian measure is studied as trigonometric functions.

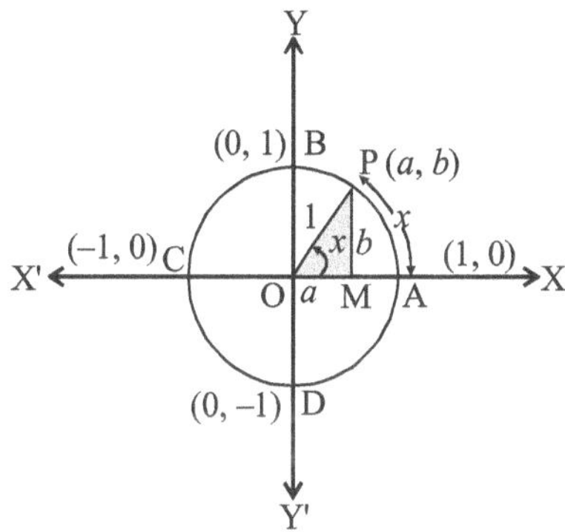

♦ Let unit circle, Here we define cos x = a and sin x = b. Since $\triangle OMP$ is a right triangle, we have $OM^2 + MP^2 = OP^2$ or $a^2 + b^2 = 1$

♦ Thus, for every point on the unit circle,
we have $a^2 + b^2 = 1$ or $\cos^2 x + \sin^2 x = 1$
Since, one complet revolution subtends an angle of 2π radian at the centre of the circle, $\triangle AOB = \pi/2$,

♦ All angles which are integral multiples of $\pi/2$ are called quadrantal angles.

♦ For quadrantal angles we have
$\cos 0° = 1,$ $\qquad \sin 0° = 0$

$\cos \dfrac{\pi}{2} = 0,$ $\qquad \sin \dfrac{\pi}{2} = 1$

$\cos \dfrac{3\pi}{2} = 0$ $\qquad \sin \dfrac{3\pi}{2} = -1$

♦ Thus,
$\sin x = 0$ implies $x = n\pi$, where n is any integer
$\cos x = 0$ implies $x = (2n + 1)\,\pi/2$, where n is any integer.

Let us see the table:

	$0°$	$\dfrac{\pi}{6}$	$\dfrac{\pi}{4}$	$\dfrac{\pi}{3}$	$\dfrac{\pi}{2}$	π	$\dfrac{3\pi}{2}$	2π
sin	0	$\dfrac{1}{2}$	$\dfrac{1}{\sqrt{2}}$	$\dfrac{\sqrt{3}}{2}$	1	0	-1	0
cos	1	$\dfrac{\sqrt{3}}{2}$	$\dfrac{1}{\sqrt{2}}$	$\dfrac{1}{2}$	0	-1	0	1
tan	0	$\dfrac{1}{\sqrt{3}}$	1	$\sqrt{3}$	not defined	0	not defined	0

♦ **Basic Formulae**

- $\sin\theta = \dfrac{1}{\operatorname{cosec}\theta},\ \theta \neq n\pi$

- $\cos\theta = \dfrac{1}{\sec\theta},\ \theta \neq (2n+1)\dfrac{\pi}{2}.$

- $\tan\theta = \dfrac{1}{\cot\theta},\ \theta \neq \dfrac{n\pi}{2}$

- $\tan\theta = \dfrac{\sin\theta}{\cos\theta},\ \theta \neq (2n+1)\dfrac{\pi}{2}.$

- $\cot\theta = \dfrac{\cos\theta}{\sin\theta},\ \theta \neq n\pi.$

A. Sign of trigonometric functions

♦ In different quadrants from the values of sin x, cos x we can find the signs of other trigonometric functions as:

	I	*II*	*III*	*IV*
sin *x*	+	+	−	−
cos *x*	+	−	−	+
tan *x*	+	−	+	−
cosce x	+	+	−	−
sec *x*	+	−	−	+
cot *x*	+	−	+	−

♦ Sign of Trigonometric Functions

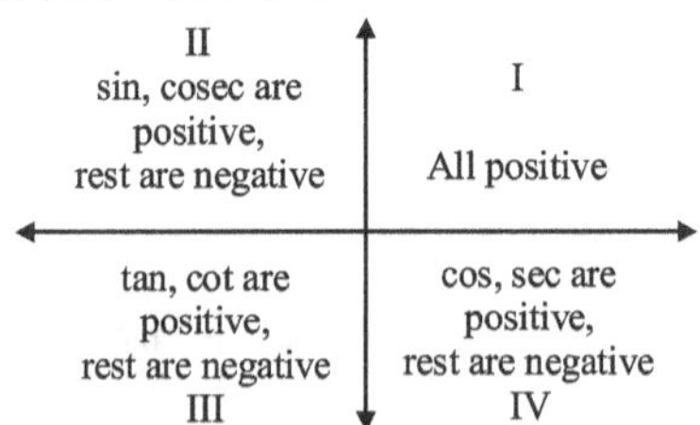

Note: Remember **ASTC** (After School to College)

B. Domain and range of trigonometric functions

♦ By the definition of sine and cosine functions, we observe that they are defined for all real numbers.

♦ Thus, domain of $y = \sin x$ and $y = \cos x$ is the set of all real numbers and range is the interval $[-1, 1]$, i.e., $-1 \le y \le 1$.

♦ Since cosec $x = 1/\sin x$, the domain of $y = \text{cosec } x$ is the set $\{x : x \in R$ and $x \ne n\pi, n \in Z\}$ and range is the set $\{y : y \in R, y \ge 1$ or $y \le -1\}$.

♦ The domain of $y = \sec x$ is the set $\{x : x \in R$ and $x \ne (2n+1)\pi/2, n \in Z\}$ and range is the set $\{y : y \in R, y \le -1$ or $y \ge 1\}$.

♦ The domain of $y = \tan x$ is the set $\{x : x \in R$ and $x \ne (2n+1)\pi/2, n \in Z\}$ and range is the set of all real numbers.

♦ The domain of $y = \cot x$ is the set $\{x : x \in R$ and $x \ne n\pi, n \in Z\}$ and the range is the set of all real numbers.

♦ Let us discuss the behaviour of other trigonometric functions through the following table as below

Domain and Range of Trigonometric Functions		
Function	**Domain**	**Range**
sin x	R	$[-1, 1]$
cos x	R	$[-1, 1]$
tan x	$R - \{(2n+1)\pi/2, n \in Z\}$	R
cosec x	$R - \{n\pi, n \in Z\}$	$(-\infty, -1] \cup [1, \infty)$
sec x	$R - \{(2n+1)\pi/2, n \in Z\}$	$(-\infty, -1] \cup [1, \infty)$
cot x	$R - \{n\pi, n \in Z\}$	R

	I quadrant	II quadrant	III quadrant	IV quadrant
sin	increases from 0 to 1	decreases from 1 to 0	decreases from 0 to -1	increases from -1 to 0
cos	decreases from 1 to 0	decreases from 0 to -1	increases from -1 to 0	increases from 0 to 1
tan	increases from 0 to ∞	increases from $-\infty$ to 0	increases from 0 to ∞	increases from $-\infty$ to 0
cot	decreases from ∞ to 0	decreases from 0 to $-\infty$	decreases from ∞ to 0	decreases from 0 to $-\infty$
sec	increases from 1 to ∞	increases from $-\infty$ to -1	decreases from -1 to $-\infty$	decreases from ∞ to 1
cosec	decreases from ∞ to 1	increases from 1 to ∞	increases from $-\infty$ to -1	decreases from -1 to $-\infty$

♦ Let us see graphs of the trigonometric functions-

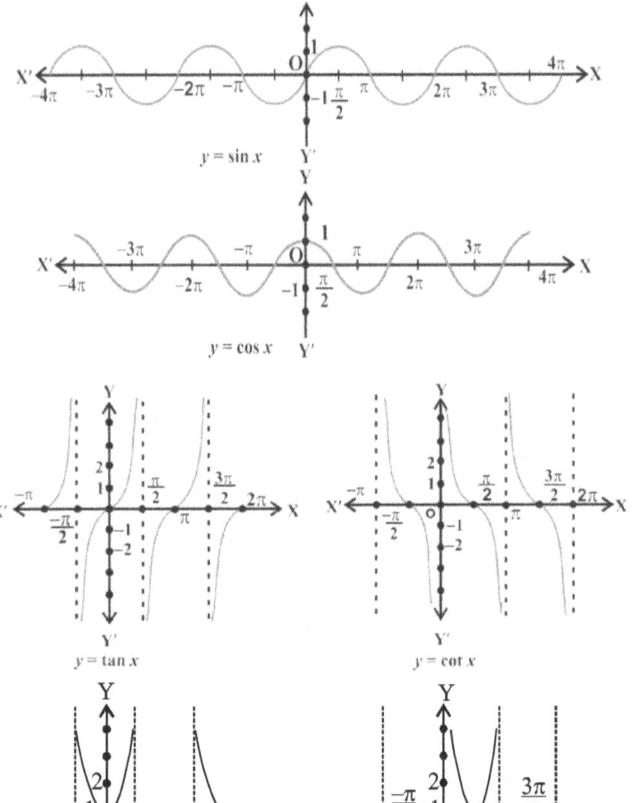

Trigonometric Functions of Sum and Difference of Two Angles

♦ sin (– x) = – sin x

♦ cos (– x) = cos x

♦ cos (x + y) = cos x cos y – sin x sin y

- $\cos(x - y) = \cos x \cos y + \sin x \sin y$
- $\cos(\pi/2 - x) = \sin x$
- $\sin(\pi/2 - x) = \cos x$
- $\sin(x + y) = \sin x \cos y + \cos x \sin y$
- $\sin(x - y) = \sin x \cos y - \cos x \sin y$
- $\cos(\pi/2 + x) = -\sin x$
- $\sin(\pi/2 + x) = \cos x$
- $\cos(\pi - x) = -\cos x$
- $\sin(\pi - x) = \sin x$
- $\cos(\pi + x) = -\cos x$
- $\sin(\pi + x) = -\sin x$
- $\cos(2\pi - x) = \cos x$
- $\sin(2\pi - x) = -\sin x$

- $\tan(x + y) = \dfrac{\tan x + \tan y}{1 - \tan x \tan y}$

- $\tan(x - y) = \dfrac{\tan x - \tan y}{1 + \tan x \tan y}$

- $\cot(x + y) = \dfrac{\cot x \cot y - 1}{\cot y + \cot x}$

- $\cot(x - y) = \dfrac{\cot x \cot y + 1}{\cot y - \cot x}$
- $\cos 2x = \cos^2 x - \sin^2 x = 2\cos^2 x - 1 = 1 - 2\sin^2 x$

$$= \dfrac{1 - \tan^2 x}{1 + \tan^2 x}$$

- $\sin 2x = 2 \sin x \cos x = \dfrac{2\tan x}{1 + \tan^2 x} \quad x \neq n\pi + \dfrac{\pi}{2}, \text{ where n is an integer}$

- $\tan 2x = \dfrac{2\tan x}{1 - \tan^2 x} \quad \text{if } 2x \neq n\pi + \dfrac{\pi}{2}, \text{ where n is an integer}$

- $\tan 3x = \dfrac{3\tan x - \tan^3 x}{1 - 3\tan^2 x} \quad \text{if } 3x \neq n\pi + \dfrac{\pi}{2}, \text{ where n is an integer}$

- $\sin 3x = 3 \sin x - 4 \sin^3 x$
- $\cos 3x = 4 \cos^3 x - 3 \cos x$

- $\tan 3x = \dfrac{3\tan x - \tan^3 x}{1 - 3\tan^2 x} \quad \text{if } 3x \neq n\pi + \dfrac{\pi}{2}, \text{ where n is an integer}$

- $\cos x + \cos y = 2\cos \dfrac{x + y}{2} \cos \dfrac{x - y}{2}$

* $\cos x - \cos y = -\, 2\sin \dfrac{x+y}{2} \sin \dfrac{x-y}{2}$

* $\sin x + \sin y = 2\sin \dfrac{x+y}{2} \cos \dfrac{x-y}{2}$

* $\sin x - \sin y = 2\cos \dfrac{x+y}{2} \sin \dfrac{x-y}{2}$

* $2 \cos x \cos y = \cos (x + y) + \cos (x - y)$
* $-2 \sin x \sin y = \cos (x + y) - \cos (x - y)$
* $2 \sin x \cos y = \sin (x + y) + \sin (x - y)$
* $2 \cos x \sin y = \sin (x + y) - \sin (x - y)$.

Trigonometric Equations

*   Equations involving trigonometric functions of a variable are called trigonometric equations.
*   The solutions of a trigonometric equation for which $0 \le x < 2\pi$ are called principal solutions.
*   The expression involving integer 'n' which gives all solutions of a trigonometric equation is called the general solution.

Principal Solutions

♦ The solutions of a trigonometric equation in the variable 'x' for which $0 \le x < 2\pi$ are called principal solutions. E.g., the principal solution of equation

$\sin x = \dfrac{1}{2}$ are $x = \dfrac{\pi}{6}, \dfrac{5\pi}{6}$.

General Solutions

♦ $\sin x = 0 \qquad \Rightarrow x = n\pi, n \in Z$

♦ $\cos x = 0 \qquad \Rightarrow x = (2n + 1)\pi/2, n \in Z$

♦ $\tan x = 0 \qquad \Rightarrow x = n\pi, n \in Z$

♦ $\sin x = \sin y \Rightarrow x = n\pi + (-1)^n y, n \in Z$

♦ $\cos x = \cos y \Rightarrow x = 2n\pi \pm y, n \in Z$

♦ $\tan x = \tan y \Rightarrow x = n\pi + y, n \in Z$

Simple Applications of Sine and Cosine Formulae

*   Sine Formulae: In any triangle, sides are proportional to the sines of the opposite angles, that is, in a triangle ABC.

$$\frac{\sin A}{a} = \frac{\sin B}{b} = \frac{\sin C}{c}$$

♦ Cosine Formulae: Let A, B and C be angles of a triangles and a, b and c be lengths of sides opposite to angles A, B and C respoctively, then
- $a^2 = b^2 + c^2 - 2bc \cos A$
- $b^2 = c^2 + a^2 - 2ca \cos B$
- $c^2 = a^2 + b^2 - 2ab \cos C$

Past Years ONE-LINERS
JEE Main/Board

♦ $\dfrac{\cos(x)}{1+\sin(x)} = |1\tan(2x)|$

♦ $\sin 2\theta = 2\sin\theta.\cos\theta$

♦ $\tan(\alpha + 2\beta) = \dfrac{\tan\alpha + \tan 2\beta}{1 - \tan\alpha \tan 2\beta}$

♦ Using A.M. – G. M. to final minimum or maximum value of Trigonomatric expressions where $\sin(x) > 0$, $\cos(x) > 0$. $\tan(x) > 0$ etc. where A. M. $\geq$ G.M.

♦ To find number of solutions of trigonometric equations try to make dissimilar trigo function as similar, ie., Let
$$\Rightarrow \ \sin x = \cos 2x \Rightarrow \sin(x) - \cos(2x) = 0$$
$$\Rightarrow \sin(x) - [1 - 2\sin^2(x)] = 0$$
$$\Rightarrow 2\sin^2(x) + \sin(x) - 1 = 0$$

♦ To find maximum value and minimum value of trigonometric expression (used concept)
$$-1 \leq \sin x \leq 1 \quad \Rightarrow 0 \leq \sin^2 x \leq 1$$
$$-1 \leq \cos x \leq 1 \quad \Rightarrow 0 \leq \cos^2 x \leq 1$$

♦ Used concept
$$\cos(C) + \cos(D) = 2\cos\left(\frac{C+D}{2}\right)\cos\left(\frac{C-D}{2}\right)$$

Tips/Tricks/Techniques ONE-LINERS
(Exam Special)

▶ **Periodic properties of trigonometric functions**
(a) $\sin x$, $\cos x$, $\sec x$ and $\operatorname{cosec} x$ are periodic functions with fundamental period 2π.
(b) $\tan x$ and $\cot x$ are periodic functions with fundamental period π.
(c) $|\sin x|$, $|\cos x|$, $|\tan x|$, $|\cot x|$, $|\sec x|$, $|\operatorname{cosec} x|$ are periodic functions with fundamental period π.
(d) $\sin^n x$, $\cos^n x$, $\sec^n x$, $\operatorname{cosec}^n x$ are periodic functions with fundamental period 2π or π according as n is odd or even.
(e) $\tan^n x$ and $\cot^n x$ are periodic function with fundamental period π whether n is odd or even.

▶ **Conditional trigonometric identities**
If $A + B + C = 180°$ (or π), or A, B, C are angles of a triangle. Then,
(a) $\sin(A + B) = \sin(\pi - C) = \sin C$, etc .

(b) $\sin\left(\dfrac{A}{2} + \dfrac{B}{2}\right) = \sin\left(\dfrac{\pi}{2} - \dfrac{C}{2}\right) = \cos\dfrac{C}{2}$, etc

(c) $\sin A + \sin B + \sin C = 4\cos\dfrac{A}{2}\cos\dfrac{B}{2}\cos\dfrac{C}{2}$

(d) $\cos A + \cos B + \cos C = 1 + 4\sin\dfrac{A}{2}\sin\dfrac{B}{2}\sin\dfrac{C}{2}$

(e) $\tan A + \tan B + \tan C = \tan A\,\tan B\,\tan C$

(f) $\cot A\cot B + \cot B\cot C + \cot C\cot A = 1$

(g) $\tan\dfrac{A}{2}\tan\dfrac{B}{2} + \tan\dfrac{B}{2}\tan\dfrac{C}{2} + \tan\dfrac{C}{2}\tan\dfrac{A}{2} = 1$

▶ **Properties of triangle**
(a) Projection formula
   (i) $a = b\cos C + c\cos B$
   (ii) $b = c\cos A + a\cos C$
   (iii) $c = a\cos B + b\cos A$
(b) Tangent rule :

$$\tan\left(\frac{B-C}{2}\right) = \frac{b-c}{b+c}\tan\left(\frac{B+C}{2}\right) = \frac{b-c}{b+c}\cot\frac{A}{2}$$

(c) Half angle formula :

   (i) $\sin\dfrac{A}{2} = \sqrt{\dfrac{(s-b)(s-c)}{bc}}$

$$\text{(ii)} \quad \cos\frac{A}{2} = \sqrt{\frac{s\,(s-a)}{bc}}$$

$$\text{(iii)} \quad \tan\frac{A}{2} = \sqrt{\frac{(s-b)\,(s-c)}{s\,(s-a)}}$$

(d) Area of a triangle :

$$\Delta = \frac{1}{2}\,bc\sin A = \frac{1}{2}\,ca\sin B = \frac{1}{2}\,ab\sin C$$

▶ **Orthocentre of the triangle and pedal triangle**

(a) The distances of the orthocentre of the triangle from the vertices are $2R\cos A$, $2R\cos B$, $2R\cos C$ and its distances from the sides are $2R\cos B\cos C$, $2R\cos C\cos A$, $2R\cos A\cos B$.

(b) Circumradius of the pedal triangle $=\dfrac{R}{2}$

(c) Area of the pedal triangle $= 2\Delta\cos A\cos B\cos C$.

(d) Circumcentre O, centroid G and orthocentre O' are collinear and G divides OO' in the ratio 1 : 2.

(e) Distance between the circumcentre O and the incentre I is

$$OI = R\sqrt{1 - 8\sin\frac{A}{2}\sin\frac{B}{2}\sin\frac{C}{2}}$$

▶ **Heights and distances**

(a) The angle of elevation or depression is the angle between the line of observation and the horizontal line according as the object is at a higher or lower level than the observer.

(b) The angle of elevation or depression is always measured from horizontal line through the point of observation.

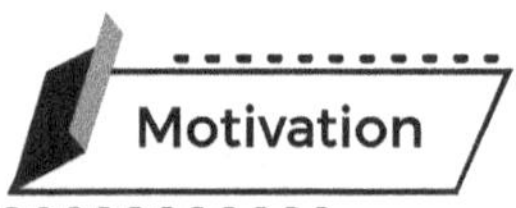

Motivation

♦ In mathematics, we use a form of complete induction called **mathematical induction**.

♦ To understand the basic principles of mathematical induction, suppose a set of thin rectangular tiles are placed as shown in Fig.

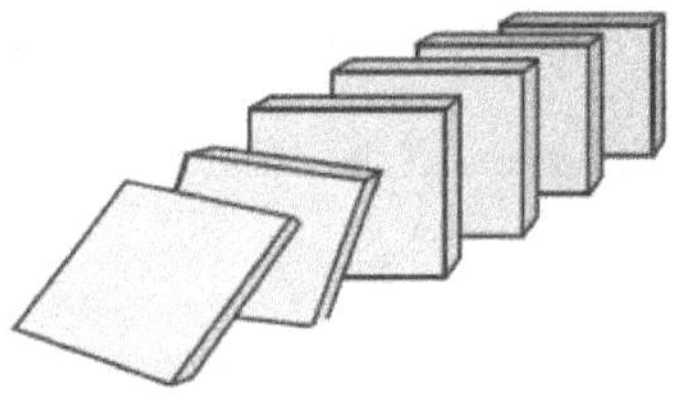

♦ When the first tile is pushed in the indicated direction, all the tiles will fall.

♦ To be absolutely sure that all the tiles will fall, it is sufficient to know that
   (a) The first tile falls, and
   (b) In the event that any tile falls its successor necessarily falls.
   This is the underlying principle of mathematical induction.

♦ We know, the set of natural numbers N is a special ordered subset of the real numbers.

♦ In fact, N is the smallest subset of R with the following property: A set S is said to be an inductive set if $1 \in S$ and $x + 1 \in S$ whenever $x \in S$. Since N is the smallest subset of R which is an inductive set, it follows that any subset of R that is an inductive set must contain N.

Illustration :

♦ Suppose we wish to find the formula for the sum of positive integers 1, 2, 3,...,n, that is, a formula which will give the value of $1 + 2 + 3$ when $n = 3$, the value $1 + 2 + 3 + 4$, when $n = 4$ and so on and suppose that in some manner we are led to believe that the formula $1 + 2 + 3 + ... + n = n(n+1)/2$ is the correct one. How can this formula actually be proved?

♦ We can, of course, verify the statement for as many positive integral values of n as we like, but this process will not prove the formula for all values of n.

- What is needed is some kind of chain reaction which will have the effect that once the formula is proved for a particular positive integer the formula will automatically follow for the next positive integer and the next indefinitely.
- Such a reaction may be considered as produced by the method of mathematical induction.

Principle of Mathematical Induction

- In algebra or in other discipline of mathematics, there are certain results or statements that are formulated in terms of n, where n is a positive integer. To prove such statements the well-suited principle that is used-based on the specific technique, is known as the **principle of mathematical induction**.
- The principle of mathematical induction is one such tool which can be used to prove a wide variety of mathematical statements. Each such statement is assumed as P(n) associated with positive integer n, for which the correctness for the case n = 1 is examined. Then assuming the truth of P(k) for some positive integer k, the truth of P (k+1) is established.
- Suppose there is a given statement P(n) involving the natural number n such that
  (i)   The statement is true for n = 1, i.e., P(1) is true, and
  (ii) If the statement is true for n = k (where k is some positive integer), then the statement is also true for n = k + 1, i.e., truth of P(k) implies the truth of P(k + 1).
  Then, P(n) is true for all natural numbers n.
- Property (i) is simply a statement of fact. There may be situations when a statement is true for all n ≥ 4. In this case, step 1 will start from n = 4 and we shall verify the result for n = 4, i.e., P(4).
- Property (ii) is a conditional property. It does not assert that the given statement is true for n = k, but only that if it is true for n = k, then it is also true for n = k +1. So, to prove that the property holds , only prove that conditional proposition:
  If the statement is true for n = k, then it is also true for n = k + 1. This is sometimes referred to as the **inductive step**.
- The assumption that the given statement is true for n = k in this inductive step is called the **inductive hypothesis**.

Past Years ONE-LINERS
JEE Main/Board

♦ Prime numbers : 2, 3, 5, 11, 13, 17, 19, 23, 29, 31, 37, 41, 43, 47, 53, 59, 61, 67, ...

P(n) is prime, put n = k, k + 1, k + 2, ...

Tips/Tricks/Techniques ONE-LINERS
(Exam Special)

For any natural number n,

♦ $1 + 2 + 3 + 4 + ... + n = \Sigma\, n = \dfrac{n(n+1)}{2}$

♦ $1^2 + 2^2 + 3^2 + 4^2 + ... + n^2 = \Sigma n^2 = \dfrac{n(n+1)\,(2n+1)}{6}$

♦ $1^3 + 2^3 + 3^3 + 4^3 + ... + n^3 = \Sigma n^3 = \left\{ \dfrac{n(n+1)}{2} \right\}^2$

♦ $1^4 + 2^4 + 3^4 + 4^4 + ... + n^4 = \dfrac{n\,(n+1)\,(2n+1)\,(3n^2+3n-1)}{30}$

♦ $1^5 + 2^5 + 3^5 + 4^5 + ... + n^5 = \dfrac{n^2(n+1)^2(2n^2+2n-1)}{12}$

♦ $2 + 4 + 6 + ... + 2n = \Sigma\, 2n = n\,(n+1)$

♦ $1 + 3 + 5 + ... + (2n-1) = \Sigma\,(2n-1) = n^2$

♦ $x^n - y^n = (x-y)\,(x^{n-1} + x^{n-2}\,y + x^{n-3}\,y^2 + ... + xy^{n-2} + y^{n-1})$
$x^n + y^n = (x+y)\,(x^{n-1} - x^{n-2}\,y + x^{n-3}\,y^2 - ... - xy^{n-2} + y^{n-1})$, when n is odd positive integer.

♦ Product of r consecutive integers is divisible by $r!$

♦ For $x \neq y$, $x^n - y^n$ is divisible by
(a) $x + y$ if n is even   (b) $x - y$ if n is even or odd

♦ For solving objective question related to natural numbers we find out the correct alternative by negative examination of this principle. If the given statement is P(n), then by putting $n = 1, 2, 3, ...$ in P (n) we decide the correct answer.

♦ When using mathematical induction to prove a summation formula, it is helpful to think of S_{k+1} as $S_{k+1} = S_k + a_{k+1}$, where a_{k+1} is the (k+1)th term of the original sum.

Complex Numbers and Quadratic Equations

Complex Numbers

- The main objective of complex numbers is to solve the equation $ax^2 + bx + c = 0$, where $D = b^2 - 4ac < 0$, which is not possible in the system of real numbers.
- Let us denote $\sqrt{-1}$ by the symbol i. Then, we have $i^2 = -1$. This means that i is a solution of the equation $x^2 + 1 = 0$.
- A number of the form a + ib , where a and b are real numbers, is defined to be a **complex number**. For example, $2+i3, (-1)+i\sqrt{3}, 4+i\left(\dfrac{-1}{11}\right)$ are complex numbers.
- For the complex number $z = a + ib$, a is called **the real part**, denoted by $Re\ z$ and b is called **the imaginary part** denoted by $Im\ z$ of the complex number z. For example, if $z = 2 + i5$, then $Re\ z = 2$ and $Im\ z = 5$.

Equality of Complex Numbers

- Two complex numbers $z_1 = a + ib$ and $z_2 = c + id$ are equal if $a = c$ and $b = d$.

Algebra of Complex Numbers

Addition of complex numbers: Let $z_1 = a + ib$ and $z_2 = c + id$ be any two complex numbers. Then, the sum $z_1 + z_2$ is defined as follows: $z_1 + z_2 = (a + c) + i\ (b + d)$, which is again a complex number.

The addition of complex numbers satisfy the following properties:

- **The closure law:** The sum of two complex numbers is a complex number, *i.e.*, $z_1 + z_2$ is a complex number for all complex numbers z_1 and z_2.
- **The commutative law:** For any two complex numbers z_1 and z_2, $z_1 + z_2 = z_2 + z_1$
- **The associative law:** For any three complex numbers z_1, z_2, z_3, $(z_1 + z_2) + z_3 = z_1 + (z_2 + z_3)$
- **The existence of additive identity:** There exists the complex number $0 + i0$ (denoted as 0), called the **additive identity** or the **zero complex number**, such that, for every complex number z, $z + 0 = z$.
- **The existence of additive inverse:** To every complex number $z = a + ib$, we

have the complex number $-a + i(-b)$ (denoted as $-z$), called **the additive inverse** or **negative of** z. We observe that $z + (-z) = 0$ (the additive identity).

♦   **Difference of two complex numbers:** Given any two complex numbers z_1 and z_2, the difference $z_1 - z_2$ is defined as follows: $z_1 - z_2 = z_1 + (-z_2)$.

Multiplication of two complex numbers : Let $z_1 = a + ib$ and $z_2 = c + id$ be any two complex numbers. Then, the product $z_1 z_2$ is defined as follows:

$$z_1 z_2 = (ac - bd) + i(ad + bc).$$

The multiplication of complex numbers possesses the following properties, which we state without proofs:

♦   **The closure law:** The product of two complex numbers is a complex number, the product $z_1 z_2$ is a complex number for all complex numbers z_1 and z_2.

♦   **The commutative law:** For any two complex numbers z_1 and z_2,
$z_1 z_2 = z_2 z_1$

♦   **The associative law:** For any three complex numbers z_1, z_2, z_3,
$(z_1 z_2) z_3 = z_1 (z_2 z_3)$.

♦   **The existence of multiplicative identity:** There exists the complex number $1 + i0$ (denoted as 1), called **the multiplicative identity** such that $z_1 = z$, for every complex number z.

♦   **The existence of multiplicative inverse:** For every non-zero complex number $z = a + ib$ or $a + bi(a \neq 0, b \neq 0)$, we have the complex number

$$\frac{a}{a^2 + b^2} + i \frac{-b}{a^2 + b^2} \quad \text{(denoted by } \frac{1}{z} \text{ or } z^{-1} \text{), called the } multiplicative\ inverse$$

of z such that $z \dfrac{1}{z} = 1$ (the multiplicative identity).

♦   **The distributive law:** For any three complex numbers z_1, z_2, z_3,
(a) $z_1 (z_2 + z_3) = z_1 z_2 + z_1 z_3$
(b) $z_3 (z_1 + z_2) = z_1 z_3 + z_2 z_3$

♦   **Division of two complex numbers:** Given any two complex numbers z_1 and z_2, where $z_2 \neq 0$, the quotient $\dfrac{z_1}{z_2}$ is defined by

$$\frac{z_1}{z_2} = z_1 \frac{1}{z_2}$$

Power of I: We know that,

♦ $i^3 = i^2 i = (-1)\, i = -i,$ $i^4 = (i^2)^2 = (-1)^2 = 1$

♦ $i^5 = (i^2)^2 i = (-1)^2\, i = i,$ $i^6 = (i^2)^3 = (-1)^3 = -1$

♦ $i^{-1} = \dfrac{1}{i} \times \dfrac{i}{i} = \dfrac{i}{-1} = -i,$ $i^{-2} = \dfrac{1}{i^2} = \dfrac{1}{-1} = -1,$

♦ $i^{-3} = \dfrac{1}{i^3} = \dfrac{1}{-i} \times \dfrac{i}{i} = \dfrac{i}{1} = -i,$ $i^{-4} = \dfrac{1}{i^4} = \dfrac{1}{1} = 1$

♦   In general, for any integer k, $i^{4k} = 1,\ i^{4k+1} = i,\ i^{4k+2} = -1,\ i^{4k+3} = -i$

The square roots of a negative real number:

♦ Note that $i^2 = -1$ and $(-i)^2 = i^2 = -1$

Therefore, the square roots of -1 are $i, -i$. However, by the symbol $\sqrt{-1}$, we would mean i only.

♦ Now, we can see that i and $-i$, both are the solutions of the equation $x^2 + 1 = 0$.

♦ Generally, if a is a positive real number, $\sqrt{-a} = \sqrt{a}\sqrt{-1} = \sqrt{a}\,i$.

Identities

♦ $(z_1 + z_2)^2 = z_1^2 + z_2^2 + 2z_1 z_2,$

♦ $(z_1 - z_2)^2 = z_1^2 - 2z_1 z_2 + z_2^2$

♦ $(z_1 + z_2)^3 = z_1^3 + 3z_1^2 z_2 + 3z_1 z_2^2 + z_2^3$

♦ $(z_1 - z_2)^3 = z_1^3 - 3z_1^2 z_2 + 3z_1 z_2^2 - z_2^3$

♦ $z_1^2 - z_2^2 = (z_1 + z_2)(z_1 - z_2)$

The Modulus and the Conjugate of a Complex Number

♦ **Modulus of complex number:** Let $z = a + ib$ be a complex number. Then, the modulus of z, denoted by $|z|$, is defined to be the non-negative real number $\sqrt{a^2 + b^2}$, i.e., $|z| = \sqrt{a^2 + b^2}$

♦ **Conjugate of complex number:** Let $z = a + ib$ be a complex number. Then, the conjugate of z denoted as $\bar{z}$, is the complex number $a - ib$, i.e., $\bar{z} = a - ib$.

Properties:

♦ $z^{-1} = \dfrac{\bar{z}}{|z|^2}$

♦ $z\bar{z} = |z|^2$

♦ $|z_1 z_2| = |z_1||z_2|$

♦ $\overline{z_1 z_2} = \bar{z_1}\,\bar{z_2}$

♦ $\left|\dfrac{z_1}{z_2}\right| = \dfrac{|z_1|}{|z_2|}$ provided $|z_2| \neq 0$

♦ $\overline{z_1 \pm z_2} = \bar{z_1} \pm \bar{z_2}$

♦ $\overline{\left(\dfrac{z_1}{z_2}\right)} = \dfrac{\bar{z_1}}{\bar{z_2}}$ provided $z_2 \neq 0$.

Argand Plane and Polar Representation

- **Argand plane:** The plane having a complex number assigned to each of its point is called **the complex plane** or **the Argand plane**.
- Let $z = x + iy$ be the complex number. Then, the modulus of complex number $z = x + iy = \sqrt{x^2 + y^2}$ is the distance between the point P(x, y) and the origin O $(0, 0)$ (Fig.).
- The points on the x-axis corresponds to the complex numbers of the form $a + i0$ and the points on the y-axis corresponds to the complex numbers of the form $0 + ib$.
- The x-axis and y-axis in the Argand plane are called, respectively, **the real axis** and the **imaginary axis**.

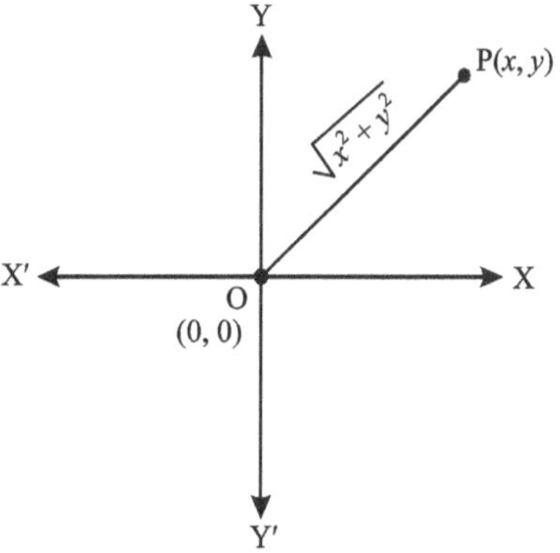

- The representation of a complex number $z = x + iy$ and its conjugate $z = x - iy$ in the Argand plane are, respectively, the points P(x, y) and Q$(x, -y)$.
- Geometrically, the point $(x, -y)$ is the mirror image of the point (x, y) on the real axis (Fig.)

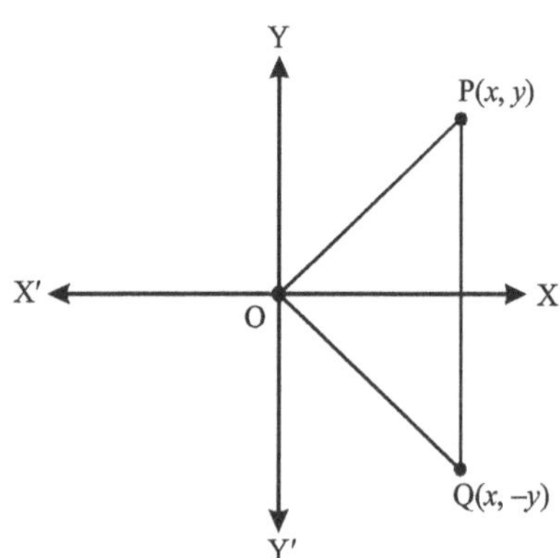

Polar Representation of a Complex Number:

- Let the point P represent the non-zero complex number $z = x + iy$. The point P is uniquely determined by the ordered pair of real numbers (r, θ), called **the polar coordinates of the point P.**
- We consider the origin as the pole and the positive direction of the x-axis as the initial line.
- We have, $x = r \cos \theta$, $y = r \sin \theta$ and therefore, $z = r (\cos \theta + i \sin \theta)$. The latter is said to be the polar form of the complex number.
- Here, $r = \sqrt{x^2 + y^2} = |z|$ is the modulus of z and θ is called **the argument (or amplitude)** of z which is denoted by arg z.
- **General argument:** When $0 \le \theta < 2\pi$.

Quadrant	Signs of x and y	Argument	Graph
I.	$x > 0, y > 0$	$0 < \theta < \dfrac{\pi}{2}$	
II.	$x < 0, y > 0$	$\dfrac{\pi}{2} < \theta < \pi$	
III.	$x < 0, y < 0$	$0 < \theta < \dfrac{3\pi}{2}$	
IV.	$x > 0, y < 0$	$\dfrac{3\pi}{2} < \theta < 2\pi$	

- **Principal argument:** The value of argument $i.e.$, θ, such that $-\pi < \theta \le \pi$ is called the principal argument.

Quadrant	Signs of x and y	Argument	Graph
I.	$x > 0, y > 0$	$\theta = \alpha$ and $0 < \theta < \dfrac{\pi}{2}$	
II.	$x < 0, y > 0$	$\theta = \pi - \alpha$ and $\dfrac{\pi}{2} < \theta < \pi$	
III.	$x < 0, y < 0$	$\theta = -(\pi - \alpha) = \alpha - \pi$ and $-\pi < \theta - \dfrac{\pi}{2}$	
IV.	$x > 0, y < 0$	$\theta - \alpha$ and $-\dfrac{\pi}{2} < \theta < 0$	

Quadratic Equation

- Let us consider the quadratic equation $ax^2 + bx + c = 0$ with real coefficients a, b, c and $a \neq 0$. Also, let us assume that $b^2 - 4ac < 0$.
- Therefore, the solutions to the above equation are

$$x = \frac{-b \pm \sqrt{b^2 - 4ac}}{2a} = \frac{-b \pm \sqrt{4ac - b^2}i}{2a}$$

- **Fundamental Theorem of Algebra:**
  "A polynomial equation has at least one root."
- As a consequence of this theorem, the following result, which is of immense importance, is arrived at:

"A polynomial equation of degree n has n roots."

Supplementary Notes of NCERT

Square-root of a Complex Number

♦   Here we explain the particular procedure for finding square root of a complex number $a + ib$ expressed in the standard form.

♦   Let a complex number $z = x + iy$,

$$x + iy = \sqrt{a + ib} \qquad \qquad \text{... (i)}$$

♦   **Step 1:** Find square of the above equation (i),
$a + ib = (x + iy)^2 = x^2 - y^2 + i2xy$

♦   **Step 2:** Equating real and imaginary parts, we have
$$x^2 - y^2 = a \qquad \qquad \text{... (ii)}$$
and $2xy = b$

♦   **Step 3:** Use the expansion given below,
$(x^2 + y^2)^2 = (x^2 - y^2)^2 + 4x^2y^2 = a^2 + b^2$
Since $x^2 + y^2$ is positive,

$$x^2 + y^2 = \sqrt{a^2 + b^2} \qquad \qquad \text{... (iii)}$$

♦   **Step 4:** Solving equations (ii) & (iii), we get

$$x = \pm\sqrt{\frac{\sqrt{a^2 + b^2} + a}{2}} \; ; y = \pm\sqrt{\frac{\sqrt{a^2 + b^2} - a}{2}}.$$

♦   **Step 5:** Check the sign dependency of x and y due to the variation in sign of b.
Since $2xy = b$, it is clear that both x and y will have the same sign when b is positive, and x and y have different signs when b is negative.

Therefore, $\sqrt{a + ib} = \pm\left(\sqrt{\dfrac{|z| + a}{2}} + i\dfrac{b}{|b|}\sqrt{\dfrac{|z| - a}{2}}\right),$

where $b \neq 0$. $(\because \operatorname{Re}(z) \leq |z|)$

Past Years ONE-LINERS
JEE Main/Board

♦ To find the number of real roots of an equation,

$$f(x) = ax^n + bx^{n-1} + \ldots + cx + d = 0$$

Find $f'(x) = 0$, with the help of $f'(x)$ check where the slope is changing and with the help of this, draw the graph where the curve intersects x-axis at various points.

♦ Complex number, $z = x + iy$

Then, Rationalize the given complex number,

$$z = x + iy = \frac{a+ib}{c+id} \times \frac{c-id}{c-id}$$

Compare both the sides & determine the values of x and y to identify the given curve.

♦ For a quadratic equation, $ax^2 + bx + c = 0$

Roots $= \alpha, \beta$; $\alpha + \beta = -b/a$; $\alpha\beta = c/a$

$$\tan(\alpha + \beta) = \frac{\tan\alpha + \tan\beta}{1 - \tan\alpha\tan\beta}$$

♦ For an equation,

$$y(y-a) = |y-b| + |y-c| \quad c > b$$

Case :I When $y > c$, if $D < 0$, No real roots will be obtained.

Case :II When $b \le y \le c$

Case :III When $y \le b$

♦ For a given complex number z,
Use the property of conjugate complex number,
$$z + \bar{z} = 0$$

♦ For a quadratic equation,

$$ax^2 + bx + c = 0 \; ; \text{Roots} = \alpha, \beta$$

Roots of quadratic equation always satisfies the quadratic equation.

$$\therefore \; a\alpha^2 + b\alpha + c = 0 \text{ and}$$

$$a\beta^2 + b\beta + c = 0$$

♦ For a quadratic equation, $ax^2 + bx + c = 0$

Roots $= \alpha, \beta$; $\alpha + \beta = -\,b/a$, $\alpha\beta = c/a$

For function to be greatest, $f'(x) = 0$, $f''(x) < 0$

$|\alpha^3 - \beta^3| = |(\alpha - \beta)(\alpha^2 + \alpha\beta + \beta^2)|$

♦ When $K = \dfrac{a + bz}{c + dz} \Rightarrow$ calculate z,

Use the value of z in $|z| > t$ (OR) $|Z| < t$

$z\bar{z} = |z|^2$

♦ For equation, $x^2 - x + 1 = 0$

$\alpha = -\,\omega$, $\beta = -\,\omega^2$ & $\omega^2 + \omega + 1 = 0$

where $\omega = \dfrac{-1 + \sqrt{3}i}{2}$, $\omega^2 = \dfrac{-1 - \sqrt{3}i}{2}$

♦ $1 + 1 + 1 + \; .... + n$ times $= n$

$1 + 3 + 5 + 7 + \; .... + 2n - 1 = n^2$

$1.2 + 2.3 + 3.4 + \; .... + (n - 1)n = \dfrac{(n-1)n(n+1)}{3}$

Two consecutive solutions $= \alpha, \alpha + 1$

Property of quadratic equations,

$$\alpha + \beta = \dfrac{-b}{a} \text{ and } \alpha\beta = \dfrac{c}{a}$$

♦ Solution of quadratic equation,

$ax^2 + bx + c = 0$; solutions $\alpha, \beta = \dfrac{-b \pm \sqrt{D}}{2a}$

$D = b^2 - 4ac$

For $(ax^2 + bx + c)^{(dx^2 + ex + f)} = K$

Case :I $ax^2 + bx + c = K$ and $dx^2 + ex + f$ can be any real number $\Rightarrow$ find value of x

Case :II $ax^2 + bx + c = -\,K$ and $dx^2 + ex + f$ has to be an even number $\Rightarrow$ find value of x

Case :III $ax^2 + bx + c$ can be any real number and $dx^2 + ex + f = 0$

Rationalize the given Complex Number

$$Z = \dfrac{a + ib}{c + id} \times \dfrac{c - id}{c - id}$$

Complex number to be purely imaginary, it's real part should be zero,

$\therefore \operatorname{Re}(z) = 0$

♦ Properties of complex number,

(i) $|z^2| = |z|^2$ (ii) $z\bar{z} = |z|^2$

(iii) $|z_1 \pm z_2|^2 = |z_1|^2 + |z_2|^2 \pm 2\,\mathrm{Re}(z_1\bar{z}_2)$

(ii) $|z_1 + z_2|^2 = (z_1 + z_2)\overline{(z_1 + z_2)} = (z_1 + z_2)(\bar{z}_1 + \bar{z}_2)$

$$= |z_1|^2 + |z_2|^2 + z_1\bar{z}_2 + \bar{z}_1 z_2$$

♦ For quadratic equation in complex number.

$ax^2 + bx + c = 0$, $D < 0$ where $D = b^2 - 4ac$

Roots of the equation, $\alpha, \beta = \dfrac{-b \pm \sqrt{-D}\,i}{2a}$

When $D > 0$, $\alpha, \beta = \dfrac{-b \pm \sqrt{D}}{2a}$

Tips/Tricks/Techniques ONE-LINERS
(Exam Special)

- -

♦ **Properties of conjugate complex number**

Let $z = a + ib \Rightarrow \bar{z} = a - ib$, then

(a) $\overline{(\bar{z})} = z$ (b) $z + \bar{z} = 2a = 2\,\mathrm{Re}\,(z) =$ purely real

(c) $z - \bar{z} = 2ib = 2i\,\mathrm{Im}(z) =$ purely imaginary

(d) $z\bar{z} = a^2 + b^2 = |z|^2$ (e) $\overline{re^{i\theta}} = re^{-i\theta}$

(f) $\overline{z^n} = (\bar{z})^n$ (g) $\overline{z_1 z_2} = \bar{z}_1\, \bar{z}_2$

(h) $|z_1 + z_2|^2 = (z_1 + z_2)\,\overline{(z_1 + z_2)} = (z_1 + z_2)\,(\bar{z}_1 + \bar{z}_2)$

$$= |z_1|^2 + |z_2|^2 + z_1\,\bar{z}_2 + \bar{z}_1\, z_2$$

(i) $z + \bar{z} = 0$ or $z = -\bar{z} \Rightarrow z = 0$ or z is purely imaginary

(j) $z = \bar{z} \Rightarrow z$ is purely real

(k) $z_1\bar{z}_2 + z_2\bar{z}_1 = 2\,\mathrm{Re}(z_1 \cdot z_2)$

♦ **Properties of modulus of a complex number**

(a) $|z| \geq 0$ and $|z| = 0$ if and only if $z = 0$, i.e., $x = 0, y = 0$

(b) $-|z| \leq \mathrm{Re}\,(z) \leq |z|$ (c) $-|z| \leq \mathrm{Im}(z) \leq |z|$

(d) $|z| = |\bar{z}| = |-z| = |-\bar{z}|$ (e) $z\bar{z} = |z|^2$

(f) $|z^2| = |z|^2$ or $|z^n| = |z|^n$, $n \in N$

also $|z_1 z_2 \ldots\ldots z_n| = |z_1|\,|z_2|\ldots\ldots\ldots|z_n|$

(g) $|z| = 1 \Leftrightarrow \bar{z} = \dfrac{1}{z}$ (h) $z^{-1} = \dfrac{\bar{z}}{|z|^2}$

(i) $|z_1 \pm z_2| \leq |z_1| + |z_2|$ (j) $|z_1 - z_2| \geq ||z_1| - |z_2||$

(k) $|z_1 + z_2| \geq ||z_1| - |z_2||$

(l) $|z_1 + z_2|^2 + |z_1 - z_2|^2 = 2(|z_1|^2 + |z_2|^2)$

(m) $|re^{i\theta}| = r$

(n) $|z_1 \pm z_2|^2 = |z_1|^2 + |z_2|^2 \pm 2\mathrm{Re}\left(z_1 \bar{z}_2\right)$

♦ **Properties of argument of a complex number**

(a) arg (any real positive number) $= 0$

(b) arg (any real negative number) $= \pi$

(c) $\arg(z - \bar{z}) = \pm \pi/2$

(d) $\arg(z_1 \cdot z_2) = \arg(z_1) + \arg(z_2)$

(e) $\arg\left(\dfrac{z_1}{z_2}\right) = \arg(z_1) - \arg(z_2)$

(f) $\arg(\bar{z}) = -\arg(z) = \arg(1/z)$

(g) $\arg(-z) = \arg(z) \pm \pi$

(h) $\arg(z^n) = n \arg(z)$

(i) $\arg(iy) = \begin{cases} \dfrac{\pi}{2}, & \text{if } y > 0 \\[2mm] -\dfrac{\pi}{2} & \text{if } y < 0 \end{cases}$

(j) $\arg(z) + \arg(\bar{z}) = 0$

♦ **Distance formula :** Let $z_1 = x_1 + iy_1$ and $z_2 = x_2 + iy_2$ be two complex numbers represented by points P and Q respectively in Argand Plane, then

$$PQ = \sqrt{(x_2 - x_1)^2 + (y_2 - y_1)^2} = |(x_2 - x_1) + i(y_2 - y_1)| = |z_2 - z_1|$$

♦ **Section formula :** If the line segment joining A (z_1) and B (z_2) is divided by the point P (z) internally in the ratio $m_1 : m_2$ then

$$z = \frac{m_1 z_2 + m_2 z_1}{m_1 + m_2}$$

But if P divides AB externally in the ratio $m_1 : m_2$, then

$$z = \frac{m_1 z_2 - m_2 z_1}{m_1 - m_2}$$

If P is mid point of AB, then $z = \dfrac{z_1 + z_2}{2}$

♦ **Area of a triangle :** Area of triangle ABC with vertices A (z_1), B (z_2) and C (z_3)

is given by $\quad \Delta = \dfrac{1}{4} \begin{Vmatrix} z_1 & \overline{z}_1 & 1 \\ z_2 & \overline{z}_2 & 1 \\ z_3 & \overline{z}_3 & 1 \end{Vmatrix}$

or $\quad \Delta = \dfrac{1}{4}\left| z_1(\overline{z}_2 - \overline{z}_3) - z_2(\overline{z}_1 - \overline{z}_3) + z_3(\overline{z}_1 - \overline{z}_2) \right|$

♦ **Equation of a circle :** The equation of a circle with centre z_0 and radius r is
$|z - z_0| = r$
The general equation of a circle is $z\overline{z} + a\overline{z} + \overline{a}z + b = 0$, where a is a complex
number and b is real number.

♦ **Euler's form of complex number:**
$e^{i\theta} = \cos\theta + i\sin\theta$ and $e^{-i\theta} = \cos\theta - i\sin\theta$

♦ **Demoivre's theorem**

(a) If n is any integer then
$$(\cos\theta + i\sin\theta)^n = \cos n\theta + i\sin n\theta$$

(b) $(\cos\theta_1 + i\sin\theta_1)(\cos\theta_2 + i\sin\theta_2)\ldots\ldots(\cos\theta_n + i\sin\theta_n)$
$$= \cos(\theta_1 + \theta_2 + \theta_3 + \ldots + \theta_n) + i\sin(\theta_1 + \theta_2 + \theta_3 + \ldots + \theta_n)$$

(c) If $p, q \in I$ and $q \neq 0$ then

$$(\cos\theta + i\sin\theta)^{p/q} = \cos\left(\frac{2k\pi + p\theta}{q}\right) + i\sin\left(\frac{2k\pi + p\theta}{q}\right)$$

where $k = 0, 1, 2, 3,\ldots\ldots\ldots, q-1$

♦ **Cube roots of unity**

$$\omega = -\frac{1}{2} + \frac{i\sqrt{3}}{2} \quad \text{then its square}$$

$$\omega^2 = -\frac{1}{2} - \frac{i\sqrt{3}}{2} \quad \text{and vice-versa}$$

Here $(1)^{1/3} = 1, \omega, \omega^2$ and $1 + \omega + \omega^2 = 0$, $\omega^3 = 1$
1 is called real root of unity ω and ω^2 are called complex roots of unity.

♦ **Condition for common roots**
Only one root common : For the two given equations
$a_1 x^2 + b_1 x + c_1 = 0$ and $a_2 x^2 + b_2 x + c_2 = 0$ then
The condition for only one Root common is
$(c_1 a_2 - c_2 a_1)^2 = (b_1 c_2 - b_2 c_1)(a_1 b_2 - a_2 b_1)$

Both roots are common : Required condition is $\dfrac{a_1}{a_2} = \dfrac{b_1}{b_2} = \dfrac{c_1}{c_2}$

♦ **Nature of the factors of the quadratic expression**
For $ax^2 + bx + c = 0$ the factors are
(a) Real and different, if $b^2 - 4ac > 0$

(b) Rational and different, if $b^2 - 4ac$ is a prefect square.

(c) Real and equal, if $b^2 - 4ac = 0$

(d) Imaginary, if $b^2 - 4ac < 0$

♦ The square root of i is $\pm \left(\dfrac{1+i}{\sqrt{2}} \right)$ (Here $b = 1$)

♦ The square root of $-i$ is $\pm \left(\dfrac{1-i}{\sqrt{2}} \right)$ (Here $b = -1$)

♦ $\arg z_1 - \arg z_2 = \arg \left(\dfrac{z_1}{z_2} \right)$

♦ If z_1, z_2, z_3 are collinear, which implies $\theta = 0$, therefore, $\dfrac{z_3 - z_1}{z_2 - z_1}$ is purely real.

♦ If z_1, z_2, z_3 are such that $PR \perp PQ$, which implies $\theta = \pi/2$, so $\dfrac{z_3 - z_1}{z_2 - z_1}$ is purely imaginary.

♦ Demoivore's theorem is not valid when n is not a rational number or the complex number is not in the form of $\cos \theta + i \sin \theta$ i.e.,

$$\left(\cos \theta + i \sin \theta \right)^{\sqrt{5}} \neq (\cos \sqrt{5}\theta + i \sin \sqrt{5}\,\theta)$$

$(\sin\theta + i \cos\theta)^n \neq \sin n\theta + i \cos n\theta$

♦ Cube root of unity are the vertices of an equilateral triangle.

♦ If $n = 4$ the fourth roots of unity are $(1)^{1/4} = \pm 1, \pm i$

♦ Fourth root of unity are vertices of a square which lies on coordinate axes.

♦ **Maximum and minimum value of quadratic expression**

In a quadratic expression $ax^2 + bx + c$

(a) If $a > 0$, quadratic expression has least value at $x = -\dfrac{b}{2a}$.

This least value is given by $\dfrac{4ac - b^2}{4a} = -\dfrac{D}{4a}$

(b) If $a < 0$, quadratic expression has greatest value at $x = -\dfrac{b}{2a}$.

This greatest value is given by $\dfrac{4ac - b^2}{4a} = -\dfrac{D}{4a}$

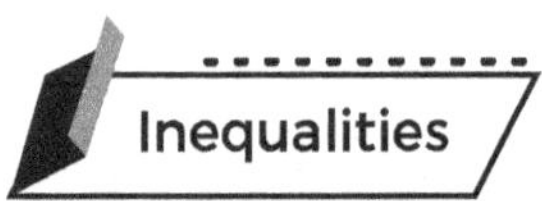

6 Linear Inequalities

Inequalities

- Two real numbers or two algebraic expressions related by the symbol '<', '>', '≤' or '≥' form an **inequality**.
- Inequalities having no variables are called numerical inequalities e.g. $3 < 5, 8 > 6$.
- Inequalities having variables are called literal inequalities e.g. $x < 5$; $y > 2$.
- Inequalities having symbols '>' or '<' are strict inequlities.
- Inequalities with symbols '≥' or '≤' are called slack inequlities.

Rules for Solving Linear Inequalities in One Variable :

- The values of the variable, which makes an inequality a true statement are called solutions of the inequality.

  Rule 1: Equal numbers may be added to (or subtracted from) both sides of an inequality without changing its sign.

  Rule 2: Both sides of an inequality can be multiplied (or divided) by the same positive number without changing its sign.

  However, on multiplying both sides by a negative number, the sign of inequality is reversed.

- $ax + by > c$ type inequation is called linear inequalities in two variables x and y, when $a \neq 0$, $b \neq 0$.
- $ax^2 + bx + c \geq 0$ type inequation is called a quadratic inequalities in one variable x, when $a \neq 0$.

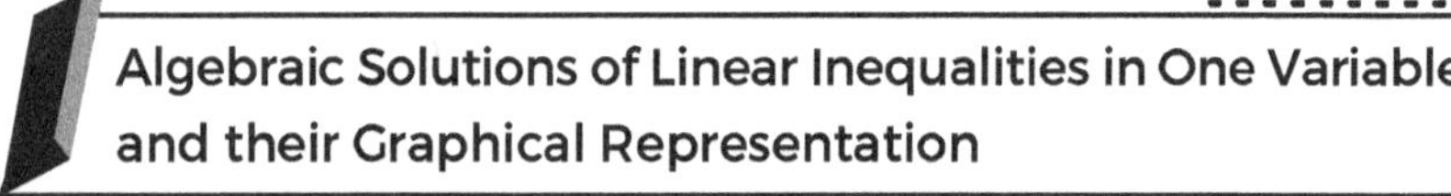

Algebraic Solutions of Linear Inequalities in One Variable and their Graphical Representation

- Any solution of an inequality in one variable is a value of the variable which makes it a true statement.
- **Rule 1:** Equal numbers may be added to (or subtracted from) both sides of an inequality without affecting the sign of inequality.
- **Rule 2:** Both sides of an inequality can be multiplied (or divided) by the same positive number. But when both sides are multiplied or divided by a negative number, then the sign of inequality is reversed.

Graphical Solution of Linear Inequalities in Two Variables

- We know that a line divides the Cartesian plane into two parts. Each part is known as a half plane.
- A vertical line will divide the plane in left and right half planes and a non-vertical line will divide the plane into lower and upper half planes.

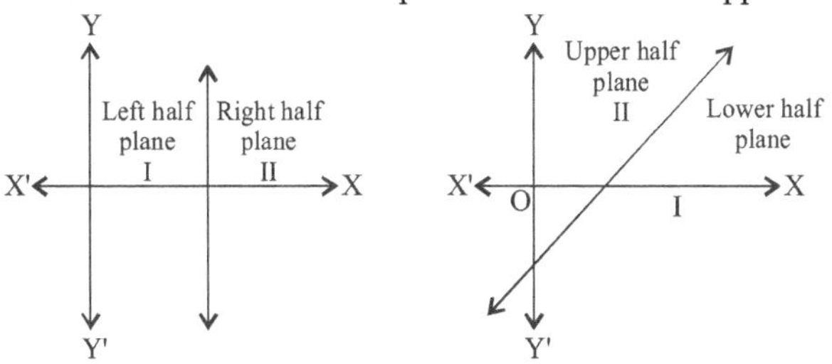

- A point in the Cartesian plane will either lie on a line or will lie in either of the half planes I or II.
- The region containing all the solutions of an inequality is called the solution region.
- In order to identify the half plane represented by an inequality, it is just sufficient to take any point (a, b) (not on line) and check whether it satisfies the inequality or not. If it satisfies, then the inequality represents the half plane and shade the region which contains the point, otherwise, the inequality represents that half plane which does not contain the point within it. For convenience, the point $(0, 0)$ is preferred.
- Let us now examine the relationship, if any, of the points in the plane and the inequalities $ax + by < c$ or $ax + by > c$. Let us consider the line $ax + by = c$, $a \neq 0, b \neq 0$.
- If an inequality is of the type $ax + by \geq c$ or $ax + by \leq c$, then the points on the line $ax + by = c$ are also included in the solution region. So draw a dark line in the solution region.
- If an inequality is of the form $ax + by > c$ or $ax + by < c$, then the points on the line $ax + b = c$ are not to be included in the solution region. So draw a broken or dotted line in the solution region.

Solution of System of Linear Inequalities in Two Variables

- Solving two or more linear inequalities in two variables x and y is called a system of linear inequalities in two variables.
- By solving inequalities we get a solution set which may be the region enclosed by straight lines or may be unbounded or may be empty set.
- The values of x, which make an inequality a true statement, are called solutions of the inequality.

- To represent $x < a$ (or $x > a$) on a number line, put a circle on the number a and dark line to the left (or right) of the number a.
- To represent $x \le a$ (or $x \ge a$) on a number line, put a dark circle on the number a and dark the line to the left (or right) of the number x.
- If an inequality is having $\le$ or $\ge$ symbol, then the points on the line are also included in the solutions of the inequality.
- If an inequality is having $<$ or $>$ symbol, then the points on the line are not included in the solutions of the inequality.
- The solution region of a system of inequalities is the region which satisfies all the given inequalities in the system simultaneously.

Past Years ONE-LINERS
JEE Main/Board

- For getting real roots, make $D \ge 0$. Thus, $b^2 - 4ac \ge 0$

Tips/Tricks/Techniques ONE-LINERS
(Exam Special)

- If $a, b \in R$ and $b \ne 0$, then

  (a) $ab > 0$ or $\dfrac{a}{b} > 0 \Rightarrow a$ and b are of the same sign.

  (b) $ab < 0$ or $\dfrac{a}{b} < 0 \Rightarrow a$ and b are of opposite sign.

- If a is any positive real number, $i.e.$, $a > 0$, then

  (a) $|x| < a \Leftrightarrow -a < x < a$

  $\quad |x| \le a \Leftrightarrow -a \le x \le a$

  (b) $|x| > a \Leftrightarrow x < -a \ \text{or} \ x > a$

  $\quad |x| \ge a \Leftrightarrow x \le -a \ \text{or} \ x \ge a$

- If 'a' be a positive real constant, then

  (a) $x^2 \le a^2 \quad \Leftrightarrow \quad |x| \le a \quad i.e., \quad -a \le x \le a$

  (b) $x^2 \ge a^2 \quad \Leftrightarrow \quad |x| \ge a \quad i.e., \quad x \le -a, x \ge a$

  (c) $x^2 < a^2 \quad \Leftrightarrow \quad |x| < a \quad i.e., \quad -a < x < a$

  (d) $x^2 > a^2 \quad \Leftrightarrow \quad |x| > a \quad i.e., \quad x < -a, x > a$

♦ If a is positive real number, x and y be the fixed real numbers, then

(a) $|x - y| < a \iff y - a < x < y + a$

(b) $|x - y| \le a \iff y - a \le x \le y + a$

(c) $|x - y| > a \iff x > y + a$ or $x < y - a$

(d) $|x - y| \ge a \iff x \ge y + a$ or $x \le y - a$

♦ An inequality of the form $\log_a f(x) > b$ is equivalent to the following systems of inequalities :

(a) $f(x) > 0, f(x) > a^b$ for $a > 1$

(b) $f(x) > 0, f(x) < a^b$ for $a < 1$.

♦ $\log_a x = \log_b x \Rightarrow a = b$ or $x = 1$

♦ $\log_c b = \dfrac{\log_a b}{\log_a c}$

♦ $\log_b a = \dfrac{1}{\log_a b}$

♦ To remove the denominator of an expression of an inequality it cannot be multiplied by denominator as its value may be positive or may be negative. We multiply the expression by the square of denominator as it is always positive. On multiplication of an inequality by a positive number the sign of inequality does not change.

♦ Triangle inequality :

(a) $|x + y| \le |x| + |y|, \ \forall \ x, y \in R$

(b) $|x - y| \ge |x| - |y|, \ \forall \ x, y \in R$

♦ $\log_a x > \log_a y \Rightarrow \begin{cases} x < y \text{, if } a > 1 \\ x > y \text{, if } 0 < a < 1 \end{cases}$

♦ $A = \dfrac{a + b}{2}, \quad G = \sqrt{ab}, \quad H = \dfrac{2ab}{a + b}$

♦ A.M. $\ge$ G.M. $\ge$ H.M

♦ Weighted A.M. $\ge$ Weighted G.M. $\ge$ Weighted H.M

7 Permutations and Combinations

- Fundamental principle of counting is also known as **Multiplication principle**.
- **Principle for 2 Events :** "If an event can occur in m different ways, following which another event can occur in n different ways, then the total number of occurrence of the events in the given order is m×n."
- **Principle for 3 Events :** "If an event can occur in m different ways, following which another event can occur in n different ways, following which a third event can occur in p different ways, then the total number of occurrence to 'the events in the given order is m × n × p."
- Hence, The Fundamental principle of counting can be generalised for any finite number of events.

- **Permutations :** A **permutation** is an arrangement in a definite order of a number of objects taken some or all at a time.
- In Permutation, Order of objects is very important.

Permutations when all the objects are distinct:

- **Theorem 1 :** The number of permutations of n different objects taken r at a time, Where $0 < r \leq n$ and the objects do not repeat is $n(n - 1)(n - 2) \ldots (n - r + 1)$, which is denoted by ^nP_r.

Factorial Notation

- The notation n! represents the product of first n natural numbers, i.e., the product
  $1 \times 2 \times 3 \times \ldots \times (n - 1) \times n$ is denoted as n!
  We read this symbol as 'n factorial'.
  Thus, $1 \times 2 \times 3 \times 4 \ldots \times (n - 1) \times n = n!$
- $1 = 1!, 1 \times 2 = 2!, 1 \times 2 \times 3 = 3!, 1 \times 2 \times 3 \times 4 = 4!$
  and so on.
  We define $0! = 1$
- We can write $5! = 5 \times 4! = 5 \times 4 \times 3! = 5 \times 4 \times 3 \times 2!$
  $= 5 \times 4 \times 3 \times 2 \times 1!$
- Clearly, for a natural number n
  $n! = n(n - 1)!$
  $= n(n - 1)(n - 2)!$ [provided $(n \geq 2)$]
  $= n(n - 1)(n - 2)(n - 3)!$ [provided $(n \geq 3)$] and so on.

Derivation of the formula for $^n\mathrm{P}_r$

$$^n\mathrm{P}_r = \frac{n!}{(n-r)!}, 0 \le r \le n$$

- In particular, when r = n,

$$^n\mathrm{P}_n = \frac{n!}{0!} = n!$$

- When r = 0,

$$^n\mathrm{P}_0 = \frac{n!}{(n-0)!} = \frac{n!}{n!} = 1$$

- **Theorem 2**: The number of permutations of n different objects taken r at a time, where repetition is allowed, is n^r.

Permutations when all the objects are not distinct objects:

- **Theorem 3 :** The number of permutations of n objects, where p objects are of the same kind and rest are all different $= \dfrac{n!}{p!}$.

- **Theorem 4 :** The number of permutations of n objects, where p_1 objects are of one kind, p_2 are of second kind, ..., p_k are of kth kind and the rest, if any, are of different kind is $\dfrac{n!}{p_1! p_2! \ldots p_k!}$.

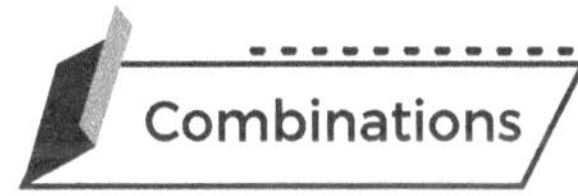

- **Combinations :** A **combination** is a selection in an indefinite order of a number of objects taken some or all at a time.
  In combination, order of objects is not important.
- The number of combinations of n different objects taken r at a time, denoted by

$$^nC_r = \frac{n!}{r!(n-r)!}, 0 \le r \le n$$

$$^n\mathrm{P}_r = {}^nC_r\, r!, \ 0 < r \le n$$

- **Theorem 5 :** In a particular, When r = n,

$$^nC_n = \frac{n!}{n!0!} = 1$$

  When r = 0,

$$^nC_0 = \frac{n!}{0!(n-0)!} = 1$$

- Selecting r objects out of n objects is same as rejecting (n − r) objects,

$$^nC_{n-r} = \frac{n!}{(n-r)!(n-(n-r))!} = \frac{n!}{(n-r)!r!} = {}^nC_r$$

- When Selection of a and b objects out of n objects are equal, Then
$$^nC_a = {}^nC_b \Rightarrow a = b \text{ or } a = n - b, \text{ i.e., } n = a + b$$

- **Theorem 6 :** The sum of selecting r and r−1 objects is equal to the selection of r objects out of n objects,
$$^nC_r + {}^nC_{r-1} = {}^{n+1}C_r$$

Past Years ONE-LINERS
JEE Main/Board

- Formulae of ^nP_r and ^nC_r are used,

$$^nP_r = \frac{n!}{(n-r)!}, \quad ^nC_r = \frac{n!}{r!(n-r)!}$$

- Digit '0' should not be placed at the first place. This should be kept in mind while Forming n-digit number because putting '0' at first place, It will convert n digit number into $(n-1)$ digits.
- Fundamental Principle of counting is used for m and n objects, Number of ways for them is decided by multiplication principle $= m \times n$
- When r objects are selected from n objects, then combinations of the objects $= {}^nC_r$
  When p_1 objects of 1st kind, p_2 objects of 2nd kind are arranged out of m objects.

  Then permutations of the objects $= \dfrac{m!}{p_1!p_2!}$

  $\therefore$ Total number of ways $= {}^nC_r \times \dfrac{m!}{p_1!p_2!}$

- Selection of objects based on combinations $= {}^nC_r$ and using the Addition principle for different cases. Thus, Total ways $= {}^nC_r \times$ sum of cases
- Selection of objects is based on combinations $= {}^nC_r$. Arrangement of objects is based on permutations $= m!$
  Thus complete problem is based on permutation and combination, then total ways $= {}^nC_r \times m!$
- Combination will be used to find the number of ways $= {}^nC_r$.
  Then use principle of Addition to find the total ways.
- For finding the number of ways of Letters as in dictionary. Then arrange all the letters according to dictionary first. Then fixing the first letter and find number of words formed with the corresponding letters. Thus, position of the word can be identified which is starting from some specific letter.
- Number of ways to arrange n objects $= n!$
  If m cases are also possible to arrange the n objects. Then total ways $= m \times n!$

Tips/Tricks/Techniques ONE-LINERS
(Exam Special)

- -

- **Principle of Addition:** If an event can be performed in m ways and there is another event which is independent of the other events, can be performed in n ways, then either of the two events can be performed in (m + n) ways.
- Number of permutations of n things taking r at a time, when a particular object is to be always included in each $= r. \, ^{n-1}P_{r-1}$.
- Number of permutations of n things taking r at a time, when a particular object is never taken in any arrangement $= \, ^{n-1}P_r$.
- Number of permutations of n different things taking all at a time, when m specified things always come together $= m!(n-m+1)!$.
- Number of permutations of n different things taking all at a time, when m specified things never come together $= n! - m!(n-m+1)!$
- Number of permutations of n different things taking r at a time, in which two specified objects always occur together $= 2! \, (r-1) \, ^{n-2}P_{r-2}$
- **Arrangement round a circular table :**
  The number of circular permutations of n different things taken all at a time is $(n-1)!$, if clockwise and anticlockwise orders are taken as different.
- **Arrangement of beads or flowers (all different) around a circular necklace or garland :**
  The number of circular permutations of n different things taken all at a time is $\dfrac{1}{2}(n-1)!$, if clockwise and anticlockwise orders are taken as not different.
- Number of combinations of n distinct things taking r $(\leq n)$ at a time, when k $(0 \leq k \leq r)$ particular objects always occur $= \, ^{n-k}C_{r-k}$.
- Number of combinations of n distinct objects taking $r(\leq n)$ at a time, when $k\,(0 \leq k \leq r)$ particular objects never occur $= \, ^{n-k}C_r$.
- Number of selections of r things from n things when p particular things are not together in any selection $= \, ^nC_r - \, ^{n-p}C_{r-p}$
- **Number of circular permutations of n different things taken r at a time :**
  Case - I : If clockwise and anticlockwise orders are taken as different, then the required number of circular permutations $= \dfrac{^nP_r}{r}$.

Case- II : If clockwise and anticlockwise orders are taken as not different, then the required number of circular permutations $= \dfrac{^n P_r}{2r}$.

- Number of selection or r consecutive things out of n things in a row $= n - r + 1$.
- Number of selection of r consecutive things out of n things along a circle

$$= \begin{cases} n, & \text{when } r < n \\ 1, & \text{when } r = n \end{cases}$$

- Number of selection of r things $(r \le n)$ out of n identical things $= 1$.
- Number of selection of zero or more things out of n identical things $= n + 1$.
- Number of selection of one or more things out of n identical things $= n$.
- If there are n points in a plane of which m $(< n)$ are collinear, then
  - (a) Total number of different straight lines obtain by joining these n points is $^nC_2 - \,^mC_2 + 1$.
  - (b) Total number of different triangles formed by joining these n points is $^nC_3 - \,^mC_3$.
- Given n points on the circumference of a circle, then
  - (a) Number of straight lines $= \,^nC_2$
  - (b) Number of triangles $= \,^nC_3$
  - (c) Number of quadrilaterals $= \,^nC_4$
- Number of diagonals in polygon of n sides is $^nC_2 - n$

  $i.e.\ \dfrac{n(n-3)}{2}$.

- If m parallel lines in a plane are intersected by a family of other n parallel lines. Then total number of parallelograms so formed is $^mC_2 \times \,^nC_2$ $i.e$

  $$\dfrac{mn(m-1)n-1)}{4}.$$

- For given n different digits $a_1, a_2, a_3, ..., a_n$ the sum of the digits at unit place of all numbers formed (if numbers are not repeated) is $(a_1 + a_2 + a_3 + ... + a_n)(n-1)!$

  $i.e.$ (sum of the digits) $(n-1)!$

- Sum of the total numbers which can be formed with given n different digits $a_1, a_2, ..., a_n$ is

  $(a_1 + a_2 + a_3 + ...+ a_n)(n-1)! . (111 ....n$ times$)$

- **Derangement Theorem :**

  If n items are arranged in a row, then the number of ways in which they can be deranged so that no one of them occupies the place assigned to it is

  $$n!\left[1 - \dfrac{1}{1!} + \dfrac{1}{2!} - \dfrac{1}{3!} + \dfrac{1}{4!} - \cdots + (-1)^n \dfrac{1}{n!}\right]$$

8 Binomial Theorem

Binomial Theorem for Positive Integral Indices

- An expression consisting of two terms is called Binomial expression.
  e.g. $(a + b)$, $(3x + 5)$ $(x - 3y)$ etc

Let us see some observations:

$$(a + b)^0 = 1$$
$$(a + b)^2 = a^2 + 2ab + b^2$$
$$(a + b)^4 = a^4 + 4a^3b + 6a^2b^2 + 4ab^3 + b^4$$

Conclusions:

- The total number of terms in the expansion is one more than the index.
- Power of the first quantity 'a' go on decreasing by 1 whereas the powers of the second quantity b in crease by 1, in the successive terms.
- In each term of the expansion, the sum of the indices of a and b is the same and is equal to the index of a + b.

Arrangement of the coefficients look like:

Index	Coefficient
0	1
1	1 1
2	1 2 1
3	1 3 3 1

Note: This array of numbers is known as Pascal's triangle. It is also known as Meru prastara by Pingla.

- These coefficients can be arranged as

$$^0C_0(=1)$$
$$^1C_0(=1) \qquad ^1C_1(=1)$$
$$^2C_0(=1) \quad ^2C_1(=0) \qquad ^2C_2(=1)$$
$$^3C_0(=1) \qquad ^3C_1(=3) \qquad ^3C_2(=3) \qquad ^3C_3(=1)$$

Binomial theorem for any positive integer n.

$$(a + b)^n = {}^nC_0\, a^n + {}^nC_1 a^{n-1}b + {}^nC_2 a^{n-2} b^2 + \ldots + {}^nC_{n-1} a.b^{n-1} + {}^nC_n b^n$$

Important observations

- The notation $\displaystyle\sum_{K=0}^{n} {}^nC_k\, a^{n-k}b^k$ stands for

$${}^nC_0 a^n b^0 + {}^nC_1 a^{n-1} b^1 + \; .... \; + {}^nC_r a^{n-r} b^r + \; .... \; + {}^nC_n a^{n-n} b^n,$$

Where $b^0 = 1 = a^{n-n}$

Hence the theorem can also be stated as

$$(a+b)^n = \sum_{K=0}^{n} {}^nC_k \, a^{n-k} b^k$$

♦   The coefficients ${}^nC_r$ are known as binomial coefficients.

Some Special Expansions:

♦ $(x-y)^n = {}^nC_0 x^n(-y)^0 + {}^nC_1 \, x^{n-1}(-y) + {}^nC_2 x^{n-2}(-y)^2 + \; ... \; + \; ..... \; + {}^nC_n(-y)^n$

      $= {}^nC_0 x^n - {}^nC_1 x^{n-1}y + {}^nC_2 x^{n-2} y^2 + \; .... \; +(-1)^n \; {}^nC_n y^n$

♦ $(1+x)^n = {}^nC_0 + {}^nC_1 x + {}^nC_2 x^2 + \; ... \; + {}^nC_n x^n$

      In particular, for $x = 1$ we have

      $2^n = {}^nC_0 + {}^nC_1 + {}^nC_2 + \; ..... \; {}^nC_n$

♦ $(1-x)^n = {}^nC_0 - {}^nC_1 x + {}^nC_2 x^2 \; ..... \; + (-1)^n \; {}^nC_n x^n.$

      In particular, for $x = 1$ we get

      $0 = {}^nC_0 - {}^nC_1 + {}^nC_2 \; .... \; + (-1)^n \; {}^nC_n$

♦ ${}^nC_0 + {}^nC_2 + {}^nC_4 + \; ...... \; = {}^nC_1 + {}^nC_3 + {}^nC_5 + \; .... \; = 2^{n-1}$

General and Middle Terms

General Term

♦   In the binomial expansion for $(a + b)^n$. The $(r + 1)^{\text{th}}$ term is called the general term of the expansion $(a + b)^n$.

♦   It is denoted by T_{r+1}. Thus $T_{r+1} = {}^nC_r a^{n-r} b^r$.

Middle Term

In the expansion $(a + b)^n$, we have

♦   If n is even, then the number of terms in the expansion will be $n + 1$. Since n is even so $n + 1$ is odd. Therefore, the middle term is $\left(\dfrac{n+1+1}{2}\right)^{\text{th}}$, i.e., $\left(\dfrac{n}{2}+1\right)^{\text{th}}$ term.

♦   If n is odd, then $n + 1$ is even, so there will be two middle terms in the expansion, namely, $\left(\dfrac{n+1}{2}\right)^{\text{th}}$ term and $\left(\dfrac{n+1}{2}+1\right)^{\text{th}}$ term.

- In the expansion of $\left(x+\dfrac{1}{x}\right)^{2n}$, where $x \neq 0$, the middle term is $\left(\dfrac{2n+1+1}{2}\right)^{th}$, i.e., $(n+1)^{th}$ term, as $2n$ is even.

It is given by $^{2n}C_n x^n \left(\dfrac{1}{x}\right)^n = {}^{2n}C_n$ (constant).

This term is called the term independent of x or the constant term.

<table>
<tr><td>

Independent Term

In the expansion of $\left(x+\dfrac{1}{x}\right)^{2n}$, where $x \neq 0$, the middle

term is $\left(\dfrac{2n+1+1}{2}\right)^{th}$, i.e., $(n+1)^{th}$ term, as $2n$ is even.

It is given by $^{2n}C_n x^n \left(\dfrac{1}{x}\right)^n = {}^{2n}C_n$ (constant)

This term is called term independent of x or the constant term. So, Independent term is the term in binomial expansion whose power of x is zero.

</td></tr>
</table>

Past Years ONE-LINERS
JEE Main/Board

- To get any number divisible by $x + a$ (used concept) $\Rightarrow x^n + a^n$ is divisible by $x + a$, where n is odd.

- To final general term (used concept) $\boxed{T_{r+1} = {}^n C_r \cdot x^{n-r}.a^r}$

- To sum of the given series like a. $^nC_0 + (a+3).\,{}^nC_1 + + ... + (a+60).\,{}^nC_n$ (used concept) $\boxed{\displaystyle\sum_{r=0}^{n}(3r+a).\,{}^nC_r}$

- To make expression simpler (used concept) take rationalization

$$\boxed{\dfrac{1}{\sqrt{x}+\sqrt{a}} \Rightarrow \dfrac{\sqrt{x}-\sqrt{a}}{\left(\sqrt{x}+\sqrt{a}\right)\left(\sqrt{x}-\sqrt{a}\right)}}$$

- For getting remainder (used concept): $x^n \div a$ break $x \Rightarrow \{(a-1)+1\}^n$ or $\{(a+1)-1\}^n$ then divide by a

- Coefficients of three successive terms (used concept) $\dfrac{{}^{n}C_{r}}{a} = \dfrac{{}^{n}C_{r+1}}{7} = \dfrac{{}^{n}C_{r+2}}{42}$

- Sum of odd terms in Binomial expansion (used concept)

$$(a+b)^{n} + (a-b)^{n} = 2[\,{}^{n}C_{0}\,a^{n}b^{0} + {}^{n}C_{2}\,a^{n-2}b^{2} + {}^{n}C_{4}a^{n-4}b^{4} + ...]$$

Tips/Tricks/Techniques ONE-LINERS
(Exam Special)

- **Number of terms in the expansion of $(x+y+z)^{n}$**

$$= \frac{(n+1)(n+2)}{2}$$

  (a) Number of terms in the expansion of
  $$(a+b+c+d)^{n} = \frac{(n+1)(n+2)(n+3)}{6}$$

  (b) The number of distinct terms in the expansion of $(x_{1} + x_{2} + x_{3} + ... x_{r})^{n}$ is given by ${}^{n+r-1}C_{r-1}$

- **Numerically greatest term in the expansion of $(x+a)^{n}$**
  Let T_{r+1} be the greatest term in $(x+a)^{n}$

  Then $\dfrac{T_{r+1}}{T_{r}} \geq 1$ and $\dfrac{T_{r+2}}{T_{r+1}} \leq 1 \quad \Rightarrow r \leq \dfrac{n+1}{\left|\dfrac{x}{a}\right|+1} - 1$

- **Binomial theorem for any index**
  When n is a negative integer or a fraction then the expansion of a binomial is possible only when
  (a) Its first term is 1, and
  (b) Its second term is numerically less than 1.
  This means that when $n \notin N$ and $|x| < 1$, then

  $$(1+x)^{n} = 1 + nx + \frac{n(n-1)}{2!}x^{2} + \frac{n(n-1)(n-2)}{3!}x^{3}$$

  $$+ .... + \frac{n(n-1)(n-r+1)}{r!}x^{r} + ...$$

  General term : $T_{r+1} = \dfrac{n(n-1)(n-2)........(n-r+1)}{r!}\,x^{r}$

- $(a+b)^{n} + (a-b)^{n} = 2[{}^{n}C_{0}a^{n} + {}^{n}C_{2}a^{n-2}b^{2} + {}^{n}C_{4}a^{n-4}b^{4} + ...]$

- $(a+b)^n - (a-b)^n = 2[{}^nC_1 a^{n-1}b + {}^nC_3 a^{n-3}b^3 + {}^nC_5 a^{n-5}b^5 + ...]$

- ${}^nC_0 + {}^nC_1 + {}^nC_2 + ... + {}^nC_n = 2^n$

- ${}^nC_0 + {}^nC_2 + ... = {}^nC_1 + {}^nC_3 + ... = 2^{n-1}$

- ${}^{2n+1}C_0 + {}^{2n+1}C_1 + ... {}^{2n+1}C_n = 2^{2n}$

- $C_0 C_r + C_1 C_{r+1} + ... + C_{n-r} C_n = {}^{2n}C_{n-r}$

- $C_0^2 + C_1^2 + C_2^2 + ... + C_n^2 = \dfrac{2n!}{n!\,n!}$

- $C_0 C_1 + C_1 C_2 + ... + C_{n-1} C_n = {}^{2n}C_{n-1}$

- $C_0 C_2 + C_1 C_3 + ... + C_{n-2} C_n = {}^{2n}C_{n-2}$

- **Greatest binomial coefficients**

  In a binomial expansion binomial coefficients of the middle terms are called as greatest binomial coefficients.

  (a) **If n is even :** ${}^nC_{n/2}$ takes maximum value.

  (b) **If n is odd :** Both ${}^nC_{\frac{n-1}{2}}$ and ${}^nC_{\frac{n+1}{2}}$ take maximum value.

- **Algorithm to find numerically greatest term :**

  Step I : Calculate $\dfrac{n+1}{\left|\dfrac{x}{a}\right|+1} = k$ (say)

  Step II : (a) If k is an integer than T_k and T_{k+1} are the numerically greatest term.

          (b) If k is not an integer. Let m is its greatest integral part then T_{m+1} is the numerically greatest term.

9. Sequences and Series

Sequences

- We denote the terms of a sequence by a_1, a_2, a_3, ..., a_n, ..., etc., the subscripts denote the position of the term.
- The nth term is the number at the nth position of the sequence and is denoted by a_n. The nth term is also called **the general term of the sequence**.
- **Finite Set :** A sequence containing finite number of terms is called a **finite sequence**. e.g. 2, 4, 8, 16, 32, ..., 1024. (i.e., Fixed number of terms = 10).
- **Infinite Set :** A sequence containing number of terms that never ends is called **infinite sequence**.
  e.g. 3, 3.3, 3.33, 3.333, ... and so on. (i.e. No fixed number of terms)
- In some cases, we see an arrangement which follows a specific formula. But in some cases, we see an arrangement in which no pattern is visible, then the sequence is generated by recurrence relation is given by
  $$a_1 = a_2 = 1$$
  $$a_3 = a_1 + a_2$$
  $$a_n = a_{n-2} + a_{n-1}, n > 2$$
  This sequence is called **Fibonacci sequence**.
- In the sequences, we find that there is no formula for the nth term. Such sequence can only be described by verbal description.
- In every sequence, we should not expect that its terms will necessarily be given by a specific formula.

Series

- **Series :** Let a_1, a_2, a_3, ..., a_n, be a given sequence. Then, the expression $a_1 + a_2 + a_3 + ...+ a_n$ is called the **series** associated with the given sequence.
- The series is finite or infinite according as the given sequence is finite or infinite.
- Series is often represented in compact form, called sigma notation, using the Greek letter Σ (sigma) as means of indicating the summation involved. Thus, the series $a_1 + a_2 + a_3 + ... + a_n$ is abbreviated as $\sum_{k=1}^{n} a_k$.

- When the series is used, it refers to the indicated sum not to the sum itself. For example, $1 + 3 + 5 + 7$ is a finite series with four terms. When we use the phrase "sum of a series," we will mean the number that results from adding the terms, the sum of the series is 16.

Arithmetic Progression

- **Arithmetic Progression :** A sequence $a_1, a_2, a_3, \ldots, a_n$, is called **arithmetic sequence** or **arithmetic progression** if $a_{n+1} = a_n + d, n \in N$ where a_1 is called the **first term** and the constant term d is called the **common difference** of the A.P.
- Let us consider an A.P. (in its standard form) with first term a and common difference d, i.e., $a, a + d, a + 2d, \ldots$ Then the nth term (general term) of the A.P. is $a_n = a + (n - 1)d$.
- The properties of an A.P. :
    (i)   If a constant is added to each term of an A.P., the resulting sequence is also an A.P.
    (ii) If a constant is subtracted from each term of an A.P., the resulting sequence is also an A.P.
    (iii) If each term of an A.P. is multiplied by a constant, then the resulting sequence is also an A.P.
    (iv) If each term of an A.P. is divided by a non-zero constant then the resulting sequence is also an A.P.
- The notations used for an arithmetic progression:
    a = the first term, l = the last term, d = common difference, n = the number of terms.
    S_n = the sum to n terms of A.P.
    Let $a, a + d, a + 2d, \ldots, a + (n - 1)d$ be an A.P. Then
    $l = a + (n - 1)d$
- Sum of an arithmetic progression is given as,

$$S_n = \frac{n}{2}[2a + (n-1)d]$$

We can also write, $S_n = \frac{n}{2}[a + l]$

Arithmetic Mean (A.M) :
- **Arithmetic Mean :** Given two numbers a and b. We can insert a number A between them so that a, A, b is an A.P. Such a number A is called the **arithmetic mean (A.M.)** of the numbers a and b.

Note that, in this case, we have $A - a = b - A$, i.e., $A = \dfrac{a+b}{2}$

- Generally, given any two numbers a and b, we can insert as many numbers as we like between them such that the resulting sequence is an A.P

♦ Let $A_1, A_2, A_3, ..., A_n$ be n numbers between a and b such that $a, A_1, A_2, A_3,$ ....., A_n, b is an A.P.

Here, b is the $(n + 2)^{th}$ term, i.e., $b = a + [(n + 2) - 1]d = a + (n + 1)d$.

This gives $d = \dfrac{b-a}{n+1}$.

♦ Thus, n numbers between a and b are as follows :

$$A_1 = a + d = a + \dfrac{b-a}{n+1}$$

$$A_2 = a + 2d = a + \dfrac{2(b-a)}{n+1}$$

$$A_3 = a + 3d = a + \dfrac{3(b-a)}{n+1}$$

$$\begin{matrix} ..... & ..... & ..... & ..... \\ ..... & ..... & ..... & ..... \end{matrix}$$

$$A_n = a + nd = a + \dfrac{n(b-a)}{n+1}$$

Geometric Progression

♦ **Geometric Progression :** A sequence in which every term except the first term bears a constant ratio to the term immediately preceding it is known as **geometric sequence** or **geometric progression** abbreviated as G.P.

♦ A sequence $a_1, a_2, a_3, ..., a_n, ...$ is called geometric progression, if each term is non-zero and $\dfrac{a_{k+1}}{a_k} = r$ (constant), for $k \geq 1$.

♦ By letting $a_1 = a$, we obtain a geometric progression,

$a, ar, ar^2, ar^3, ...$ where a is called the **first term** and r is called the **common ratio** of the G.P.

♦ The notations used in geometric progression are :

a = the first term, r = the common ratio, l = the last term,

n = the numbers of terms, S_n = the sum of first n terms.

General term of G.P. :

♦ Let us consider a G.P. with first non-zero term 'a' and common ratio 'r'. Write a few terms of it. The second term is obtained by multiplying a by r, thus $a_2 = ar$. Similarly, third term is obtained by multiplying a_2 by r. Thus, $a_3 = a_2r = ar^2$, and so on.

♦ Therefore, the pattern suggests that the nth term of a G.P. is given by $a_n = ar^{n-1}$. Thus, a, G.P. can be written as $a, ar, ar^2, ar^3, ..., ar^{n-1}; a, ar, ar^2, ..., ar^{n-1}....$ according as G.P. is finite or infinite, respectively.

♦ The series $a + ar + ar^2 + ... + ar^{n-1}$ or $a + ar + ar^2 + ... + ar^{n-1} + ...$ are called **finite** or **infinite geometric series**, respectively.

Sum to n terms of a G.P. :

♦　　Let the first term of a G.P. be a and the common ratio be r. Let us denote S_n by the sum to first n terms of G.P. Then

$$S_n = a + ar + ar^2 + ... + ar^{n-1} \qquad ..... \text{(i)}$$

Case 1 : If $r = 1$, we have

$$S_n = a + a + a + ... + a\ (n \text{ terms}) = na$$

Case 2 : If $r \neq 1$, multiplying (i) by r, we have

$$rS_n = ar + ar^2 + ar^3 + ... + ar^n \qquad .... \text{(ii)}$$

Subtracting (ii) from (i), we get $(1 - r)S_n = a - ar^n = a\ (1 - r^n)$

This gives　$S_n = \dfrac{a(1 - r^n)}{1 - r}$　or　$S_n = \dfrac{a(r^n - 1)}{r - 1}$

Geometric Mean (G.M.) :

♦　　**Geometric Mean:** The geometric mean of two positive numbers a and b is the number $\sqrt{ab}$.

♦　　Given any two positive numbers a and b, we can insert as many numbers as we like between them to make the resulting sequence in a G.P.

♦　　Let $G_1, G_2, ..., G_n$ be n numbers between positive numbers a and b such that $a, G_1, G_2, G_3,....., G_n, b$ is a G.P. Thus, b being the $(n + 2)^{\text{th}}$ term, we have

$$b = ar^{n+1}\ \text{ or }\ r = \left(\frac{b}{a}\right)^{\frac{1}{n+1}}$$

Hence,　$G_1 = ar = a\left(\frac{b}{a}\right)^{\frac{1}{n+1}}, G_2 = ar^2 = a\left(\frac{b}{a}\right)^{\frac{2}{n+1}},$

$$G_3 = ar^3 = a\left(\frac{b}{a}\right)^{\frac{3}{n+1}}$$

$$G_n = ar^n = a\left(\frac{b}{a}\right)^{\frac{n}{n+1}}$$

Supplementary Material of NCERT :

Infinite G.P. and its Sum :

♦　　**Infinite G.P. :** G.P. of the form $a, ar, ar^2, ar^3, ...$ is called infinite G.P.

♦　　Now, for a geometric progression, $a, ar, ar^2, ar^3, ...$ if numerical value of common ratio r is less than 1, then

$$S_n = \frac{a(1 - r^n)}{(1 - r)} = \frac{a}{1 - r} - \frac{ar^n}{1 - r}$$

♦　　In this case as, $n \to \infty$, $r^n \to 0$ since $|\,r\,| < 1$. Therefore

$$S_n \to \frac{a}{1 - r}$$

- Symbolically sum to infinity is denoted by S_∞ or S.

  Thus, we have $S = \dfrac{a}{1-r}$.

Relationship between A.M. and G.M.

- Let A and G be A.M. and G.M. of two given positive real numbers a and b, respectively. Then

$$A = \frac{a+b}{2} \text{ and } G = \sqrt{ab}$$

- Thus, we have

$$A - G = \frac{a+b}{2} - \sqrt{ab} = \frac{a+b-2\sqrt{ab}}{2}$$

$$= \frac{(\sqrt{a}-\sqrt{b})^2}{2} \geq 0 \qquad \qquad ..... (i)$$

From (i), we obtain the relationship $A \geq G$.

Sum to n Terms of Special Series

- Sum of first n natural numbers,

$$S_n = 1+2+3+.....+n = \frac{n(n+1)}{2}$$

- Sum of squares of the first n natural numbers,

$$S_n = 1^2 + 2^2 + 3^2 +.....+n^2 = \frac{n(n+1)(2n+1)}{6}$$

- Sum of cubes of the first n natural numbers,

$$S_n = 1^3 + 2^3 + 3^3 +.....+n^3 = \frac{n^2(n+1)^2}{4} = \frac{[n(n+1)]^2}{4}$$

Past Years ONE-LINERS
JEE Main/Board

- Three terms a_1, a_2 and a_3 are in A.P.,

  $\therefore \quad 2a_2 = a_1 + a_3$

- Sum of n terms of G.P., $S_n = \dfrac{a(r^n - 1)}{r - 1} = \displaystyle\sum_{k=1}^{n} a_k$

- When 5 terms are in A.P., then terms are $a - 2d, a - d, a, a + d, a + 2d$

- $S_n = 1^2 + 2^2 + 3^2 + ... + n^2 = \displaystyle\sum_{k=1}^{n} k^2 = \dfrac{n(n+1)(2n+1)}{6}$

  $S_n = \displaystyle\sum_{k=1}^{n} t_n = \sum_{k=1}^{n}(ak^2 + bk + c) = a\sum_{k=1}^{n} k^2 + b\sum_{k=1}^{n} k + c\sum_{k=1}^{n} 1$

- For the conditions $\displaystyle\sum_{k=1}^{n} f(a+k)$ and $f(x+y) = f(x).f(y)$.

  Assume $f(x)$ according to the above conditions satisfying for all the values of x and y.

- For the sequence $a_1, a_2, a_3, a_4, ... a_n$ are in A.P.

  Sum of n terms of A.P., $S_n = \displaystyle\sum_{k=1}^{n} a_n = \dfrac{n}{2}[a_1 + a_n]$

- Three terms are in G.P. $\Rightarrow q^2 = pr$ (i.e., p, q and r)

  Sum of n terms in G.P. $\Rightarrow S_n = \dfrac{a(r^n - 1)}{r - 1}$

- Sum of square of odd terms $= \displaystyle\sum_{k=1}^{n}(2k - 1)^2$

  Sum of square of even terms $= \displaystyle\sum_{k=1}^{n}(2k)^2$

- General term of A.P. $\Rightarrow a_n = a_1 + (n-1)d$

  Sum of n terms of A.P. $\Rightarrow S_n = \dfrac{n}{2}[2a_1 + (n-1)d]$

  Assume a_k term according to the given condition and sum of a_k terms will give the desired solution.

- $f(x) = ax^2 + bx + c, f(x+y) = f(x) + f(y) + xy.$

  Put the values of x & y and find all the terms according to $\displaystyle\sum_{n=1}^{k} a_n$. Then find the sum of a_n terms.

- For the three terms p, q and r, in A. P. $\Rightarrow 2q = p + r$ for G.P. $\Rightarrow q^2 = pr$

- Sum of square of n natural terms,

$$S_n = 1^2 + 2^2 + 3^2 + ... + n^2 = \frac{n(n+1)(2n+1)}{6}$$

  Generate a_k term & sum of a_k terms will give the desired solution.

- Non-constant A.P. $\Rightarrow$ common difference d will be other than zero constant A.P. $\Rightarrow d = 0$

  when sequence is in G.P., it follows

  $a_n = a_1 r^{n-1}$

  when sequence is in A.P., it follows

  $a_n = a_1 + (n-1)d$

- A.M. of two numbers a & $b \Rightarrow$ A.M. $= \dfrac{a+b}{2}$ when $G_1, G_2, G_3, ..., G_n$ are

  geometric means between a & b, then $G_n = ar^n = a\left(\dfrac{b}{a}\right)^{\frac{n}{n+1}}$

- Sum of cube of n natural terms, $S_n = 1^3 + 2^3 + 3^3 + ... + n^3 = \dfrac{n^2(n+1)^2}{4}$.

  Sum of odd terms, $S_n = \displaystyle\sum_{k=1}^{n} (2k-1)$

Tips/Tricks/Techniques ONE-LINERS
(Exam Special)

- -

♦ For Arithmetic Progression,
  (i) Any three numbers are in A.P. can be taken as
  $a - d, a, a + d$
  (ii) Any four numbers in A.P.
  $\Rightarrow a - 3d, a - d, a + d, a + 3d$
  (iii) Any five numbers in A.P.
  $\Rightarrow a - 2d, a - d, a, a + d, a + 2d$

♦ For every sequence, it is not always possible to write a specific formula.

♦ Sum of first n odd natural numbers, $\displaystyle\sum_{r=1}^{n} (2r - 1) = n^2$

  Sum of first n even natural numbers, $\displaystyle\sum_{r=1}^{n} 2r = n\,(n + 1)$

♦ Sum of n arithmetic means $A_1, A_2, A_3, \ldots, A_n$ inserted between a and b is equal
  to n times the single A.M. between a and b i.e. $\displaystyle\sum_{r=1}^{n} A_r = nA$ where $A = \dfrac{a+b}{2}$

♦ Between any two numbers, $\dfrac{\text{sum of } m \text{ AM's}}{\text{sum of } n \text{ AM's}} = \dfrac{m}{n}$

♦ For Geometric Progression,

  (i) Three numbers in G.P. can be taken as $\dfrac{a}{r}, a, ar.$

  (ii) Four numbers in G.P. $\Rightarrow \dfrac{a}{r^3}, \dfrac{a}{r}, ar, ar^3$

  (iii) Five numbers in G.P $\Rightarrow \dfrac{a}{r^2}, \dfrac{a}{r}, a, ar, ar^2$

♦ G.M. of n positive numbers $a_1, a_2, a_3, \ldots\ldots, a_n$ is
  $(a_1 \cdot a_2 \cdot a_3 \ldots\ldots\ldots a_n)^{1/n}.$

♦ If a and b are two numbers of opposite signs, then G.M. between them does
  not exist.

◆ **Harmonic progression (H.P.)**

The sequence $\langle x_1, x_2, x_3, \ldots\ldots, x_n, \ldots\rangle$ where each $x_i \neq 0$ is said to be a harmonic progression (H.P.), if the sequence formed by the reciprocals of its terms is an A.P.

That is, the sequence $\left\langle \dfrac{1}{x_1}, \dfrac{1}{x_2}, \dfrac{1}{x_3}, \ldots\ldots, \dfrac{1}{x_n}, \ldots\ldots \right\rangle$ is an A.P.

The standard form of H.P. is $\left\langle \dfrac{1}{a}, \dfrac{1}{a+d}, \dfrac{1}{a+2d}, \ldots\ldots\ldots \right\rangle$

General term n^{th} term of a H.P. is given by

$$T_n = \frac{1}{a+(n-1)d}$$

◆ **Relations between A.M., G.M. and H.M.**

If a and b are positive numbers, then

$$A = \frac{a+b}{2}; \quad G = \sqrt{ab}; \quad H = \frac{2ab}{a+b}. \quad \text{We have}$$

(a) A.M., G.M., H.M. are in G.P., i.e. $G^2 = AH$

(b) A.M. $\geq$ G.M. $\geq$ H.M., i.e., $A \geq G \geq H$. Equality holds if and only if $a = b$

◆ **Arithmetico-geometric sequence (A.G.S.)**

If each term of a sequence is the product of the corresponding terms of an A.P. and a G.P., then it is called arithmetico-geometric sequence (A.G.S.)

e.g. $a, (a+d)r, (a+2d)r^2, \ldots\ldots$

The general term (n^{th} term) of an A.G.S. is

$$T_n = [a + (n-1)d]\, r^{n-1}$$

$$S_n = \frac{a}{1-r} + \frac{r.d\left(1 - r^{n-1}\right)}{(1-r)^2} \quad \text{and} \quad S_\infty = \frac{a}{1-r} + \frac{dr}{(1-r)^2}$$

◆ If r^{th} term of an A.P.,
$T_r = Ar^3 + Br^2 + Cr + D$, then sum of first n term of this AP,

$$S_n = \sum_{r=1}^{n} T_r = A \sum_{r=1}^{n} r^3 + B \sum_{r=1}^{n} r^2 + C \sum_{r=1}^{n} r + D \sum_{r=1}^{n} 1$$

◆ If for an A.P. ; p^{th} term is q, q^{th} term is p then m^{th} term is $= p + q - m$.

◆ If for the different A.P.'s

$$\frac{S_n}{S'_n} = \frac{f_n}{\phi_n} \quad \text{then} \quad \frac{T_n}{T'_n} = \frac{f(2n-1)}{\phi(2n-1)}$$

- If for two A.P.'s $\dfrac{T_n}{T'_n} = \dfrac{An+B}{Cn+D}$ then $\dfrac{S_n}{S'_n} = \dfrac{A\left(\dfrac{n+1}{2}\right)+B}{C\left(\dfrac{n+1}{2}\right)+D}$.

- If no. of terms n in any series is odd then only one middle term is exist which is $\left(\dfrac{n+1}{2}\right)^{\text{th}}$ term.

- If no. of terms n in any series is even then $(n/2)^{\text{th}}$ term and $\left\{\left(\dfrac{n}{2}\right)+1\right\}^{\text{th}}$ term are two middle terms, where n is even.

- Product of n GM's inserted between 'a' and 'b' is equal to n^{th} power of the single GM between 'a' and 'b' i.e.

$$\prod_{r=1}^{n} G_r = (G)^n \text{ where } G = \sqrt{ab}$$

- a, b, c are in A.P. and H.P. $\Rightarrow a, b, c$ are in G.P.

- If a, b, c are in A.P. then $\dfrac{1}{bc}, \dfrac{1}{ac}, \dfrac{1}{ab}$ are in A.P.

- If a^2, b^2, c^2 are in A.P. then $\dfrac{1}{b+c}, \dfrac{1}{c+a}, \dfrac{1}{a+b}$ are in A.P.

- If a, b, c are in G.P. then a^2, b^2, c^2 are in G.P.

- If a, b, c, d are in G.P. then $a+b, b+c, c+d$ are in G.P.

- If a, b, c are in H.P. then $\dfrac{b+c}{a}, \dfrac{c+a}{b}, \dfrac{a+b}{c}$ are in A.P.

- **Sum of series by method of difference**

  Sometimes, the nth term of a series cannot be determined by the methods discussed so far. If a series is such that the difference between successive terms are either in A.P. or in G.P., then we determine its nth term by the method of difference and then find the sum of the series by using the formulas for Σn, Σn^2, and Σn^3.

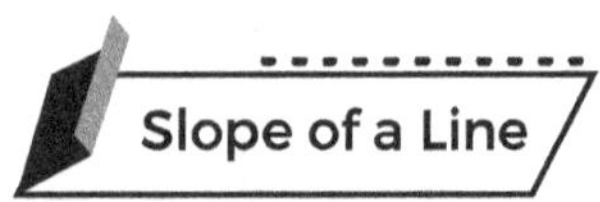

Slope of a Line

- A line in a coordinate plane forms two angles with the x-axis, which are supplementary.
- **Inclination of Line:** The angle (say) θ made by the line l with positive direction of x-axis and measured anti clockwise is called **the inclination of the line**. Obviously $0° \leq \theta \leq 180°$.

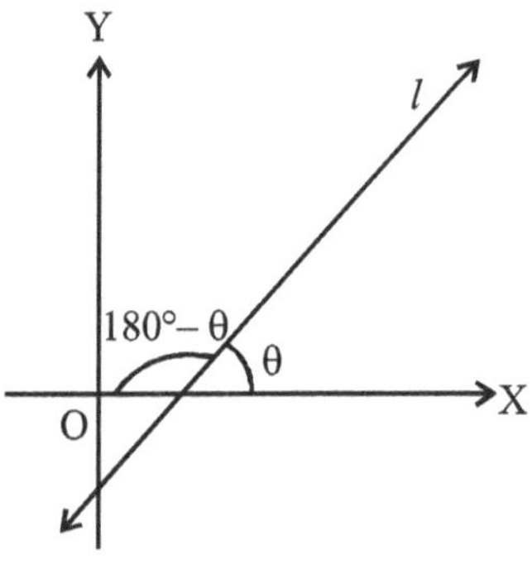

- We observe that lines parallel to x-axis, or coinciding with x-axis, have inclination of $0°$. The inclination of a vertical line (parallel to or coinciding with y-axis) is $90°$.
- **Slope:** If θ is the inclination of a line l, then $\tan \theta$ is called the slope or gradient of the line l.
- The slope of a line whose inclination is $90°$ is not defined. The slope of a line is denoted by m. Thus, $m = \tan \theta$ and $\theta \neq 90°$.
- It may be observed that the slope of x-axis is zero and slope of y-axis is not defined.

Slope of a line when coordinates of any two points on the line are given :

- We know that a line is completely determined when we are given two points on it.
- Let $P(x_1, y_1)$ and $Q(x_2, y_2)$ be two points on non-vertical line l whose inclination is θ.
  The inclination of the line l may be acute or obtuse.

♦ **Case-1:** When angle θ is acute,

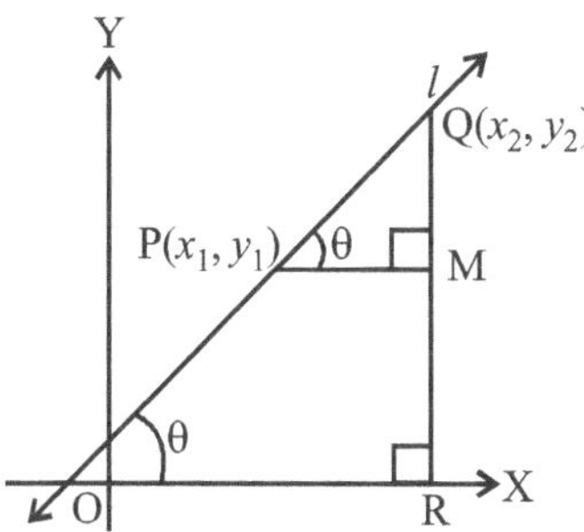

In Figure, $\angle MPQ = \theta$. ... (i)
Therefore, slope of line $l = m = \tan\theta$.

But in $\angle MPQ$, we have $\tan\theta = \dfrac{MQ}{MP} = \dfrac{y_2 - y_1}{x_2 - x_1}$ ...(ii)

From equations (i) and (ii), we have $m = \dfrac{y_2 - y_1}{x_2 - x_1}$

♦ **Case-2:** When angle θ is obtuse,
In Figure, we have $\angle MPQ = 180° - \theta$.
Therefore, $\theta = 180° - \angle MPQ$.
Now, slope of the line l
$m = \tan\theta = \tan(180° - \angle MPQ) = -\tan\angle MPQ$

$= -\dfrac{MQ}{MP} = -\dfrac{y_2 - y_1}{x_1 - x_2} = \dfrac{y_2 - y_1}{x_2 - x_1}$

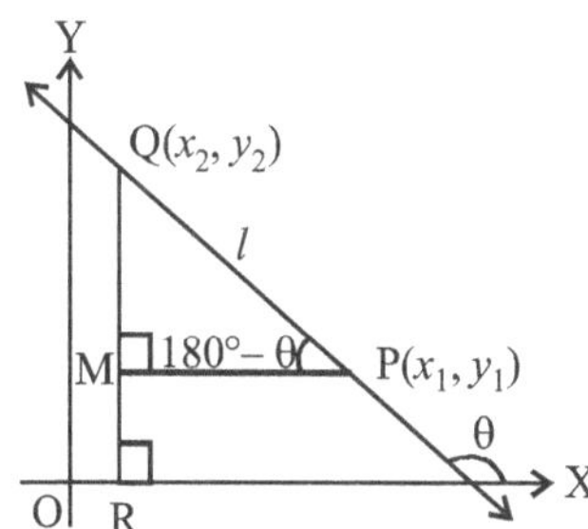

♦ Consequently, we see that in both the cases the slope m of the line through

the points (x_1, y_1) and (x_2, y_2) is given by $m = \dfrac{y_2 - y_1}{x_2 - x_1}$.

Conditions for parallelism and perpendicularity of lines in terms of their slopes:

♦ In a coordinate plane, suppose that non-vertical lines l_1 and l_2 have slopes m_1 and m_2, respectively & their inclinations be α and β, respectively.

♦ **Parallelism :** If the line l_1 is parallel to l_2, then their inclinations are equal, i.e., $\alpha = \beta$, and hence, $\tan \alpha = \tan \beta$. Therefore $m_1 = m_2$, i.e., their slopes are equal.

♦ Conversely, if the slope of two lines l_1 and l_2 is same, i.e., $m_1 = m_2$. Then $\tan \alpha = \tan \beta$.

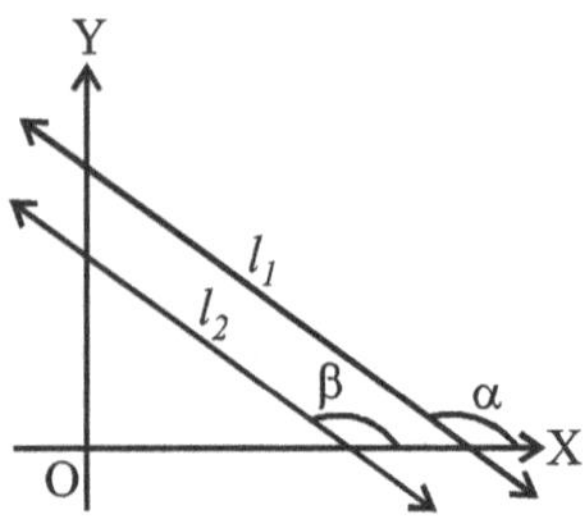

♦ **Perpendicularity:** If the lines l_1 and l_2 are perpendicular, then $\beta = \alpha + 90°$. Therefore, $\tan \beta = \tan (\alpha + 90°)$

$$= -\cot \alpha = -\frac{1}{\tan \alpha}$$

i.e., $m_2 = -\dfrac{1}{m_1}$ or $m_1 m_2 = -1$

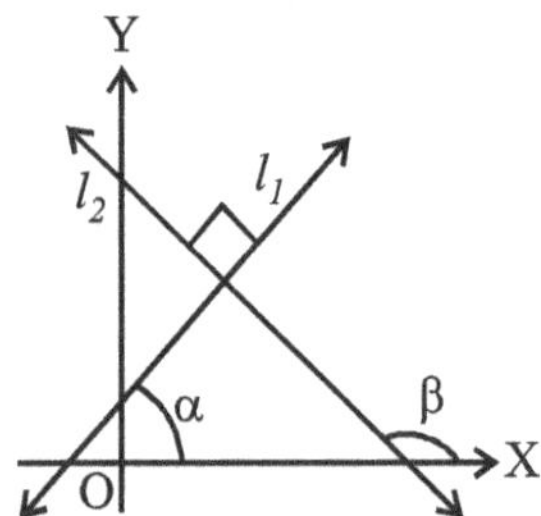

♦ Conversely, if $m_1 m_2 = -1$, i.e., $\tan \alpha \tan \beta = -1$.

Angle between two lines :

♦ Let l_1 and l_2 be two non-vertical lines with slopes m_1 and m_2, respectively. If α_1 and α_2 are the inclinations of lines l_1 and l_2, respectively. Then,
$$m_1 = \tan \alpha_1 \text{ and } m_2 = \tan \alpha_2.$$

♦ When two lines intersect each other, they make two pairs of vertically opposite angles such that sum of any two adjacent angles is $180°$.

♦ Let θ and ϕ be the adjacent angles between the lines l_1 and l_2 .Then,
$\theta = \alpha_2 - \alpha_1$ and $\alpha_1, \alpha_2 \neq 90°$.

Therefore,

$$\tan \theta = \tan (\alpha_2 - \alpha_1) = \frac{\tan \alpha_2 - \tan \alpha_1}{1 + \tan \alpha_1 \tan \alpha_2} = \frac{m_2 - m_1}{1 + m_1 m_2} \text{ (as } 1 + m_1 m_2 \neq 0)$$

$$\tan \phi = \tan (180° - \theta) = -\tan \theta - \frac{m_2 - m_1}{1 + m_1 m_2}, \text{ (as } 1 + m_1 m_2 \neq 0)$$

and $\phi = 180° - \theta$ so that

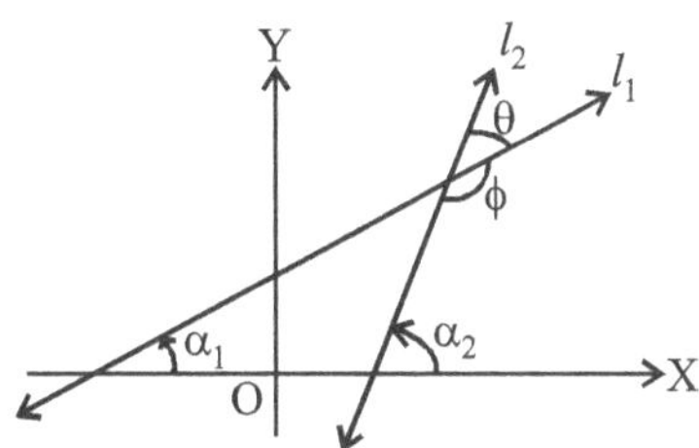

♦ Now, there arise two cases:

♦ **Case-1:** If $\dfrac{m_2 - m_1}{1 + m_1 m_2}$ is positive, then tan θ will be positive and tan ϕ will be negative, which means θ will be acute and ϕ will be obtuse.

♦ **Case-2:** If $\dfrac{m_2 - m_1}{1 + m_1 m_2}$ is negative, then tan θ will be negative and tan ϕ will be positive, which means that θ will be obtuse and ϕ will be acute.

Thus, the acute angle (say θ) between lines l_1 and l_2 with slopes m_1 and m_2, respectively, is given by

$$\tan \theta = \left| \frac{m_2 - m_1}{1 + m_1 m_2} \right|, \text{ as } 1 + m_1 m_2 \neq 0$$

♦ The obtuse angle (say ϕ) can be found by using $\phi = 180° - \theta$.

Collinearity of three points :

♦ Three points A,B and C are **collinear** if and only if
Slope of AB = Slope of BC.

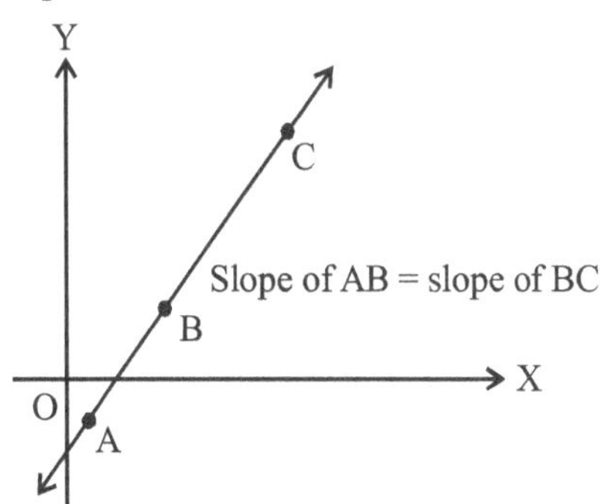

Various Forms of the Equation of a Line

Horizontal and vertical lines :

- If a horizontal line L is at a distance a from the x-axis then coordinate of every point lyingon the line is either a or $-a$. Therefore, equation of the line L is either $y = a$ or $y = -a$.

- Similarly, If a vertical line L is at a distance b from the y-axis then equation of the line L is
either $x = b$ or $x = -b$.

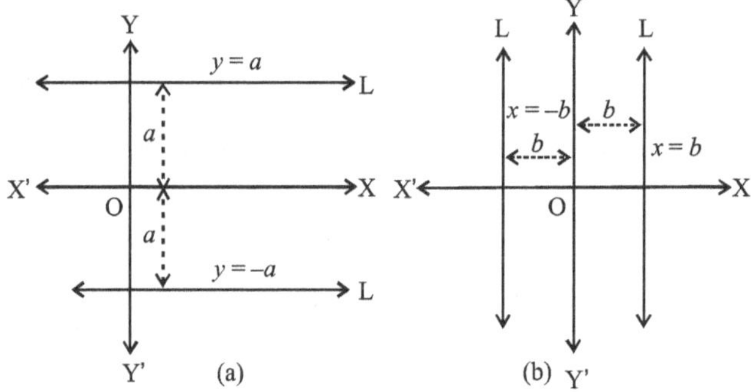

Point-Slope Form :

- Suppose that $P_0(x_0, y_0)$ is a fixed point on a non-vertical line L, whose slope is m.

- Let P (x, y) be an arbitrary point on line L. Then, by the definition, the slope of Line L is given by

$$m = \frac{y - y_0}{x - x_0}, \text{ i.e., } y - y_0 = m(x - x_0)$$

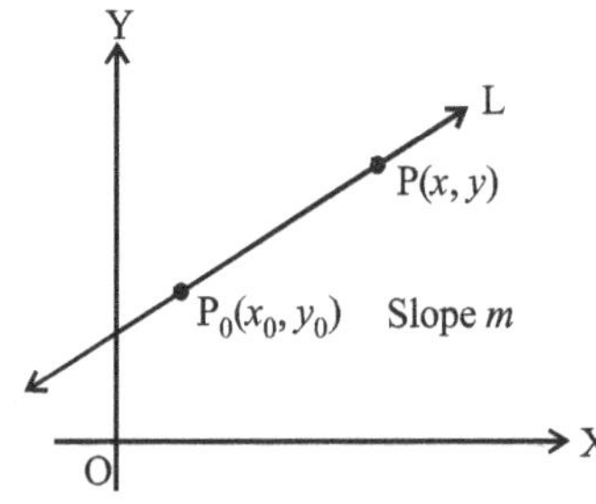

Two-Point Form :

- Let the line L passes through two given points $P_1(x_1, y_1)$ and $P_2(x_2, y_2)$.

- Let P (x, y) be a general point on L. Three Points P_1, P_2 and P are collinear, therefore, we have slope of P_1

$$P = \text{slope of } P_1 P_2 \quad \text{i.e.,} \quad \frac{y - y_1}{x - x_1} = \frac{y_2 - y_1}{x_2 - x_1}$$

♦ Thus, equation of the line passing through the points (x_1, y_1) and (x_2, y_2) is given by

$$y - y_1 = \frac{y_2 - y_1}{x_2 - x_1}(x - x_1)$$

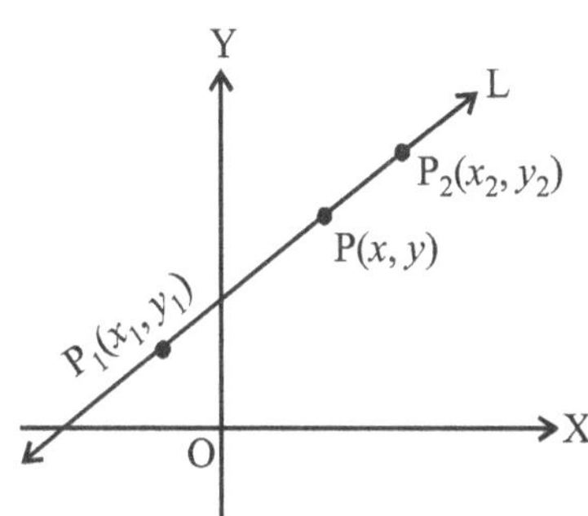

Slope-Intercept Form :

♦ Sometimes a line is known to us with its slope and an intercept on one of the axes.

♦ **Case-1:** Suppose a line L with slope m cuts the y-axis at a distance c from the origin,

The distance c is called the y intercept of the line L. Obviously, coordinates of the point where the line meet the y-axis are (0, c).

Thus, L has slope m and passes through a fixed point (0, c). Therefore, by point-slope form, the equation of L is,

$$y - c = m(x - 0) \text{ or } y = mx + c$$

♦ Note that the value of c will be positive or negative according as the intercept is made on the positive or negative side of the y-axis, respectively.

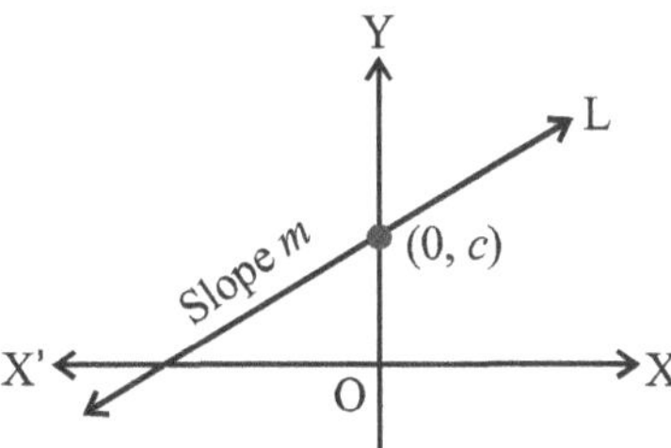

♦ **Case-2:** Suppose a line L with slope m cuts the x-axis at a distance d from the origin,

The distance d is called the x intercept of the line L. Obviously, coordinates of the point where the line meet the x-axis are (d,0).

Thus, L has slope m and passes through a fixed point $(d, 0)$. Therefore, by point-slope form, the equation of L is,
$$y = m(x - d)$$

Intercept Form :

♦ Suppose a line L makes x-intercept a and y-intercept b on the axes.

♦ Obviously L meets x-axis at the point $(a, 0)$ and y-axis at the point $(0, b)$.

♦ By two-point form of the equation of the line, we have the equation

$$y - 0 = \frac{b - 0}{0 - a}(x - a) \text{ or } ay = -bx + ab$$

♦ Thus, equation of the line making intercepts a and b on x-and y-axis, respectively, is

$$\frac{x}{a} + \frac{y}{b} = 1$$

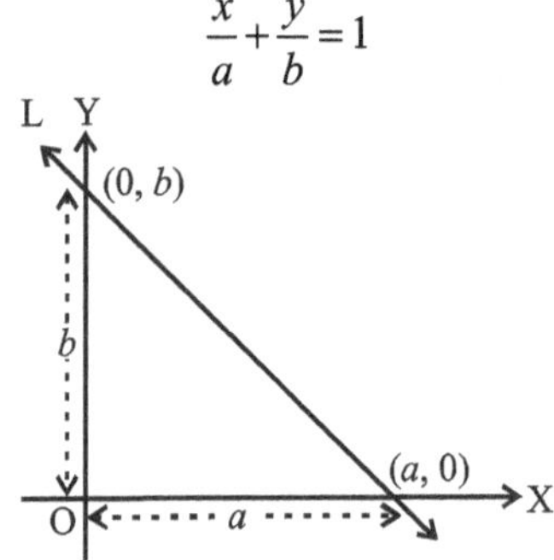

Normal Form :

♦ Suppose a non-vertical line is known to us with following data:

   (i)   Length of the perpendicular (normal) from origin to the line.

   (ii)   Angle which normal makes with the positive direction of x-axis.

♦ Let L be the line, whose perpendicular distance from origin O be OA = p and the angle between the positive x-axis and OA be $\angle$XOA = ω.

♦ The possible positions of line L in the Cartesian plane are shown in the Figure, Now, our purpose is to find slope of L and a point on it. Draw perpendicular AM on the x-axis in each case.

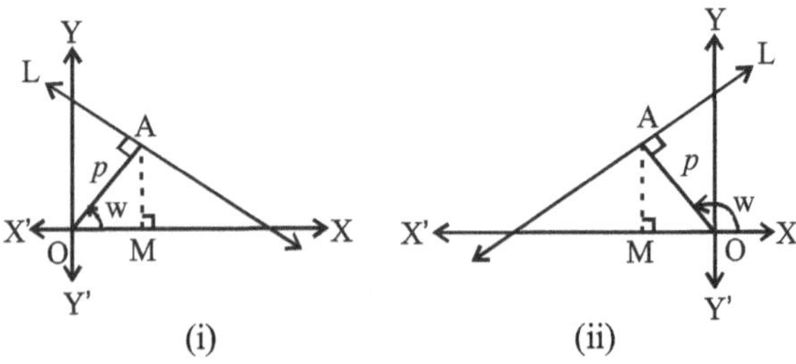

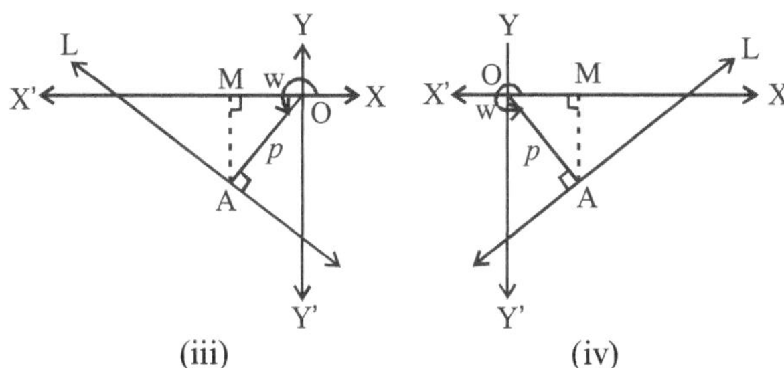

(iii)   (iv)

♦ In each case, we have OM = p cos ω and MA = p sin ω, so that the coordinates of the point A are (p cos ω, p sin ω).

♦ Further, line L is perpendicular to OA. Therefore,

$$\text{The slope of the line L} = -\frac{1}{\text{slope of OA}} = -\frac{1}{\tan\omega} = -\frac{\cos\omega}{\sin\omega}$$

♦ Thus, the line L has slope $-\dfrac{\cos\omega}{\sin\omega}$ and point A (p cos ω, p sin ω) on it.

Therefore, by point-slope form, the equation of the line L is

$$y - p\sin\omega = -\frac{\cos\omega}{\sin\omega}(x - p\cos\omega)$$

or $x\cos\omega + y\sin\omega = p(\sin^2\omega + \cos^2\omega)$

♦ Hence, the equation of the line having normal distance p from the origin and angle ω which the normal makes with the positive direction of x-axis is given by

$$x\cos\omega + y\sin\omega = p$$

General Equation of a Line

♦ Any equation of the form Ax + By + C = 0, where A and B are not zero simultaneously is called **general linear equation** or **general equation of a line**.

Different forms of Ax + By + C = 0 :

    (a)   **Slope-Intercept Form :** If B ≠ 0, then Ax + By + C = 0 can be written as

$$y = -\frac{A}{B}x - \frac{C}{B} \text{ or } y = mx + c \qquad ...(1)$$

We know that Equation (1) is the slope-intercept form of the equation of a line whose slope is $-\dfrac{A}{B}$, and y-intercept is $-\dfrac{C}{B}$.

♦ If B = 0, then $x = -\dfrac{C}{A}$, which is a vertical line whose slope is undefined & x-intercept is $-\dfrac{C}{A}$.

(b) **Intercept Form** : If $C \neq 0$, then $Ax + By + C = 0$ can be written as

$$\frac{x}{-\dfrac{C}{A}} + \frac{y}{-\dfrac{C}{B}} = 1 \text{ or } \frac{x}{a} + \frac{y}{b} = 1 \qquad \ldots(2)$$

We know that equation (2) is intercept form of the equation of a line whose

x-intercept is $-\dfrac{C}{A}$ and y-intercept is $-\dfrac{C}{B}$.

♦ If $C = 0$, then $Ax + By + C = 0$ can be written as $Ax + By = 0$, which is a line passing through the origin and, therefore, has zero intercepts on the axes.

(c) **Normal Form** : Let $x \cos \omega + y \sin \omega = p$ be the normal form of the line represented by the equation $Ax + By + C = 0$ or $Ax + By = -C$. Thus, both the equations are same and therefore,

$$\frac{A}{\cos \omega} = \frac{B}{\sin \omega} = -\frac{C}{p}$$

Which gives $\cos \omega = -\dfrac{Ap}{C}$ and $\sin \omega = -\dfrac{Bp}{C}$.

♦ Now, $\sin^2 \omega + \cos^2 \omega = \left(-\dfrac{Ap}{C}\right)^2 + \left(-\dfrac{Bp}{C}\right)^2 = 1$

Or $p^2 = \dfrac{C^2}{A^2 + B^2}$ or $p = \pm \dfrac{C}{\sqrt{A^2 + B^2}}$

Therefore $\cos \omega = \pm \dfrac{A}{\sqrt{A^2 + B^2}}$ and $\sin \omega = \pm \dfrac{B}{\sqrt{A^2 + B^2}}$

♦ Thus, the normal form of the equation $Ax + By + C = 0$ is $x\cos \omega + y \sin \omega = p$,

where $\cos \omega = \pm \dfrac{A}{\sqrt{A^2 + B^2}}$, $\sin \omega = \pm \dfrac{B}{\sqrt{A^2 + B^2}}$,

and $p = \pm \dfrac{C}{\sqrt{A^2 + B^2}}$.

Note that Proper choice of signs is made so that p should be positive.

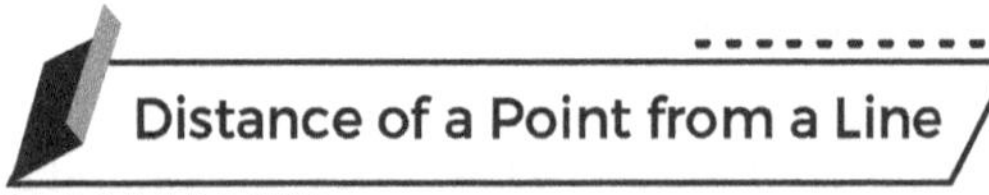

Distance of a Point from a Line

♦ The distance of a point from a line is the length of the perpendicular drawn from the point to the line.

♦ Let $L : Ax + By + C = 0$ be a line, whose distance from the point $P\ (x_1, y_1)$ is d.

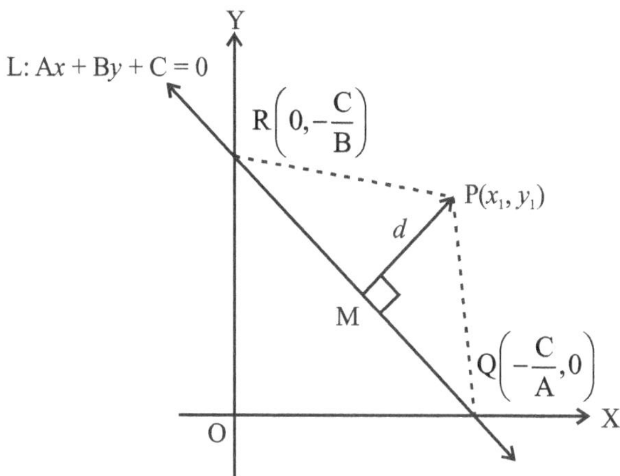

♦ The perpendicular distance (d) of a line $Ax + By + C = 0$ from a point (x_1, y_1) is given by,

$$d = \frac{|Ax_1 + By_1 + C|}{\sqrt{A^2 + B^2}}$$

Distance between two parallel lines :

♦ As we know that slopes of two parallel lines are equal. Therefore, two parallel lines can be taken in the form

$y = mx + c_1 \ldots (1)$ and $y = mx + c_2 \ldots (2)$

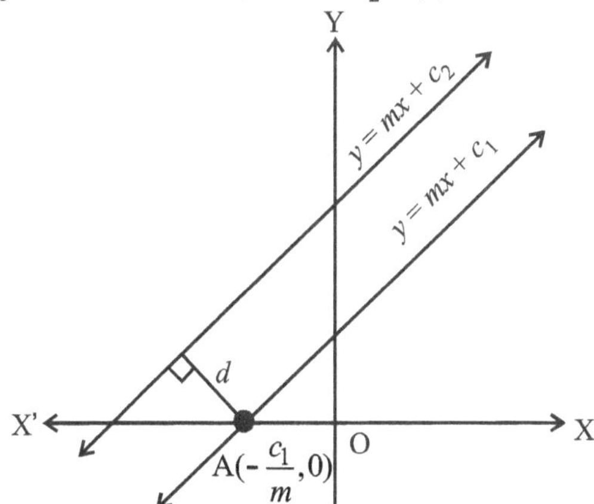

♦ The distance d between two parallel lines $y = mx + c_1$ and $y = mx + c_2$ is given by,

$$d = \frac{|c_1 - c_2|}{\sqrt{1 + m^2}}$$

♦ If lines are given in general form, i.e., $Ax + By + C_1 = 0$ and $Ax + By + C_2 = 0$, then above formula will take the form

$$d = \frac{|c_1 - c_2|}{\sqrt{A^2 + B^2}}$$

Supplementary Notes of NCERT

Equation of Family of Lines Passing through the Point of Intersection of Two Lines & Shifting of Origin

Equation of Family of Lines Passing Through the Point of Intersection of Two Lines :

♦ Let the two intersecting lines l_1 and l_2 be given by ,

$$A_1 x + B_1 y + C_1 = 0 \qquad \ldots\ldots\ldots(1)$$
$$\text{and} \qquad A_2 x + B_2 y + C_2 = 0 \qquad \ldots\ldots\ldots(2)$$

♦ From the equations (1) and (2), we can form an equation,

$$A_1 x + B_1 y + C_1 + k(A_2 x + B_2 y + C_2) = 0 \ldots\ldots\ldots(3)$$

where k is an arbitrary constant called parameter.

♦ For any value of k, the equation (3) is of first degree in x and y. Hence it represents a family of lines. A particular member of this family can be obtained for some value of k. This value of k may be obtained from other conditions.

Shifting of Origin :

♦ An equation corresponding to a set of points with reference to a system of coordinate axes may be simplified by taking the set of points in some other suitable coordinate system such that all geometric properties remain unchanged.

♦ One such transformation is that in which the new axes are transformed parallel to the original axes and origin is shifted to a new point. A transformation of this kind is called a **translation of axes**.

♦ To see how the coordinates of a point of the plane changed under a translation of axes, let us take a point P (x, y) referred to the axes OX and OY.

♦ Let O'X' and O'Y' be new axes parallel to OX and OY respectively, where O' is the new origin. Let (h, k) be the coordinates of O' referred to the old axes, i.e., OL = h and LO' = k. Also, OM = x and MP = y.

♦ Let O'M' = x' and M'P = y' be respectively, the abscissa and ordinates of a point P referred to the new axes O' X' and O' Y'

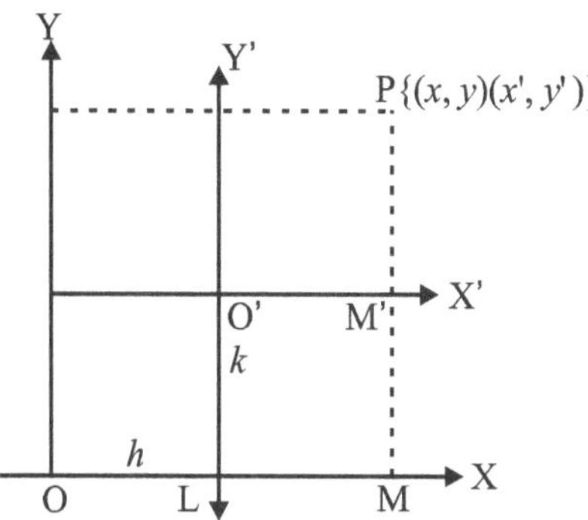

- From Figure, it can be easily seen that

  OM = OL + LM,

  i.e., x = h + x' and MP = MM' + M' P, i.e., y = k + y'.

  Hence, x = x' + h, y = y' + k

- These formulae give the relations between the old and new coordinates.

Past Years ONE-LINERS
JEE Main/Board

- Solution of system of equations, $a_1x + b_1y + c_1 = 0$, $a_2x + b_2y + c_2 = 0$, $a_3x + b_3y + c_3 = 0$,

  ❖ Area of triangle, $\Delta = \dfrac{1}{2}\begin{vmatrix} x_1 & y_1 & 1 \\ x_2 & y_2 & 1 \\ x_3 & y_3 & 1 \end{vmatrix}$

- Centroid of coordinates,

  $$C_1 = \left(\frac{x_1 + x_2 + x_3}{3}, \frac{y_1 + y_2 + y_3}{3} \right)$$

  ❖ Method of eliminating variables by using two equations of line also.

- Method of eliminating variables by using the two equations of line,

  $$a_1x + b_1y + c_1 = 0, \ a_2x + b_2y + c_2 = 0$$

- Condition of centroid, orthocentre and circumcentre (i.e., centroid divides orthocentre and circumcentre in the ratio of 2 : 1)

- Equation of line in intercept form, $\dfrac{x}{a} + \dfrac{y}{b} = 1$

♦ Intersecting point of both diagonals is equidistant from all the sides of rhombus.

❖ Distance of a point from a line $= \left| \dfrac{Ax_1 + By_1 + C}{\sqrt{A^2 + B^2}} \right|$

Tips/Tricks/Techniques ONE-LINERS
(Exam Special)

♦ Let $A(x_1, y_1)$, $B(x_2, y_2)$ and $C(x_3, y_3)$ be vertices of any triangle ABC, then

Co-ordinates of centroid, $G = \left(\dfrac{x_1 + x_2 + x_3}{3}, \dfrac{y_1 + y_2 + y_3}{3} \right)$

Co-ordinates of incentre, $= 0 \left(\dfrac{ax_1 + bx_2 + cx_3}{a+b+c}, \dfrac{ay_1 + by_2 + cy_3}{a+b+c} \right)$,

where a, b, c are length of the sides BC, AC and AB respectively of triangle ABC.

♦ Point of intersection of two lines $a_1x + b_1y + c_1 = 0$ and

$a_2x + b_2y + c_2 = 0$ is given by $\left(\dfrac{b_1c_2 - b_2c_1}{a_1b_2 - a_2b_1}, \dfrac{c_1a_2 - c_2a_1}{a_1b_2 - a_2b_1} \right)$

♦ Coodinates of foot of perpendicular (h, k) from the point (x_1, y_1) on the line $ax + by + c = 0$ or $L(x, y) = 0$ may be given by

$$\dfrac{h - x_1}{a} = \dfrac{k - y_1}{b} = -\dfrac{ax_1 + by_1 + c}{a^2 + b^2} = -\dfrac{L(x_1, y_1)}{a^2 + b^2}$$

♦ Coordinates of the image of (x_2, y_2) of the point (x_1, y_1) in the line mirror $ax + by + c = 0$ or $L(x, y) = 0$ may be given by

$$\dfrac{x_2 - x_1}{a} = \dfrac{y_2 - y_1}{b} = -\dfrac{2(ax_1 + by_1 + c)}{a^2 + b^2} = -\dfrac{2L(x_1, y_1)}{a^2 + b^2}$$

♦ The condition for three lines $a_1x + b_1y + c_1 = 0$, $a_2x + b_2y + c_2 = 0$ and $a_3x + b_3y + c_3 = 0$ to be concurrent i.e., they pass through the same point is

$$\begin{vmatrix} a_1 & b_1 & c_1 \\ a_2 & b_2 & c_2 \\ a_3 & b_3 & c_3 \end{vmatrix} = 0.$$

i.e., $a_1(b_2c_3 - b_3c_2) + a_2(b_3c_1 - b_1c_3) + a_3(b_1c_2 - b_2c_1) = 0$

♦ A homogeneous equation of degree two of the type, $ax^2 + 2hxy + by^2 = 0$ always represents a pair of straight lines passing through the origin and

(a) $h^2 > ab \Rightarrow$ Lines are real and distinct

(b) $h^2 = ab \Rightarrow$ Lines are real and coincident

(c) $h^2 < ab \Rightarrow$ Lines are imaginary with real point of intersection $(0, 0)$

♦ If the triangle is equilateral, the centroid, incentre, orthocentre, circumcentre, coincides.

♦ Orthocentre, centroid and circumcentre are always colinear and centroid divides the line joining orthocentre and circumcentre in the ratio $2 : 1$.

♦ In an isosceles triangle centroid, orthocentre, incentre, circumcentre lies on the same line.

♦ The point (x_1, y_1) lies on the line $ax + by + c = 0$ if,
$$ax_1 + by_1 + c = 0$$

♦ Let the given line be $ax + by + c = 0$

A point $P(x_1, y_1)$ will lie above or below this line according as $\dfrac{ax_1 + by_1 + c}{b}$ is positive or negative respectively.

♦ Lines $a_1x + b_1y + c_1 = 0$ and $a_2x + b_2y + c_2 = 0$ are parallel

if $\dfrac{a_1}{a_2} = \dfrac{b_1}{b_2}$

♦ Lines $a_1 x + b_1y + c_1 = 0$ and $a_2 x + b_2 y + c_2 = 0$ are perpendicular then $a_1a_2 + b_1b_2 = 0$.

♦ Two lines $a_1x + b_1y + c_1 = 0$ and
$a_1x + b_2y + c_2 = 0$ are coincident if
$$\dfrac{a_1}{a_2} = \dfrac{b_1}{b_2} = \dfrac{c_1}{c_2}$$

♦ Area of the triangle formed by the lines $y = m_1x + c_1$, $y = m_2x + c_2$, $y = m_3x + c_3$ is $\dfrac{1}{2}\left|\sum \dfrac{(c_1 - c_2)^2}{m_1 - m_2}\right|$.

Sections of a Cone

- Conic sections are the curves obtained by intersecting a right circular cone by a plane.

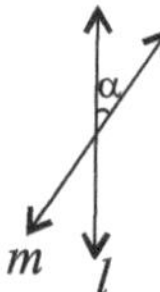

- Let α be fixed angle between a fixed vertical line l (say) and another line m(say) inclined to it.

Circle, Ellipse, Parabola and Hyperbola:

When the plane cuts the nappe (other than the vertex) of the cone, we have following curves:

- Let β be the angle made by the intersecting plane with the vertical axis of the cone.
- If $\beta = 90°$, Obtained conic section is a circle.
- If $\alpha < \beta < 90°$, obtained conic section is an ellipse.
- If $\beta = \alpha$, obtained conic section is a parabola.
- If $0 \leq \beta < \alpha$; the palne cuts through both the nappes and obtained curve is a hyperbola.

Degenerated Conic Sections

When the plane cuts at the vertex of the cone, we have

- If $\alpha < \beta \leq 90°$, then the section is a point.
- If $\beta = \alpha$, then the section is a straight line.
  (**Note:** It is the degenerated case of a parabola.)
- If $0 \leq \beta < \alpha$, then the section is a pair of intersecting straight lines.
  Note: It is the degenerated case of a hyperbola.

- A circle is the set of all points in a plane that are equidistant from a fixed point in the plane.
- The fixed point is called the centre of the circle and the distance from the centre to a point on the circle is called the radius of the circle.

Standard Equation of a Circle

- The equation of a circle having centre (h, k) & radius r is

$$(x - h)^2 + (y - k)^2 = r^2$$

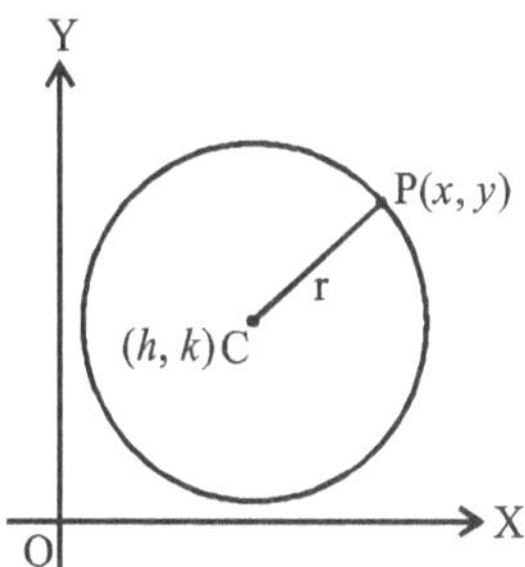

- A parabola is the set of all points in a plane that are equidistant from a fixed line and a fixed point (not on the line) in the plane.
- The fixed line is **called** the **directrix** of the parabola and the fixed point is called the **focus**.

<table>
<tr><td colspan="5" align="center">Four Standard Forms of the Parabola</td></tr>
<tr><td>Standard Equation</td><td>$y^2 = 4ax\ (a > 0)$</td><td>$y^2 = -4ax\ (a > 0)$</td><td>$x^2 = 4ay\ (a > 0)$</td><td>$x^2 = -4ay\ (a > 0)$</td></tr>
<tr><td>Shape of Parabola</td><td colspan="4"></td></tr>
<tr><td>Vertex</td><td></td><td></td><td></td><td></td></tr>
<tr><td>Focus</td><td></td><td></td><td></td><td></td></tr>
<tr><td>Equation of directrix</td><td>$O\ (0, 0)$</td><td>$O\ (0, 0)$</td><td>$O\ (0, 0)$</td><td>$O\ (0, 0)$</td></tr>
<tr><td>Equation of axis</td><td>$S\ (a, 0)$</td><td>$S\ (-a, 0)$</td><td>$S\ (0, a)$</td><td>$S\ (0, -a)$</td></tr>
<tr><td>Length of latus rectum</td><td>$x = -a$</td><td>$x = a$</td><td>$y = -a$</td><td>$y = a$</td></tr>
<tr><td></td><td>$y = 0$</td><td>$y = 0$</td><td>$x = 0$</td><td>$x = 0$</td></tr>
<tr><td></td><td>$4a$</td><td>$4a$</td><td>$4a$</td><td>$4a$</td></tr>
</table>

Observations:

- Parabola is symmetric with respect to axis of the parabola.

- If the equation has a y^2 term, then the axis of symmetry is along the x-axis and if the equation has an x^2 term then the axis of symmetry is along the y-axis.
- If the taxis of symmetry is along the x-axis, the parabola opens to the
  - right if the coefficient of x is positive.
  - left if the coefficient of x is negative.
- If the axis of symmetry is along the y-axis, the parabola opens
  - upwards if the coefficient of y is positive.
  - downwards if the coefficient of y is negative.

Latus Rectum:

- Latus rectum of a parabola is a line segment perpendicular to the axis of the parabola, through the focus and whose end points lie on the parabola.
- Length of the latus rectum of the parabola is $4a$.

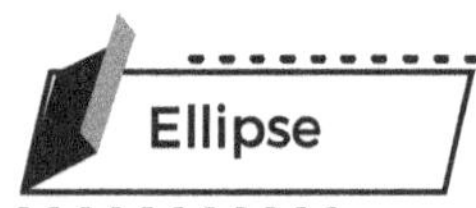

- An ellipse is the set of all points in a plane, the sum of whose distances from two fixed points in the plane is a constant.
- The two fixed points are called the **foci** of the ellipse.
- The constant which is the sum of the distances of a point on the distances of a point on the ellipse from the two fixed points is always greater than the distance between the two fixed points.
- The **mid point** of the line segment joining the foci is called the **centre** of the ellipse.
- The line segment through the foci of the ellipse is called the **major axis**.
- The line segment through the centre and perpendicular to the major axis is called the minor axis.
- The end points of the major axis are called the **vertices** of the ellipse.
- Length of the major axis is denoted as 2a.
- Length of the minor axis is denoted as 2b.
- Distance between the foci is denoted by 2c.
- Length of the semi major axis is a and length of the semi minor axis is b.

Relationship between semi-major axis, semi-minor axis and the distance of the focus from the centre of the ellipse:

- $a^2 = b^2 + c^2$ i.e., $c = \sqrt{a^2 - b^2}$

Special Cases of an Ellipse:

- In the equation $c^2 = a^2 - b^2$ if we keep a fixed and vary c from 0 to a, the resulting ellipse will vary in shape.
  Case (i) When $c = 0$, both foci merge together with the centre of the ellipse and $a^2 = b^2$ i.e., $a = b$. So, the ellipse becomes circle.
  Case (ii) When $c = a$, then $b = 0$. The ellipse reduces to the line segment joining the two foci.

Eccentricity:

♦ The eccentricity of an ellipse is the ratio of the distances from the centre of the ellipse to one of the foci and to one of the vertices of the ellipse (denoted by e).

$$\text{i.e., } \boxed{e = \frac{c}{a}}$$

♦ In terms of the eccentricity the focus is at a distance of ae from the centre.

♦ The standard equations of ellipses have centre at the origin and the major and minor axis are coordinate axes.

Latus Rectum

♦ Latus rectum of an ellipse is a one segment perpendicular to the major axis through any of the foci and whose end points lie on the ellipse.

<table>
<tr><td colspan="3" align="center">Two Standard Length of the Datus Rectum is $\dfrac{2b^2}{a}$ Ellipse</td></tr>
<tr>
<td>Standard equation</td>
<td>$\dfrac{x^2}{a^2}+\dfrac{y^2}{b^2}=1$ (a > b), where a and b are constants
(Horizontal Form of an Ellipse)</td>
<td>$\dfrac{y^2}{a^2}+\dfrac{x^2}{b^2}=1$ (a > b), where a and b are constants
(Vertical Form of an Ellipse)</td>
</tr>
<tr>
<td>Shape of the ellipse</td>
<td colspan="2">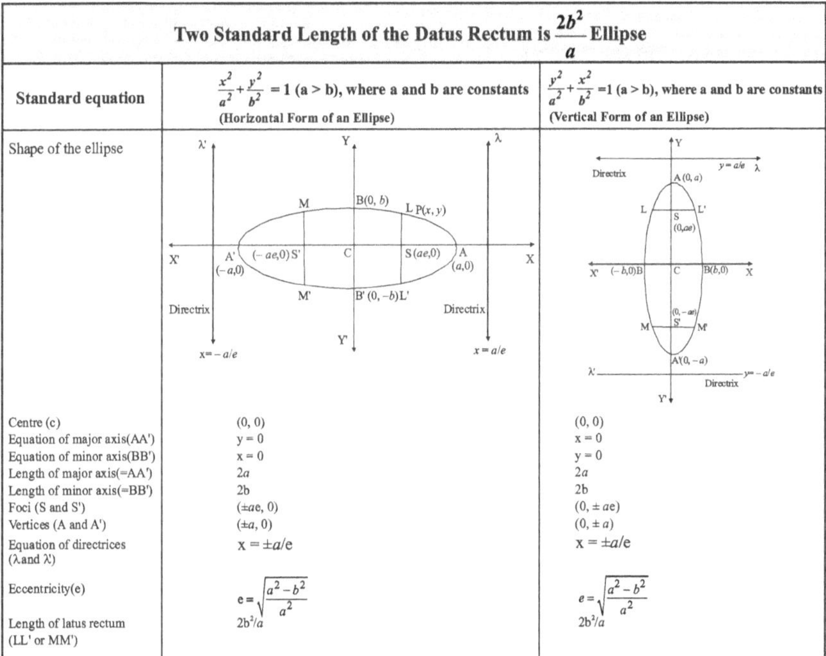</td>
</tr>
<tr><td>Centre (c)</td><td>(0, 0)</td><td>(0, 0)</td></tr>
<tr><td>Equation of major axis(AA')</td><td>y = 0</td><td>x = 0</td></tr>
<tr><td>Equation of minor axis(BB')</td><td>x = 0</td><td>y = 0</td></tr>
<tr><td>Length of major axis(=AA')</td><td>2a</td><td>2a</td></tr>
<tr><td>Length of minor axis(=BB')</td><td>2b</td><td>2b</td></tr>
<tr><td>Foci (S and S')</td><td>(±ae, 0)</td><td>(0, ± ae)</td></tr>
<tr><td>Vertices (A and A')</td><td>(±a, 0)</td><td>(0, ± a)</td></tr>
<tr><td>Equation of directrices (λ and λ')</td><td>x = ±a/e</td><td>x = ±a/e</td></tr>
<tr><td>Eccentricity(e)</td><td>$e=\sqrt{\dfrac{a^2-b^2}{a^2}}$</td><td>$e=\sqrt{\dfrac{a^2-b^2}{a^2}}$</td></tr>
<tr><td>Length of latus rectum (LL' or MM')</td><td>$2b^2/a$</td><td>$2b^2/a$</td></tr>
</table>

Important Observations:

♦ Ellipse is symmetric with respect to both the coordinate axes.

♦ The foci always lie on the major axis.

♦ Length of the latus rectum of an ellipse is $\dfrac{2b^2}{a}$.

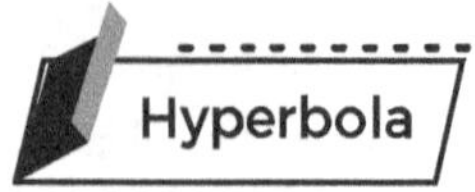

Hyperbola

- A hyperbola is the set of all points in a plane, the difference of whose distances from two fixed points in the plane is a constant.

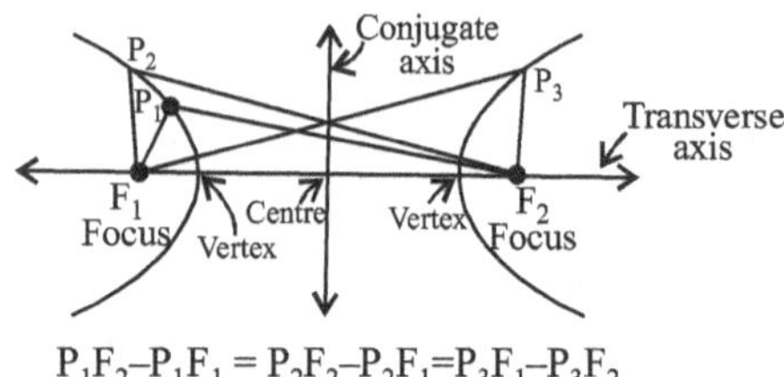

$$P_1F_2 - P_1F_1 = P_2F_2 - P_2F_1 = P_3F_1 - P_3F_2$$

- The term **"difference"** that is used in the definition means the distance to the farther point minus the distance to the closer point.

- The two fixed points are called the foci of the hyperbola.

- The mid-point of the line segment joining the foci is called the **centre of the hyperbola**.

- The line through the foci is called the transverse axis and the line through the centre and perpendicular to the transverse axis is called the **conjugate axis**.

- The points at which the hyperbola intersects the transverse axis are called the **vertices of the hyperbola**.

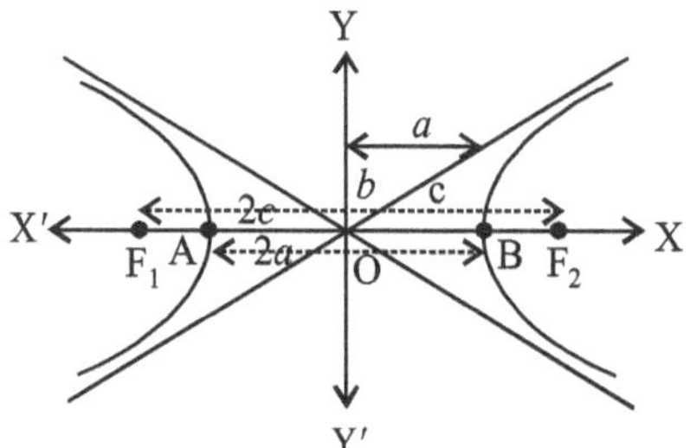

- We denote the distance between the two foci by $2c$.

- The distance between two vertices (the length of the transverse axis) by $2a$ and we define the quantity b as

$$b = \sqrt{c^2 - a^2} \cdot$$

- Also $2b$ is the length of the conjugate axis

Eccentricity:

♦ The ratio $e = \dfrac{c}{a}$ is called the eccentricity of the hyperbola.

♦ Since $c \geq a$, the eccentricity is never less than one.

♦ In terms of the eccentricity, the foci are at a distance of ae from the centre.

Standard equation of Hyperbola

Hyperbola and its Conjugate		
	Hyperbola	**Conjugate Hyperbola**
Standard Equation	$\dfrac{x^2}{a^2} - \dfrac{y^2}{b^2} = 1$	$\dfrac{y^2}{b^2} - \dfrac{x^2}{a^2} = 1$ or $\dfrac{x^2}{a^2} - \dfrac{y^2}{b^2} = -1$
Centre	$(0, 0)$	$(0, 0)$
Eq. of transverse axis	$y=0$	$x=0$
Eq. of conjugate axis	$x=0$	$y=0$
Length of transverse axis	$2a$	$2b$
Length of conjugate axis	$2b$	$2a$
Foci	$(\pm ae, 0)$	$(0, \pm be)$
Equation of directrices	$y = \pm a/e$	$y = \pm b/e$
Vertices	$(\pm a, 0)$	$(0, \pm b)$
Eccentricity	$e = \sqrt{\dfrac{a^2 - b^2}{a^2}}$	$e = \sqrt{\dfrac{a^2 - b^2}{b^2}}$
Length of latus rectum	$2b^2/a$	$2a^2/b$

♦ A hyperbola in which $a = b$ is called an equilateral hyperbola.

♦ The standard equations of hyperbolas have transverse and conjugate axes as the coordinate axes and the centre at the origin.

Latus rectum:

♦ Latus rectum of hyperbola is a line segment perpendicular to the transverse axis through any of the foci and whose end points lie on the hyperbola.

♦ The latus rectum in hyperbola is $\dfrac{2b^2}{a}$.

Past Years ONE-LINERS
JEE Main/Board

- Equation of circle whose ends of diameter are (x_1, y_1) and (x_2, y_2) is
$(x - x_1)(x - x_2) + (y - y_1)(y - y_2) = 0$

- Normal to the ellipse $\dfrac{x^2}{a^2} + \dfrac{y^2}{b^2} = 1$ at $\left(ae, \dfrac{b^2}{a}\right)$ is $\dfrac{a^2 x}{ae} - \dfrac{b^2 y}{b^2/a} = a^2 - b^2$.

- The condition for the line $y = mx + c$ to be a tangent to the ellipse

  $\dfrac{x^2}{a^2} + \dfrac{y^2}{b^2} = 1$ is $C^2 = a^2 m^2 + b^2$.

- Equation of family of circles be $S_1 + \lambda S_2 = 0$
- Distance between centres $> r_1 + r_2 \Rightarrow$ circles are separated

- If ellipse is $\dfrac{x^2}{a^2} + \dfrac{y^2}{b^2} = 1$ then end point of latus rectum in first quadrant is

  $\left(ae, \dfrac{b^2}{a}\right)$.

Tips/Tricks/Techniques ONE-LINERS
(Exam Special)

Circles

- A point (x_1, y_1) lies outside, on or inside a circle
$S \equiv x^2 + y^2 + 2gx + 2fy + c = 0$ according as
$S_1 \equiv x_1^2 + y_1^2 + 2gx_1 + 2fy_1 + c$ is positive, zero or negative respectively.
- Let $S = 0$ be a circle and $A\,(x_1, y_1)$ be a point. If the diameter of the circle through point A which is passing through the circle at P and Q then
$AP = AC - r =$ least distance
$AQ = AC + r =$ greatest distance where 'r' is the
radius and C is the centre of circle

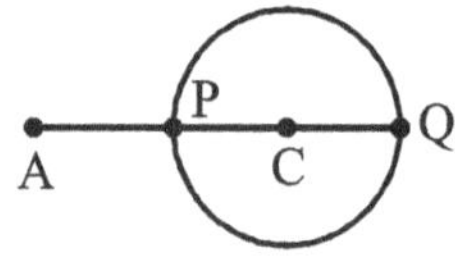

- The equation of tangent to the circle
$x^2 + y^2 + 2gx + 2fy + c = 0$ at a point (x_1, y_1) is
$xx_1 + yy_1 + g\,(x + x_1) + f\,(y + y_1) + c = 0$ or $T = 0$
- The equation of normal to the circle
$x^2 + y^2 + 2gx + 2fy + c = 0$ at any point (x_1, y_1) is

$$y - y_1 = \dfrac{y_1 + f}{x_1 + g}\,(x - x_1)$$

- Let PQ and PR be two tangents drawn from $P(x_1, y_1)$ to the circle $x^2 + y^2 + 2gx + 2fy + c = 0$. Then, PQ = PR is called the length of tangent drawn from point P and is given by

$$PQ = PR = \sqrt{x_1^2 + y_1^2 + 2gx_1 + 2fy_1 + c} = \sqrt{S_1}$$

- Equation of chord of contact of the tangent from a point (x_1, y_1) to the circle $x^2 + y^2 + 2gx + 2fy + c = 0$ is

$$xx_1 + yy_1 + g(x + x_1) + f(y + y_1) + c = 0$$

- The length of chord of contact $= 2\sqrt{r^2 - p^2}$

where 'r' is the radius of the circle and 'p' is the length of perpendicular from the centre to the chord of contact.

- If the equation of two circles are

$$S_1 \equiv x^2 + y^2 + 2g_1x + 2f_1y + c_1 = 0 \text{ and}$$
$$S_2 \equiv x^2 + y^2 + 2g_2x + 2f_2y + c_2 = 0,$$

then equation of common chord is $S_1 - S_2 = 0$

$$\Rightarrow 2x(g_1 - g_2) + 2y(f_1 - f_2) + c_1 - c_2 = 0$$

- The length of the common chord is $2\sqrt{r_1^2 - p_1^2} = 2\sqrt{r_2^2 - p_2^2}$ where r_1, r_2

and p_1, p_2 are radii and length of perpendiculars drawn from the centres to the chord.

- Consider two circles with centres c_1 and c_2 and radii r_1 and r_2.

  Case 1: If $c_1c_2 > r_1 + r_2$ then the circles neither touch nor intersect and have four common tangents.

  Case 2: If $c_1c_2 = r_1 + r_2$ then the circles touch each other externally and have three common tangents.

  Case 3: If $r_2 - r_1 < c_1c_2 < r_1 + r_2$ then the circles intersect in two distinct points and have two common tangents.

  Case 4: If $c_1c_2 = r_2 - r_1$ then circle touch one another internally and have one common tangent.

  Case 5: If $c_1c_2 < r_2 - r_1$ then the smaller circle completely lies inside the bigger circle and have no common tangent.

Parabola

- A point (x_1, y_1) lies inside, on or outside of the region of the parabola $y^2 = 4ax$ according as $y_1^2 - 4ax_1 <, = \text{ or } > 0$

Equations of parabola	Tangent at (x_1, y_1)
$y^2 = 4ax$	$yy_1 = 2a(x + x_1)$
$y^2 = -4ax$	$yy_1 = -2a(x + x_1)$
$x^2 = 4ay$	$xx_1 = 2a(y + y_1)$
$x^2 = -4ay$	$xx_1 = -2a(y + y_1)$

Equations of normals of all standard parabolas at (x_1, y_1)

Equations of parabola	Normal at (x_1, y_1)
$y^2 = 4ax$	$y - y_1 = \dfrac{-y_1}{2a}(x - x_1)$
$y^2 = -4ax$	$y - y_1 = \dfrac{y_1}{2a}(x - x_1)$
$x^2 = 4ay$	$y - y_1 = -\dfrac{2a}{x_1}(x - x_1)$
$x^2 = -4ay$	$y - y_1 = \dfrac{2a}{x_1}(x - x_1)$

♦ The equation of chord of contact of tangents drawn from a point (x_1, y_1) to the parabola $y^2 = 4ax$ is $yy_1 = 2a(x + x_1)$.

♦ Length of the chord of contact is $\dfrac{1}{a}\sqrt{(y_1^2 - 4ax_1)(y_1^2 + 4a^2)}$

♦ **Condition of tangency :** A line $y = mx + c$ touches a parabola $y^2 = 4ax$, if $c = a/m$

♦ (a) The line $y = mx + c$ touches parabola $x^2 = 4ay$ if $c = -am^2$

  (b) The line $x\cos\alpha + y\sin\alpha = p$ touches the parabola $y^2 = 4ax$ if $a\sin^2\alpha + p\cos\alpha = 0$

♦ The chord of contact joining the point of contact of two perpendicular tangents always passes through focus.

Ellipse

♦ The point P (x_1, y_1) lies outside, on or inside the ellipse $\dfrac{x^2}{a^2} + \dfrac{y^2}{b^2} = 1$ according

as $\dfrac{x_1^2}{a^2} + \dfrac{y_1^2}{b^2} - 1 > 0, = 0$ or < 0

♦ The equation of the tangent to the ellipse $\dfrac{x^2}{a^2} + \dfrac{y^2}{b^2} = 1$ at the point (x_1, y_1) is

$\dfrac{xx_1}{a^2} + \dfrac{yy_1}{b^2} = 1$

♦ The equation of the normal to the ellipse $\dfrac{x^2}{a^2} + \dfrac{y^2}{b^2} = 1$ at the point (x_1, y_1) is

$\dfrac{a^2 x}{x_1} - \dfrac{b^2 y}{y_1} = a^2 - b^2$

♦ The equation of chord of contact of tangent drawn from a point $P(x_1, y_1)$ to

the ellipse $\dfrac{x^2}{a^2} + \dfrac{y^2}{b^2} = 1$ is $T = 0$ where $T \equiv \dfrac{xx_1}{a^2} + \dfrac{yy_1}{b^2} - 1$

Hyperbola

♦ The point $P(x_1, y_1)$ lies outside, on or inside the hyperbola

$\dfrac{x^2}{a^2} - \dfrac{y^2}{b^2} = 1$ according as $\dfrac{x_1^2}{a^2} - \dfrac{y_1^2}{b^2} - 1 > 0, = 0$ or < 0

♦ The equation of the tangent to the hyperbola $\dfrac{x^2}{a^2} - \dfrac{y^2}{b^2} = 1$ at the point (x_1, y_1)

is $\dfrac{xx_1}{a^2} - \dfrac{yy_1}{b^2} = 1$.

♦ The equation of the normal to the hyperbola $\dfrac{x^2}{a^2} - \dfrac{y^2}{b^2} = 1$ at the point (x_1, y_1)

is $\dfrac{a^2 x}{x_1} + \dfrac{b^2 y}{y_1} = a^2 + b^2$

♦ The equation of chord of contact of tangent drawn from a point $P(x_1, y_1)$ to

the hyperbola $\dfrac{x^2}{a^2} - \dfrac{y^2}{b^2} = 1$ is $T = 0$ where $T \equiv \dfrac{xx_1}{a^2} - \dfrac{yy_1}{b^2} - 1$.

♦ If asymptotes of the standard hyperbola are perpendicular to each other, then it is known as Rectangular Hyperbola. Then

$$2 \tan^{-1} \dfrac{b}{a} = \dfrac{\pi}{2} \Rightarrow b = a \text{ or } x^2 - y^2 = a^2$$

is general form of the equation of the rectangular hyperbola.

♦ **Number of tangents from a point :** Two tangents can be drawn from a point to a hyperbola. The two tangents are real and distinct, coincident or imaginary according as the given point lies outside, on or inside the hyperbola.

♦ (a) The angle between the asymptotes of $\dfrac{x^2}{a^2} - \dfrac{y^2}{b^2} = 1$ is $2 \tan^{-1} (b/a)$.

    (b) A hyperbola and its conjugate hyperbola have the same asymptotes.
    (c) The asymptotes pass through the centre of the hyperbola.
    (d) The bisector of the angle between the asymptotes are the coordinate axes.

12 Introduction to Three Dimensional Geometry

♦ To locate the position of a point in a space, we need three intersecting mutually perpendicular lines in the space. These lines are called the **coordinate axes** and the three numbers are called the **coordinates of the point** with respect to the axes.

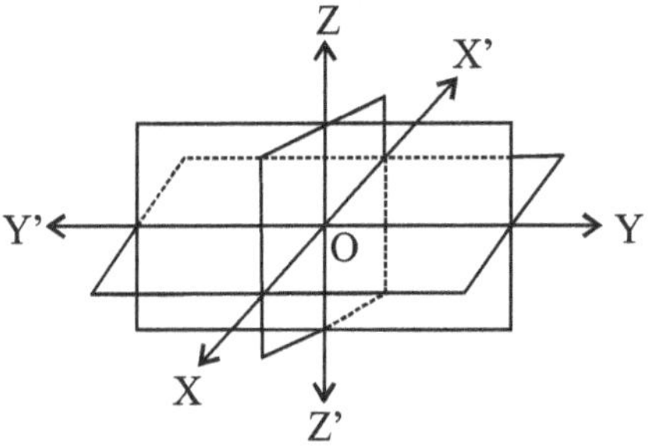

♦ Consider three planes intersecting at a point O such that these three planes are mutually perpendicular to each other as shown in figure.

♦ These three planes intersect along the lines X'OX, Y'OY and Z'OZ, called the x, y and z-axes, respectively. We may note that these lines are mutually perpendicular to each other. These lines constitute the **"rectangular coordinate system."**

♦ The planes XOY, YOZ and ZOX, called, respectively the XY-plane, YZ-plane and the ZX-plane, are known as the **three coordinate planes**.

♦ We take the XOY plane as the plane of the paper and the line Z'OZ as perpendicular to the plane XOY. If the plane of the paper is considered as horizontal, then the line Z'OZ will be vertical.

♦ The distances measured from XY-plane upwards in the direction of OZ are taken as positive and those measured downwards in the direction of OZ' are taken as negative.

♦ Similarly, the distance measured to the right of ZX-plane along OY are taken as positive, to the left of ZX-plane and along OY' as negative, in front of the YZ-plane along OX as positive and to the back of it along OX' as negative.

- The point O is called the origin of the coordinate system.
- The three coordinate planes divide the space into eight parts known as **octants**. These octants could be named as XOYZ, X'OYZ, X'OY'Z, XOY'Z, XOYZ', X'OYZ', X'OY'Z' and XOY'Z' and denoted by I, II, III, ..., VIII , respectively.

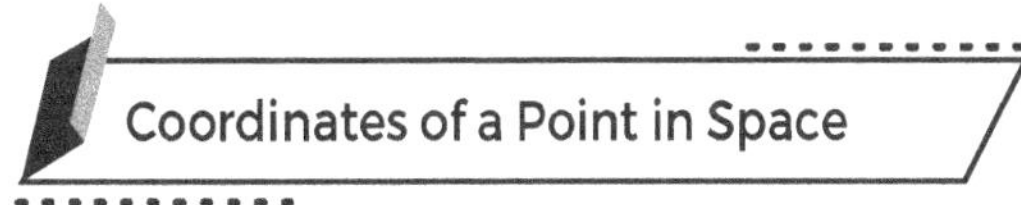

Coordinates of a Point in Space

- Let the point P be in a space and OA = x, OB = y and OC = z. Then, the point P will have the coordinates x, y and z and we write P (x, y, z).
- Given x, y and z, we locate the three points A, B and C on the three coordinate axes. Through the points A, B and C we draw planes parallel to the YZ-plane, ZX-plane and XY-plane, respectively.

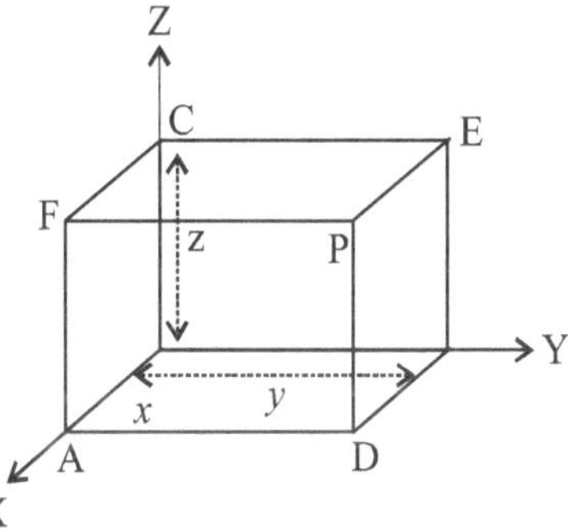

- The point of intersection of these three planes, namely, ADPF, BDPE and CEPF is obviously the point P, corresponding to the ordered triplet (x, y, z). We observe that if P (x, y, z) is any point in the space, then x, y and z are perpendicular distances from YZ, ZX and XY planes, respectively.
- **Note :** The coordinates of the origin O are (0,0,0). The coordinates of any point on the x-axis will be as $(x,0,0)$ and the coordinates of any point in the YZ-plane will be as $(0, y, z)$.
- The sign of the coordinates of a point determine the octant in which the point lies. The following table shows the signs of the coordinates in eight octants.

Octants / Coordinates	I	II	III	IV	V	VI	VII	VIII
x	+	−	−	+	+	−	−	+
y	+	+	−	−	+	+	−	−
z	+	+	+	+	−	−	−	−

Distance Between Two Points

- Let $P(x_1, y_1, z_1)$ and $Q(x_2, y_2, z_2)$ be two points referred to a system of rectangular axes OX, OY and OZ.
- Through the points P and Q draw planes parallel to the coordinate planes so as to form a rectangular parallelopiped with one diagonal PQ.

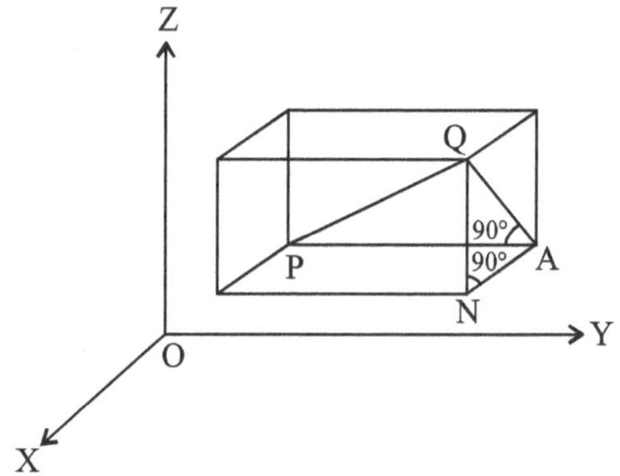

- Now, $PA = y_2 - y_1$, $AN = x_2 - x_1$ and $NQ = z_2 - z_1$

  And $PQ^2 = (x_2 - x_1)^2 + (y_2 - y_1)^2 + (z_2 - z_1)^2$

  Therefore, $PQ = \sqrt{(x_2 - x_1)^2 + (y_2 - y_1)^2 + (z_2 - z_1)^2}$

  This gives us the distance between two points (x_1, y_1, z_1) and (x_2, y_2, z_2)

  $$OQ = \sqrt{x_2^2 + y_2^2 + z_2^2}\,.$$

- In particular, if $x_1 = y_1 = z_1 = 0$, i.e., point P is origin O, then which gives the distance between the origin O and any point $Q(x_2, y_2, z_2)$.

Section Formula

- Let the two given points be $P(x_1, y_1, z_1)$ and $Q(x_2, y_2, z_2)$. Let the point R (x, y, z) divide PQ in the given ratio m : n internally.
- Draw PL, QM and RN perpendicular to the XY-plane. Obviously PL || RN || QM and feet of these perpendiculars lie in a XY-plane.

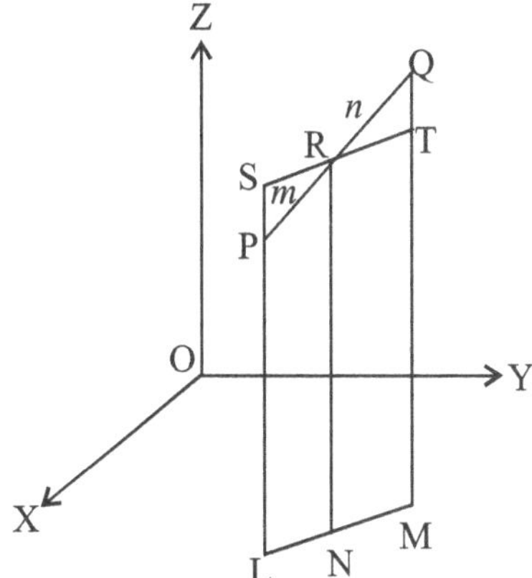

♦   Note that quadrilaterals LNRS and NMTR are parallelograms. The triangles PSR and QTR are similar. Therefore,

$$\frac{m}{n} = \frac{PR}{QR} = \frac{SP}{QT} = \frac{SL - PL}{QM - TM} = \frac{NR - PL}{QM - NR} = \frac{z - z_1}{z_2 - z}$$

♦   This implies, $z = \dfrac{mz_2 + nz_1}{m + n}$

♦   Similarly, by drawing perpendiculars to the XZ and YZ-planes, we get

$$y = \frac{my_2 + ny_1}{m + n} \text{ and } x = \frac{mx_2 + nx_1}{m + n}$$

♦   Hence, the coordinates of the point R which divides the line segment joining two points P (x_1, y_1, z_1) and Q (x_2, y_2, z_2) internally in the ratio m : n are,

$$\left(\frac{mx_2 + nx_1}{m + n}, \frac{my_2 + ny_1}{m + n}, \frac{mz_2 + nz_1}{m + n} \right)$$

♦   If the point R divides PQ externally in the ratio m : n, then its coordinates are obtained by replacing n by - n so that coordinates of point R will be,

$$\left(\frac{mx_2 - nx_1}{m - n}, \frac{my_2 - ny_1}{m - n}, \frac{mz_2 - nz_1}{m - n} \right)$$

♦   **Case 1:** Coordinates of the mid-point: In case R is the mid-point of PQ, then

$$m : n = 1 : 1 \text{ so that } x = \frac{x_1 + x_2}{2}, y = \frac{y_1 + y_2}{2} \text{ and } z = \frac{z_1 + z_2}{2}$$

These are the coordinates of the mid point of the segment joining P (x_1, y_1, z_1) and Q (x_2, y_2, z_2).

♦   **Case 2:** The coordinates of the point R which divides PQ in the ratio k : 1 are obtained by taking $k = \dfrac{m}{n}$ which are as given below,

$$\left(\frac{kx_2 + x_1}{1 + k}, \frac{ky_2 + y_1}{1 + k}, \frac{kz_2 + z_1}{1 + k} \right)$$

♦   Generally, this result is used in solving problems involving a general point on the line passing through two given points.

Tips/Tricks/Techniques ONE-LINERS
(Exam Special)

- **Properties of Distance:-**
  - ❖ When three points A, B and C are collinear, Then AC = AB + BC
  - ❖ When three vertices A, B and C represents right angled triangle, Then
    $AC^2 = AB^2 + BC^2$

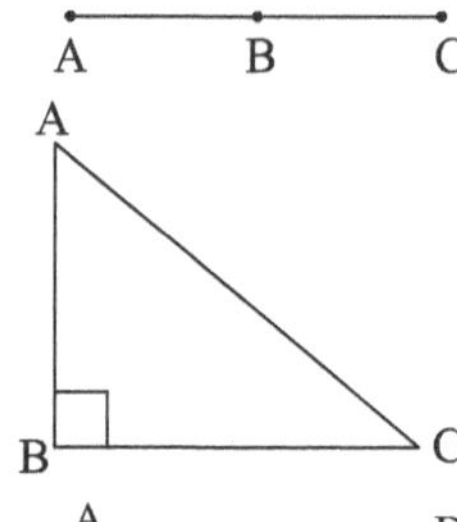

  - ❖ When four vertices A, B, C and D represents parallelogram, Then AB = CD, BC = AD and mid point of AC is equal to mid point of BD

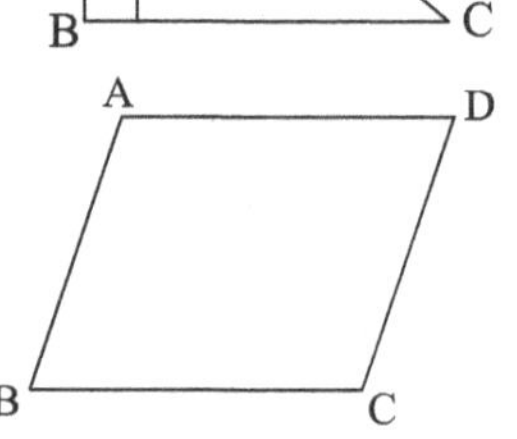

  - ❖ When four vertices A, B, C and D represents Rectangle, Then AB = CD and BC = AD & AC = BD

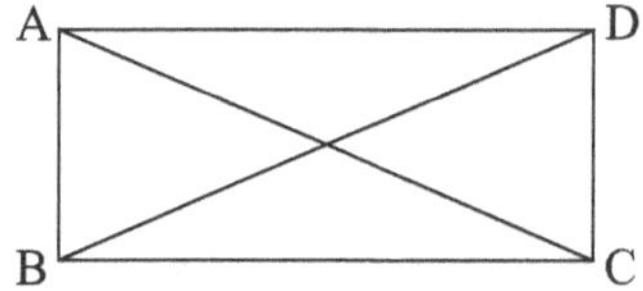

  - ❖ When four vertices A, B, C and D represents rhombus, Then AB = BC = CD = AD But AC ≠ BD

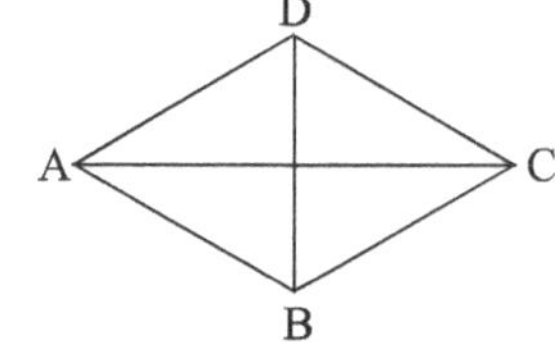

  - ❖ When four vertices A, B, C and D represents square, Then AB = BC = CD = AD and AC = BD

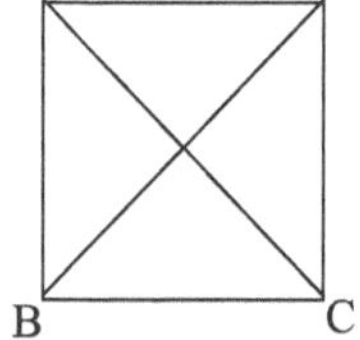

- **Centroid of Triangle:-** The centroid of the triangle whose coordinates are (x_1, y_1, z_1), (x_2, y_2, z_2) and (x_3, y_3, z_3), Then

  Centroid, $G = \left(\dfrac{x_1 + x_2 + x_3}{3}, \dfrac{y_1 + y_2 + y_3}{3}, \dfrac{z_1 + z_2 + z_3}{3} \right)$

- In parallelogram, rectangle, square and rhombus, diagonals bisect each other.

13 Limits and Derivatives

Intuitive Idea of Derivatives

- Physical experiments have confirmed that the body dropped from a tall cliff covers a distance of $4.9t^2$ metres in t seconds.
- Distance s in metres covered by the body as a function of time t in seconds is given by $s = 4.9t^2$
- *Velocity is the rate of change of displacement.*

Limits

- In general as $x \to a$, $f(x) \to l$, then l is called *limit of the function $f(x)$* which is symbolically written as $\lim_{x \to a} f(x) = l$.

- We say $\lim_{x \to a^-} f(x)$ is the expected value of f at $x = a$ given the values of f near x to the left of a. This value is called the *left hand limit* of f at a.

- We say $\lim_{x \to a^+} f(x)$ is the expected value of f at $x = a$ given the values of f near x to the right of a. This value is called the *right hand limit* of $f(x)$ at a.

- If the right and left hand limits coincide, we call that common value as the limit of $f(x)$ at $x = a$ and denote it by $\lim_{x \to a} f(x)$.

Algebra of Limits

- Let f and g be two functions such that both $\lim_{x \to a} f(x)$ and $\lim_{x \to a} g(x)$ exist.

(i) $\lim_{x \to a}[f(x) + g(x)] = \lim_{x \to a} f(x) + \lim_{x \to a} g(x).$

(ii) $\lim_{x \to a}[f(x) - g(x)] = \lim_{x \to a} f(x) - \lim_{x \to a} g(x).$

(iii) $\quad \lim\limits_{x \to a} [f(x).g(x)] = \lim\limits_{x \to a} f(x) . \lim\limits_{x \to a} g(x).$

(iv) $\quad \lim\limits_{x \to a} \dfrac{f(x)}{g(x)} = \dfrac{\lim\limits_{x \to a} f(x)}{\lim\limits_{x \to a} g(x)}$ [Whenever the denominator is non zero]

$$\lim\limits_{x \to a} [(\lambda.f)(x)] = \lambda. \lim\limits_{x \to a} f(x).$$

Limits of Polynomials and Rational Functions

- A function f is said to be a polynomial function of degree n $f(x) = a_0 + a_1 x + a_2 x^2 + \ldots + a_n x^n$, where $a_i s$ are real numbers such that $a_n \neq 0$ for some natural number n.

- Let $f(x) = a_0 + a_1 x + a_2 x^2 + \ldots + a_n x^n$

    then, $\lim\limits_{x \to a} f(x) = \lim\limits_{x \to a} [a_0 + a_1 x + a_2 x^2 + \ldots + a_n x^n]$

    $= a_0 + a_1 a + a_2 a^2 + \ldots + a_n a^n = f(a)$

- A function f is said to be a rational function, if $f(x) = \dfrac{g(x)}{h(x)}$, where $g(x)$ and $h(x)$

    are polynomials such that $h(x) \neq 0$.

    Then, $\lim\limits_{x \to a} f(x) = \lim\limits_{x \to a} \dfrac{g(x)}{h(x)} = \dfrac{\lim\limits_{x \to a} g(x)}{\lim\limits_{x \to a} h(x)} = \dfrac{g(a)}{h(a)}$

- $\lim\limits_{x \to a} f(x) = \dfrac{\lim\limits_{x \to a} g(x)}{\lim\limits_{x \to a} h(x)} = \dfrac{\lim\limits_{x \to a} (x-a)^k g_1(x)}{\lim\limits_{x \to a} (x-a)^l h_1(x)}$

- For any positive integer n,

    $$\lim\limits_{x \to a} \dfrac{x^n - a^n}{x - a} = na^{n-1}.$$

Limits of Trigonometric Functions

- Let f and g be two real valued functions with the same domain such that $f(x) \leq g(x)$ for all x in the domain of definition, For some a, if both $\lim\limits_{x \to a} f(x)$ and

    $\lim\limits_{x \to a} g(x)$ exist, then $\lim\limits_{x \to a} f(x) \leq \lim\limits_{x \to a} g(x).$

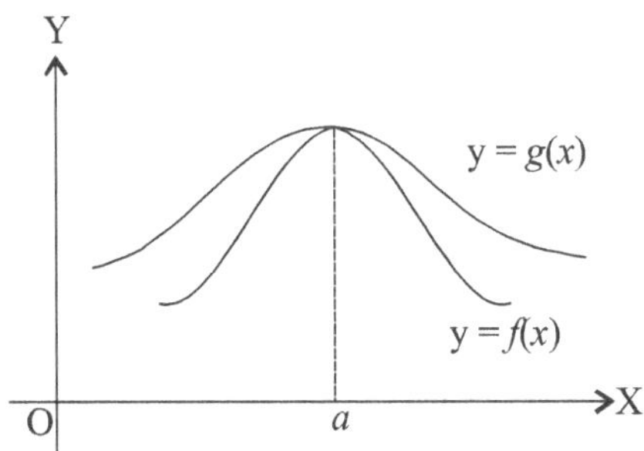

(Sandwich Theorem) Let f, g and h be real functions such that $f(x) \le g(x) \le h(x)$ for all x in the common domain of definition. For some real number a, if

$$\lim_{x \to a} f(x) = l = \lim_{x \to a} h(x), \text{ then } \lim_{x \to a} g(x) = l. \text{ This is illustrated in Fig 13.9.}$$

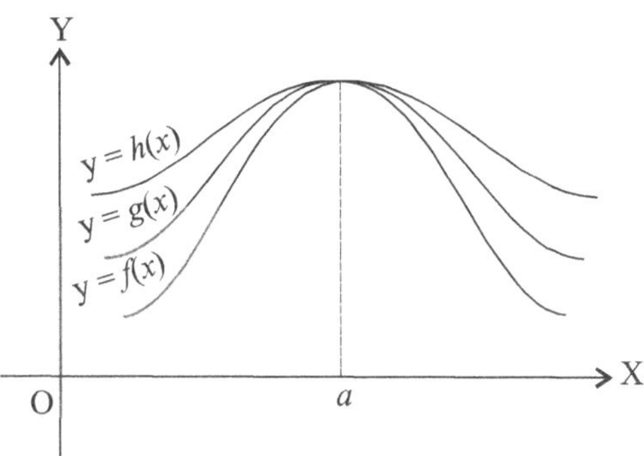

♦ The following are two important limits.

(i) $\displaystyle \lim_{x \to 0} \frac{\sin x}{x} = 1.$ (ii) $\displaystyle \lim_{x \to 0} \frac{1 - \cos x}{x} = 0.$

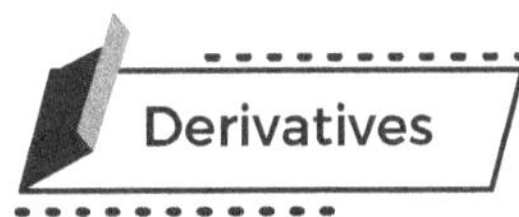

♦ *Suppose f is a real valued function and a is a point in its domain of definition. The derivative of f at a is defined by* $\displaystyle \lim_{h \to 0} \frac{f(a+h) - f(a)}{h}$
provided this limit exists.

♦ *Derivative of $f(x)$ at a is denoted by $f'(a)$.*

First Principle of Derivative

♦ *Suppose f is a real valued function, the function defined by* $\displaystyle \lim_{h \to 0} \frac{f(x+h) - f(x)}{h}$

wherever the limit exists is defined to be the derivative of f at x and is denoted by f'(x).

$$f'(x) = \lim_{h \to 0} \frac{f(x+h) - f(x)}{h}$$

♦ Sometimes $f'(x)$ is denoted by $\frac{d}{dx}(f(x))$ or if $y = f(x)$, it is denoted by $\frac{dy}{dx}$.

♦ This is referred to as derivative of $f(x)$ or y with respect to x.

♦ It is also denoted by D $(f(x))$.

Algebra of Derivative of Functions

♦ Let f and g be two functions such that their derivatives are defined in a common domain. Then

(i) Derivative of sum of two functions is sum of the derivatives of the functions.

$$\frac{d}{dx}[f(x) + g(x)] = \frac{d}{dx}f(x) + \frac{d}{dx}g(x).$$

(ii) Derivative of difference of two functions is difference of the derivatives of the functions.

$$\frac{d}{dx}[f(x) - g(x)] = \frac{d}{dx}f(x) - \frac{d}{dx}g(x).$$

(iii) Derivative of product of two functions is given by the following *product rule.*

$$\frac{d}{dx}[f(x).g(x)] = \frac{d}{dx}f(x).g(x) + f(x).\frac{d}{dx}g(x).$$

(iv) Derivative of quotient of two functions is given by the following *quotient rule* (whenever the denominator is non-zero).

$$\frac{d}{dx}\left(\frac{f(x)}{g(x)}\right) = \frac{\frac{d}{dx}f(x).g(x) - f(x)\frac{d}{dx}g(x)}{(g(x))^2}$$

Derivative of Polynomials and Trigonometric Functions

♦ Let $f(x) = a_n x^n + a_{n-1}x^{n-1} + \ldots + a_1 x + a_0$ be a polynomial function, where a_is are all real numbers and $a_n \neq 0$. Then, the derivative function is given by

$$\frac{df(x)}{dx} = n a_n x^{n-1} + (n-1)a_{n-1}x^{x-2} + \ldots + 2a_2 x + a_1.$$

Past Years ONE-LINERS
JEE Main/Board

- If $\lim\limits_{x \to a} \dfrac{f(x)}{g(x)}$, reduces to $\dfrac{0}{0}$ or $\dfrac{\infty}{\infty}$. Then, $\lim\limits_{x \to a} \dfrac{f(x)}{g(x)} = \lim\limits_{x \to a} \dfrac{f'(x)}{g'(x)}$

  and continue until $\dfrac{0}{0}$ or $\dfrac{\infty}{\infty}$ form is removed.

- For 1^∞ form $\lim\limits_{x \to a}[f(x)]^{g(x)} = e^{\lim\limits_{x \to a}(f(x)-1)g(x)}$

- Using Rationalisation like

$$\frac{1}{\sqrt{a}+\sqrt{b}} = \frac{1}{\left(\sqrt{a}+\sqrt{b}\right)}\frac{\left(\sqrt{a}-\sqrt{b}\right)}{\left(\sqrt{a}-\sqrt{b}\right)}$$

- Using trigonometric identities and ratios, e.g.

$$\frac{\tan^3 x}{\sin^4 x \times (1-\tan^2 x)} = \frac{\dfrac{\sin^3(x)}{\cos^3(x)}}{\sin^4 x \times \left(\dfrac{\cos^2 x - \sin^2 x}{\cos^2 x}\right)}$$

Tips/Tricks/Techniques ONE-LINERS
(Exam Special)

- **The algebra of limits**

  If $\lim\limits_{x \to a} f(x)$ and $\lim\limits_{x \to a} g(x)$ both exist and $\lim\limits_{x \to a} g(x) = m$, then, $\lim\limits_{x \to a} f(x) = \ell$,

  (a) $\lim\limits_{x \to a} k f(x) = k. \lim\limits_{x \to a} f(x) = k\ell$, where k is constant

  (b) $\lim\limits_{x \to a} [f(x)+k] = \lim\limits_{x \to a} f(x)+k = \ell + k$, where k is a constant

  (c) $\lim\limits_{x \to a} |f(x)| = |\lim\limits_{x \to a} f(x)| = |\ell|$

  (d) $\lim\limits_{x \to a} (f(x))^{g(x)} = \ell^m$

  (e) If $f(x) \le g(x)$ for every x in the neighbourhood of a, then $\lim\limits_{x \to a} f(x) \le$

  $\lim\limits_{x \to a} g(x)$

- **Methods of evaluation of limits**
  - **(a) When x → ∞ :**

    In this case expression should be expressed as a function of $1/x$ and then after removing indeterminate form (if it is there any), replace $1/x$ by 0.
  - **(b) Evaluation of limits by using L- Hospital's rule :**

    This result states that if $\lim\limits_{x\to a}\dfrac{f(x)}{g(x)}$ reduces to $\dfrac{0}{0}$ or $\dfrac{\infty}{\infty}$ (only these two indeterminate forms)

    Then, differentiate both numerator and denominator until and unless this form is removed.

    i.e., $\lim\limits_{x\to a}\dfrac{f(x)}{g(x)} = \lim\limits_{x\to a}\dfrac{f'(x)}{g'(x)}$, provided the later limit exists.

    But if it again take the form $\dfrac{0}{0}$ or $\dfrac{\infty}{\infty}$, then

    $\lim\limits_{x\to a}\dfrac{f(x)}{g(x)} = \lim\limits_{x\to a}\dfrac{f'(x)}{g'(x)} = \lim\limits_{x\to a}\dfrac{f''(x)}{g''(x)}$ and this process is continued till

    $\dfrac{0}{0}$ or $\dfrac{\infty}{\infty}$ form is removed.

- **Some standard limits**

  (a) $\lim\limits_{x\to 0} \sin x = 0$ (b) $\lim\limits_{x\to 0} \cos x = \lim\limits_{x\to 0}\left(\dfrac{1}{\cos x}\right) = 1$

  (c) $\lim\limits_{x\to 0} \tan x = 0$ (d) $\lim\limits_{x\to 0}\dfrac{\sin^{-1} x}{x} = \lim\limits_{x\to 0}\dfrac{x}{\sin^{-1} x} = 1$

  (e) $\lim\limits_{x\to 0}\dfrac{\tan^{-1} x}{x} = \lim\limits_{x\to 0}\dfrac{x}{\tan^{-1} x} = 1$

  (f) $\lim\limits_{x\to\infty}\left(1+\dfrac{a}{x}\right)^{x} = \lim\limits_{x\to 0}(1+ax)^{1/x} = e^{a}$

  (g) $\lim\limits_{x\to 0}\dfrac{a^{x}-1}{x} = \log_e a \quad (a>0)$

  (h) $\lim\limits_{x\to 0}\dfrac{e^{x}-1}{x} = 1$ (i) $\lim\limits_{x\to a}\dfrac{x^{n}-a^{n}}{x-a} = n\,a^{n-1}$

  (j) $\lim\limits_{x\to 0}\dfrac{\log(1+x)}{x} = 1$ (k) $\lim\limits_{x\to 0}\dfrac{(1+x)^{n}-1}{x} = n$

  (l) $\lim\limits_{x\to\infty}\dfrac{\sin x}{x} = \lim\limits_{x\to\infty}\dfrac{\cos x}{x} = 0$

  (m) $\lim\limits_{x\to\infty}\dfrac{\sin 1/x}{1/x} = 1$ (n) $\lim\limits_{x\to\infty} 1/x = 0$

♦ **Some limits which do not exist**

(a) $\lim\limits_{x\to 0}\left(\dfrac{1}{x}\right)$ (b) $\lim\limits_{x\to 0} x^{1/x}$

(c) $\lim\limits_{x\to 0}\dfrac{|x|}{x}$ (d) $\lim\limits_{x\to a}\dfrac{|x-a|}{x-a}$

(e) $\lim\limits_{x\to 0}\sin\left(\dfrac{1}{x}\right)$ (f) $\lim\limits_{x\to 0}\cos\left(\dfrac{1}{x}\right)$

(g) $\lim\limits_{x\to 0} e^{1/x}$ (h) $\lim\limits_{x\to\infty}\sin x$

(i) $\lim\limits_{x\to\infty}\cos x$

♦ $\lim\limits_{x\to a}\log f(x) = \log\left(\lim\limits_{x\to a} f(x)\right) = \log \ell,\ \text{where}\ \ell = \lim\limits_{x\to a} f(x)$

♦ $\lim\limits_{x\to a} e^{f(x)} = e^{\lim\limits_{x\to a} f(x)} = e^{\ell},\ \text{where}\ \ell = \lim\limits_{x\to a} f(x)$

♦ If $\lim\limits_{x\to a} f(x) = +\infty \text{ or} -\infty$, then $\lim\limits_{x\to a}\dfrac{1}{f(x)} = 0$

♦ $\lim\limits_{x\to\infty} a^x = \begin{cases} 0, & \text{if}\quad |a|<1 \\ 1, & \text{if}\quad a=1 \\ \infty & \text{if}\quad a>1 \\ \text{does not exist} & \text{if}\quad a\le -1 \end{cases}$

The derivative of the product of more than two functions as given below

$$(fgh)' = (fgh)\left(\dfrac{f'}{f}+\dfrac{g'}{g}+\dfrac{h'}{h}\right)$$

♦ **An important formula for evaluating limits of 1^{∞} forms**

$$= \underset{x\to a}{\text{Lim}} \left[f(x)\right]^{g(x)} = e^{\underset{x\to a}{\text{Lim}}[f(x)-1]g(x)}$$

Where $\underset{x\to a}{\text{Lim}} f(x) = 1$ and $\underset{x\to a}{\text{Lim}} g(x) = \infty$

♦ **Limit of the form ∞^{0}**

When $\lim\limits_{x\to a} f(x) \ne 1$ but $f(x)$ is positive in the

neighbourhood of $x = a$.

In this case, we write, $\{(f(x)\}^{g(x)} = e^{\log_e \{f(x)\}^{g(x)}}$

$\Rightarrow \quad \lim\limits_{x\to a}[f(x)]^{g(x)} = e^{\lim\limits_{x\to a} g(x)\log_e f(x)}$

14 Mathematical Reasoning

- The basic unit involved in mathematical reasoning is a mathematical statement.

- Let us start with two sentences:

  In 2003, the president of India was a woman.

  An elephant weighs more than a human being.

  When we read these sentences, we immediately decide that the first sentence is false and the second is correct. There is no confusion regarding these. In mathematics such sentences are called statements.

- On the other hand, consider the sentence:

  Women are more intelligent than men.

  Some people may think it is true while others may disagree. Regarding this sentence we cannot say whether it is always true or false . That means this sentence is ambiguous. Such a sentence is not acceptable as a statement in mathematics.

- A **sentence** is called a mathematically acceptable statement if it is either true or false but not both.

- Now, consider the following sentences :

  How beautiful!

  Open the door.

  Where are you going?

  Are they statements? No, because the first one is an exclamation, the second an order and the third a question. None of these is considered as a statement in mathematical language.

- Sentences involving variable time such as "today", "tomorrow" or "yesterday" are not statements. This is because it is not known what time is referred here. For example, the sentence

  Tomorrow is Friday.

  This is not a statement. The sentence is correct (true) on a Thursday but not on other days.

- The sentences with pronouns unless a particular person is referred to and for variable places such as "here", "there" etc. are also not a statement. For example,

She is a mathematics graduate.
Kashmir is far from here.
are not statements.

♦ Here is another sentence,
There are 40 days in a month.
Would you call this a statement? Note that the period mentioned in the sentence above is a "variable time" that is any of 12 months. But we know that the sentence is always false (irrespective of the month) since the maximum number of days in a month can never exceed 31. Therefore, this sentence is a statement.

♦ While dealing with statements, we usually denote them by small letters $p, q, r,...$ For example, we denote the statement "Fire is always hot" by p. This is also written as
p: Fire is always hot.

New Statements From Old

♦ We now look into method for producing new statements from those that we already have.
♦ This technique is to ask not only what it means to say that a given statement is true but also what it would mean to say that the given statement is not true.

Negation of a statement
♦ The denial of a statement is called the **negation of the statement.**
♦ Let us consider the statement:
p : New Delhi is a city.
The negation of this statement is
~"p : New Delhi is not a city.
♦ **Definition 1:** If p is a statement, then the negation of p is also a statement and is denoted by ~" p and read as 'not p'.
♦ **Note:** While forming the negation of a statement, phrases like, "It is not the case" or "It is false that" are also used.

Compound statements
♦ Many mathematical statements are obtained by combining one or more statements using some connecting words like "and", "or", etc.
♦ Consider the following statement
p: There is something wrong with the bulb or with the wiring.
This statement tells us that there is something wrong with the bulb or there is something wrong with the wiring. That means the given statement is actually made up of two smaller statements:
q: There is something wrong with the bulb.
r: There is something wrong with the wiring.
connected by "or".
♦ **Definition 2 :** A **compound statement** is a statement which is made up of two or more statements. In this case, each statement is called a **component statement**.

Special Words/Phrases

- Some of the connecting words which are found in compound statements like "And","Or", etc. are often used in Mathematical Statements. These are called **connectives.**
- When we use these words in compound statements, it is necessary to understand the role of these words.

The word "And" :

- Let us look at a compound statement with "And",

  p: A point occupies a position and its location can be determined.

  The statement can be broken into two component statements as,

  q: A point occupies a position.

  r: Its location can be determined.

  Here, we observe that both statements are true.
- We have the following rules regarding the connective "And",

  1. The compound statement with 'And' is true if all its component statements are true.

  2. The component statement with 'And' is false if any of its component statements is false (this includes the case that some of its component statements are false or all of its component statements are false).
- Do not think that a statement with "And" is always a compound statement. Therefore, the word "And" is not used as a connective.

The word "Or" :

- Let us look at the following statement,

  p: Two lines in a plane either intersect at one point or they are parallel.

  We know that this is a true statement. What does this mean? This means that if two lines in a plane intersect, then they are not parallel. Alternatively, if the two lines are not parallel, then they intersect at a point. That is this statement is true in both the situations.
- In order to understand statements with "Or" we first notice that the word "Or" is used in two ways in English language.
- Let us first look at the following statement.

  p: An ice-cream or pepsi is available with a Thali in a restaurant.

  This means that a person who does not want ice-cream can have a pepsi along with Thali or one does not want pepsi can have an ice-cream along with Thali. That is, who do not want a pepsi can have an ice-cream. A person cannot have both ice-cream and pepsi. This is called an exclusive "Or".
- Here is another statement.

  p: A student who has taken biology or chemistry can apply for M.Sc. microbiology.

  Here we mean that the students who have taken both biology and chemistry can apply for the microbiology programme, as well as the students who have taken only one of these subjects. In this case, we are using inclusive "Or".

♦ It is important to note the difference between these two ways because we require this when we check whether the statement is true or not.

Examples: For each of the following statements, determine whether an inclusive "Or" or exclusive "Or" is used.

(i) To enter a country, you need a passport or a voter registration card.

(ii) The school is closed if it is a holiday or a Sunday.

(iii) Two lines intersect at a point or are parallel.

(iv) Students can take French or Sanskrit as their third language.

Solutions:

(i) Here "Or" is inclusive since a person can have both a passport and a voter registration card to enter a country.

(ii) Here also "Or" is inclusive since school is closed on holiday as well as on Sunday.

(iii) Here "Or" is exclusive because it is not possible for two lines to intersect and parallel together.

(iv) Here also "Or" is exclusive because a student cannot take both French and Sanskrit.

♦ Rule for the compound statement with 'Or' ,

1. A compound statement with an 'Or' is true when one component statement is true or both the component statements are true.

2. A compound statement with an 'Or' is false when both the component statements are false.

Quantifiers

♦ **Quantifiers** are phrases like, "There exists" and "For all".

♦ For example, consider the statement.

p: There exists a rectangle whose all sides are equal.

This means that there is atleast one rectangle whose all sides are equal.

♦ A word closely connected with "there exists" is "for every" (or for all). Consider a statement.

p: For every prime number p, $\sqrt{p}$ is an irrational number.

This means that if S denotes the set of all prime numbers, then for all the members p of the set S, p is an irrational number.

♦ In general, a mathematical statement that says "for every" can be interpreted as saying that all the members of the given set S where the property applies must satisfy that property.

♦ We should also observe that it is important to know precisely where in the sentence a given connecting word is introduced. For example, compare the following two sentences:

1. For every positive number x there exists a positive number y such that $y < x$.

2. There exists a positive number y such that for every positive number x, we have $y < x$.

♦ Although these statements may look similar, they do not say the same thing. As a matter of fact, (1) is true and (2) is false.

♦ Thus, in order for a piece of mathematical writing to make sense, all of the symbols must be carefully introduced and each symbol must be introduced precisely at the right place – not too early and not too late.

♦ The words "And" and "Or" are called **connectives** and "There exists" and "For all" are called **quantifiers.**

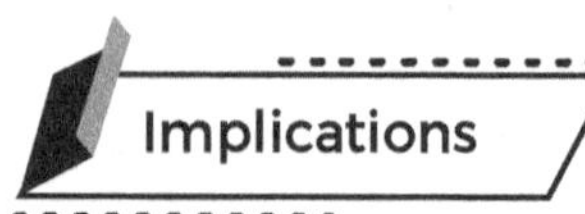

♦ In this section, we shall discuss the **implications** of "if-then", "only if" and "if and only if".

♦ The statements with "if-then" are very common in mathematics. For example, consider the statement.

r: If you are born in some country, then you are a citizen of that country.

When we look at this statement, we observe that it corresponds to two statements p and q given by

p: you are born in some country.

q: you are citizen of that country.

Then the sentence "if p then q" says that in the event if p is true, then q must be true.

♦ One of the most important facts about the sentence "if p then q" is that it does not say any thing (or places no demand) on q when p is false. For example, if you are not born in the country, then you cannot say anything about q.

♦ Another point to be noted for the statement "if p then q" is that the statement does not imply that p happens.

♦ There are several ways of understanding "if p then q" statements. We shall illustrate these ways in the context of the following statement.

r: If a number is a multiple of 9, then it is a multiple of 3.

Let p and q denote the statements

p: a number is a multiple of 9.

q: a number is a multiple of 3.

Then, if p then q is the same as the following:

(i) p implies q is denoted by $p \Rightarrow q$. The symbol $\Rightarrow$ stands for implies. This says that a number is a multiple of 9 implies that it is a multiple of 3.

(ii) p is a sufficient condition for q. This says that knowing that a number as a multiple of 9 is sufficient to conclude that it is a multiple of 3.

(iii) p only if q. This says that a number is a multiple of 9 only if it is a multiple of 3.

(iv) q is a necessary condition for p. This says that when a number is a multiple of 9, it is necessarily a multiple of 3.

(v) $\sim q$ implies $\sim p$. This represents that if a number is not a multiple of 3, then it is not a multiple of 9.

Contrapositive and Converse :

♦ **Contrapositive** and **converse** are certain other statements which can be formed from a given statement with "if-then".

♦ For example, let us consider the following "if-then" statement.

If the physical environment changes, then the biological environment changes.

Then the contrapositive of this statement is If the biological environment does not change, then the physical environment does not change.

Note that both these statements convey the same meaning.

Validating Statements

♦ In this section, we will discuss when a statement is true. To answer this question, one must answer all the following questions.

♦ The answer to these questions depend upon which of the special words and phrases "and", "or", and which of the implications "if and only", "if-then", and which of the quantifiers "for every", "there exists", appear in the given statement.

♦ Here, we shall list some general rules for checking whether a statement is true or not.

♦ **Rule 1:** If p and q are mathematical statements, then in order to show that the statement "p and q" is true, the following steps are followed.

    Step-1: Show that the statement p is true.

    Step-2: Show that the statement q is true.

♦ **Rule 2:** Statements with "Or"

If p and q are mathematical statements, then in order to show that the statement "p or q" is true, one must consider the following.

Case 1: By assuming that p is false, show that q must be true.

Case 2: By assuming that q is false, show that p must be true.

♦ **Rule 3:** Statements with "If-then"

In order to prove the statement "if p then q" we need to show that any one of the following case is true.

Case 1: By assuming that p is true, prove that q must be true. (Direct method)

Case 2: By assuming that q is false, prove that p must be false. (Contrapositive method)

♦ **Rule 4:** Statements with "if and only if"

In order to prove the statement "p if and only if q", we need to show.

  (i)   If p is true, then q is true and

  (ii)   If q is true, then p is true

♦ **Note:** To prove $p \Rightarrow q$, it is enough to show $\sim q \Rightarrow \sim p$ which is the contrapositive of the statement $p \Rightarrow q$.

By Contradiction

♦   Here to check whether a statement p is true, we assume that p is not true i.e. $\sim p$ is true. Then, we arrive at some result which contradicts our assumption. Therefore, we conclude that p is true.

♦   A method by which we may show that a statement is false. The method involves giving an example of a situation where the statement is not valid. Such an example is called a **counter example.** The name itself suggests that this is an example to counter the given statement.

♦   **Note:** In mathematics, counter examples are used to disprove the statement. However, generating examples in favour of a statement do not provide validity of the statement.

Past Years ONE-LINERS
JEE Main/Board

♦   De Morgan's law $\Rightarrow$ (i) $\sim(p \wedge q) \equiv \sim p \vee \sim q$

(ii) $\sim(p \vee q) \equiv \sim p \wedge \sim q$

Distributive law $\Rightarrow$ (i) $p \wedge (q \vee r) \equiv (p \wedge q) \vee (p \wedge r)$

(ii) $p \vee (q \wedge r) \equiv (p \vee q) \wedge (p \vee r)$

$p \Rightarrow q \equiv \sim p \vee q$ (Implications)

♦ $\wedge = $ and, $\vee = $ or

$p \Rightarrow q \equiv \sim p \vee q$ and $q \Rightarrow p \equiv \sim q \vee p$

♦   Negation $\Rightarrow \sim(p \wedge q) \equiv \sim p \vee \sim q$

De Morgan's law $\Rightarrow$ (i) $\sim(p \wedge q) \equiv \sim p \vee \sim q$

(ii) $\sim(p \vee q) \equiv \sim p \wedge \sim q$

♦   Distributive law $\Rightarrow$ (i) $p \wedge (q \vee r) \equiv (p \wedge q) \vee (p \wedge r)$

(ii) $p \vee (q \wedge r) \equiv (p \vee q) \wedge (p \vee r)$

♦   Negation $\Rightarrow \sim(p \vee q) \equiv \sim p \wedge \sim q$

Distributive law $\Rightarrow$ $p \wedge (q \vee r) \equiv (p \wedge q) \vee (p \wedge r)$

♦   In truth table of

$(p \Rightarrow q) \Rightarrow [(\sim p \Rightarrow q) \Rightarrow q] = $ T, T, T, T

(i.e. All the possibilities are true)

$\therefore$ It is tautology.

$p \Rightarrow q \equiv \sim p \vee q,$

- Distributive law $\Rightarrow$ (i) $p \wedge (q \vee r) \equiv (p \wedge q) \vee (p \wedge r)$

  (ii) $p \vee (q \wedge r) \equiv (p \vee q) \wedge (p \vee r)$

  Complement law $\Rightarrow p \wedge \sim p \equiv F$ and $\sim T = F$

- Negation of conditional statement $\Rightarrow \sim (p \wedge q) \equiv \sim p \vee \sim q$

  De Morgan's law (i) $\sim (p \wedge q) \equiv \sim p \vee \sim q$

  (ii) $\sim (p \vee q) \equiv \sim p \wedge \sim q$

Tips/Tricks/Techniques ONE-LINERS
(Exam Special)

Truth Table

A table that shows the relationship between the truth value of compound statement. S $(p, q, r, ...)$ and the truth values of its sub-statements $p, q, r, ...,$ etc., is called the truth table of statement S.

If p and q are two simple statements then truth table for basic logical connectives of :

Conjunction :

p	q	$p \wedge q$
T	T	T
T	F	F
F	T	F
F	F	F

Disjunction :

p	q	$p \vee q$
T	T	T
T	F	T
F	T	T
F	F	F

Negation :

p	$\sim p$
T	F
F	T

Conditional :

p	q	$p \Rightarrow q$
T	T	T
T	F	F
F	T	T
F	F	T

Biconditional :

p	q	$p \Rightarrow q$	$q \Rightarrow p$	$p \Leftrightarrow q$ or $(p \Rightarrow q) \wedge (q \Rightarrow p)$
T	T	T	T	T
T	F	F	T	F
F	T	T	F	F
F	F	T	T	T

♦ **Logical equivalence**

Two compound statements S_1 $(p, q, r, ...)$ and S_2 $(p, q, r, ...)$ are said to be logically equivalent if they have the same truth values for all logical possibilities.

In other words, two statements S_1 and S_2 are equivalent if they have identical truth table *i.e.* the entries in the last column of the truth tables are same.

If statements S_1 and S_2 are equivalent then we write $S_1 \equiv S_2$

Tautology : A statement is said to be a tautology if it is true for all logical possibilities.

Contradiction : A statement is a contradiction if it is false for all logical possibilities *i.e.* its truth value is always F.

♦ **Duality**

Two compound statements S_1 and S_2 are said to be duals of each other if one can be obtained from the other by replacing $\wedge$ by $\vee$ and $\vee$ by $\wedge$.

Converse: The converse of the conditional statement $p \to q$ is defined as $q \to p$.

Inverse : The inverse of the conditional statement $p \to q$ is defined as $\sim p \to \sim q$

Contrapositive : The contrapositive of the conditional statement $p \to q$ is defined as $\sim q \to \sim p$

♦ **Negation of compound statements**

(a) **Negation of conjunction :**

If p and q are two statements then
$$\sim (p \wedge q) \equiv \sim p \vee \sim q$$

(b) **Negation of disconjunction :**

If p and q are two statements then $\sim (p \vee q) \equiv \sim p \wedge \sim q$

(c) **Negation of implication :**

If p and q are two statements, then $\sim (p \Rightarrow q) \equiv p \wedge \sim q$

(d) **Negation of Biconditional :**

If p and q are two statements, then
$$\sim (p \Leftrightarrow q) \equiv (p \wedge \sim q) \vee (q \wedge \sim p)$$

Algebra of statements

If p, q, r are any three statements then the some law of algebra of statements are as follow :

(a) **Idempotent Laws**

(i) $p \vee p \equiv p$ (ii) $p \wedge p \equiv p$

(b) **Commutative Laws**

(i) $p \vee q \equiv q \vee p$ (ii) $p \wedge q \equiv q \wedge p$

(c) **Associative Law**

(i) $(p \vee q) \vee r \equiv p \vee (q \vee r)$ (ii) $(p \wedge q) \wedge r \equiv p \wedge (q \wedge r)$

(d) **Distributive Laws**

(i) $p \wedge (q \vee r) \equiv (p \wedge q) \vee (p \wedge r)$

(ii) $p \vee (q \wedge r) \equiv (p \vee q) \wedge (p \vee r)$

(e) **De 'Morgan's Law**

(i) $\sim (p \wedge q) \equiv \sim p \vee \sim q$

(ii) $\sim (p \vee q) \equiv \sim p \wedge \sim q$

(f)   Contrapositive Laws

For any statement p, we have

$$p \Rightarrow q \equiv \sim q \Rightarrow \sim p$$

(g)   Involution Laws (Double Negation Laws)

$$\sim (\sim p) \equiv p$$

♦ The truth value of compound statement is determined by the truth value of each of its sub-statements,

♦ If the compound statement is made up of n sub-statements then its truth table will contain 2^n rows.

♦ The negation of a tautology is a contradiction and vice-versa.

♦ The connectives $\wedge$ and $\vee$ are also called dual of each other

♦ If $S^*(p,q)$ is the dual of the compound statement $S(p, q)$ then

(a) $S^* (\sim p, \sim q) \equiv \sim S (p, q)$ (b) $\sim S^* (p, q) \equiv S (\sim p, \sim q)$

For ex : The duals of the following statements.

(i) $(p \wedge q) \vee (r \vee s)$

(ii) $(p \vee t) \wedge (p \vee c)$

(iii) $\sim (p \wedge q) \vee [p \wedge \sim (q \vee \sim s)]$

are as given below :

(i) $(p \vee q) \wedge (r \wedge s)$

(ii) $(p \wedge t) \vee (p \wedge c)$

(iii) $\sim (p \vee q) \wedge [p \vee \sim (q \wedge \sim s)]$

Statistics

- Variability is a factor which is required to be studied under statistics. Like 'measures of central tendency' we want to have a single number to describe variability. This single number is called a 'measure of dispersion'.
- The dispersion or scatter in a data is measured on the basis of the observations and the types of the measure of central tendency, used there.
- There are following measures of dispersion:
  (i) Range, (ii) Quartile deviation, (iii) Mean deviation, (iv) Standard deviation.

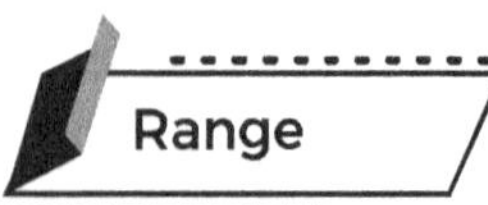

- Range is the difference between maximum value and minimum value.
  $\therefore$ Range = Maximum Value – Minimum Value
- The range of data gives us a rough idea of variability or scatter but does not tell about the dispersion of the data from a measure of central tendency.
- For this purpose, The important measures of dispersion, which depend upon the deviations of the observations from a central tendency are mean deviation and standard deviation.

- The deviation of an observation x from a fixed value 'a' is the difference x – a. The measure of central tendency lies between the maximum and the minimum values of the set of observations. Therefore, some of the deviations will be negative and some positive. Thus, the sum of deviations may vanish. Moreover, the sum of the deviations from mean (x) is zero.

$$\text{Also Mean of deviations} = \frac{\text{Sum of deviations}}{\text{Number of observations}}$$

$$= \frac{0}{n} = 0$$

♦ The mean deviation from 'a' is denoted as M.D. (a). Therefore,

$$\text{M.D.(a)} = \frac{\text{Sum of absolute values of deviations from 'a'}}{\text{Number of observations}}$$

♦ **Remark:** Mean deviation may be obtained from any measure of central tendency. However, mean deviation from mean and median are commonly used in statistical studies.

Mean deviation for ungrouped data :

♦ Let n observations be x_1 , x_2 , x_3 , ..., xn and $\bar{x}$ = Mean and M = Median. Then,
1. Mean deviation about mean is

$$\text{M.D.}(\bar{x}) = \frac{1}{n}\sum_{i=1}^{n} |x_i - \bar{x}|, \text{ where } \bar{x} = \text{Mean}$$

2. Mean deviation about median is

$$\text{M.D.(M)} = \frac{1}{n}\sum_{i=1}^{n} |x_i - M|, \text{ where M = Median}$$

Mean deviation for grouped data :

♦ Data can be grouped into two ways :

(a) Discrete frequency distribution: Let the given data consist of n distinct values $x_1, x_2, ..., x_n$ occurring with frequencies $f_1, f_2, ..., f_n$ respectively. This data can be represented in the tabular form as given below, and is called discrete frequency distribution:

$$x : x_1 \quad x_2 \quad x_3 \,.... \, x_n$$
$$f : f_1 \quad f_2 \quad f_3 \,.... \, f_n$$

   (i) Mean deviation about mean :

$$\text{M.D.}(\bar{x}) = \frac{\sum_{i=1}^{n} f_i |x_i - \bar{x}|}{\sum_{i=1}^{n} f_i} = \frac{1}{N}\sum_{i=1}^{n} f_i |x_i - \bar{x}|$$

   (ii) Mean deviation about median :

$$\text{M.D.(M)} = \frac{1}{N}\sum_{i=1}^{n} f_i |x_i - M|$$

(b) Continuous frequency distribution: A continuous frequency distribution is a series in which the data are classified into different class-intervals without gaps along with their respective frequencies.

   (i) Mean deviation about mean :

$$\text{M.D.}(\bar{x}) = \frac{1}{N}\sum_{i=1}^{n} f_i |x_i - \bar{x}|$$

Shortcut method for calculating mean deviation about mean :

$$\overline{x} = a + \frac{\sum\limits_{i=1}^{n} f_i\, d_i}{N} \times h \quad \text{Where } d_i = \frac{x_i - a}{h} \quad \&\ a \text{ is the assumed mean and}$$

h is the common factor.

$$\text{Now, M.D.}(\overline{x}) = \frac{1}{N} \sum\limits_{i=1}^{n} f_i \,|\, x_i - \overline{x}\,|$$

(ii)   Mean deviation about median :

$$\text{M.D.(M)} = \frac{1}{N} \sum\limits_{i=1}^{n} f_i \,|\, x_i - M\,|$$

$$\text{and Median} = l + \frac{\dfrac{N}{2} - C}{f} \times h$$

Where median class is the class interval whose cumulative frequency is just

greater than or equal to $\dfrac{N}{2}$, N is the sum of frequencies, l, f, h and C are,

respectively the lower limit , the frequency, the width of the median class and
C the cumulative frequency of the class just preceding the median class.

Limitations of mean deviation:

♦   In a series, where the degree of variability is very high, the median is not a
representative central tendency. Thus, the mean deviation about median
calculated for such series can not be fully relied.

♦   The sum of the deviations from the mean (minus signs ignored) is more than
the sum of the deviations from median. Therefore, the mean deviation about
the mean is not very scientific.

♦   Thus, in many cases, mean deviation may give unsatisfactory results. Also
mean deviation is calculated on the basis of absolute values of the deviations
and therefore, cannot be subjected to further algebraic treatment.

♦   This implies that we must have some other measure of dispersion. Standard
deviation is such a measure of dispersion.

Variance and Standard Deviation

Variance : Mean of the squares of the deviations from mean is called the variance.
It is denoted by σ^2 (read as sigma square).

♦ Therefore, the variance of n observations x_1, x_2, ..., x_n is given by

$$\sigma^2 = \frac{1}{n} \sum_{i=1}^{n} (x_i - \overline{x})^2$$

Standard Deviation :

♦ In the calculation of variance, we find that the units of individual observations xi and the unit of their mean x are different from that of variance, since variance involves the sum of squares of (xi – x).

♦ For this reason, the proper measure of dispersion about the mean of a set of observations is expressed as positive square-root of the variance and is called standard deviation.

♦ Therefore, the standard deviation, usually denoted by σ, is given by

$$\sigma = \sqrt{\frac{1}{n} \sum_{i=1}^{n} (x_i - \overline{x})^2}$$

Standard deviation of a discrete frequency distribution :

♦ $$\sigma = \sqrt{\frac{1}{N} \sum_{i=1}^{n} f_i (x_i - \overline{x})^2},$$

where $\overline{x}$ is the mean of the distribution and $N = \sum_{i=1}^{n} f_i$.

Standard deviation of a continuous frequency distribution :

♦ $$\sigma = \sqrt{\frac{1}{N} \sum_{i=1}^{n} f_i (x_i - \overline{x})^2},$$

where $\overline{x}$ is the mean of the distribution and $N = \sum_{i=1}^{n} f_i$.

♦ Another formula for standard deviation :

$$\text{standard deviation } (\sigma) = \frac{1}{N} \sqrt{N \sum_{i=1}^{n} f_i x_i^2 - \left(\sum_{i=1}^{n} f_i x_i \right)^2}$$

Shortcut method to find Variance and Standard deviation :

♦ Sometimes the values of xi in a discrete distribution or the mid points xi of different classes in a continuous distribution are large and so the calculation of mean and variance becomes tedious and time consuming.

◆ By using step-deviation method, it is possible to simplify the procedure.

◆ Let 'A' be the assumed mean, Then

$$\text{Variance, } \sigma^2 = \frac{h^2}{N^2}\left[N\sum f_i y_i - \left(\sum f_i y_i\right)^2\right] \text{ and}$$

$$\text{Standard Deviation, } \sigma_x = \frac{h}{N}\left[N\sum_{i=1}^{n} f_i y_i^2 - \left(\sum_{i=1}^{n} f_i y_i\right)^2\right] \text{ Where } y_i = \frac{x_i - A}{h}.$$

Analysis of Frequency Distributions

◆ The mean deviation and the standard deviation have the same units in which the data are given.

◆ Whenever we want to compare the variability of two series with same mean, which are measured in different units, we do not merely calculate the measures of dispersion but we require such measures which are independent of the units.

◆ **Coefficient of Variation :** The measure of variability which is independent of units is called coefficient of variation (denoted as C.V.) .The coefficient of variation is defined as

$$\text{C.V.} = \frac{\sigma}{\bar{x}} \times 100, \ \bar{x} \neq 0,$$

where σ and $\bar{x}$ are the standard deviation and mean of the data.

◆ For comparing the variability or dispersion of two series, we calculate the coefficient of variance for each series. The series having greater C.V. is said to be more variable than the other. The series having lesser C.V. is said to be more consistent than the other.

Comparison of two frequency distributions with same mean :

◆ Let $\bar{x}_1$ and σ_1 be the mean and standard deviation of the first distribution, $\bar{x}_2$ and σ_2 be the mean and standard deviation of the second distribution.

$$\text{Then} \quad \text{C.V. (1st distribution)} = \frac{\sigma_1}{\bar{x}_1} \times 100$$

$$\text{and} \quad \text{C.V. (2nd distribution)} = \frac{\sigma_2}{\bar{x}_2} \times 100$$

$$\text{Given } \bar{x}_1 = \bar{x}_2 = \bar{x} \text{ (say)}$$

$$\text{Therefore } \text{C.V. (1st distribution)} = \frac{\sigma_1}{\bar{x}} \times 100 \qquad \text{...(i)}$$

and $\qquad \text{C.V.} \, (2\text{nd distribution}) = \dfrac{\sigma_2}{\overline{x}} \times 100 \qquad \text{...(ii)}$

♦ It is clear from (i) and (ii) that the two C.Vs. can be compared on the basis of values of σ_1 and σ_2 only.

♦ Thus, we say that for two series with equal means, the series with greater standard deviation (or variance) is called more variable or dispersed than the other.

♦ Also, the series with lesser value of standard deviation (or variance) is said to be more consistent than the other.

Past Years ONE-LINERS
JEE Main/Board

♦ Mean, $\overline{x} = \dfrac{\sum f_i x_i}{N}$ where $N = \sum f_i$

Median, $M = l + \dfrac{\dfrac{N}{2} - C}{f} \times h$

♦ Let correct observation $= b$
Incorrect observation $= a$

$\underset{(\overline{x})}{\text{Old Mean}} = \dfrac{\sum x_i}{N},$

$\underset{(v)}{\text{Old Variance}} = \dfrac{\sum x_i^2}{N} - (\overline{x})^2$

$\underset{(\overline{y})}{\text{New Mean}} = \dfrac{N\overline{x} - a + b}{N},$

$\underset{(V')}{\text{New Variance}} = \dfrac{[V + (\overline{x})^2]N - a^2 + b^2}{N} - (\overline{y})^2$

♦ Mean, $\overline{x} = \dfrac{\sum x_i}{N}$

Standard deviation, $\sigma = \sqrt{\dfrac{\sum (x_i - \overline{x})^2}{N}}$

♦ Old Number of observations $= N$, Added observation $= a$
New number of observations $= N' = N + n$
Number of Added observations $= n$

Old Mean, $\bar{x} = \dfrac{\sum x_i}{N}$; Old variance, $V = \dfrac{\sum x_i^2}{N} - (\bar{x})^2$

New Mean, $\bar{y} = \dfrac{N\bar{x} + a}{N'}$;

New Variance, $V' = \dfrac{[V + (\bar{x})^2]N + a^2}{N'} - (\bar{y})^2$

♦ For observations $x_1, x_2, x_3 \ldots x_n$;

$$\text{Mean} = \bar{x}, \quad \text{variance} = V = \dfrac{\sum x_i^2}{n} - (\bar{x})^2 = \dfrac{\sum x_i}{n}$$

→ By multiplying by a in the observations $x_1, x_2, x_3, \ldots x_n$; we get
$$y_1 = ax_1, y_2 = ax_2 \ldots y_n = ax_n$$

∴ $\text{Mean} = \bar{y} = \dfrac{\sum y_i}{n}$ and Variance $= V'$

$$V' = \dfrac{a^2 \in x_i^2}{n} - (\bar{x})^2 a^2$$

∴ $\boxed{\bar{y} = a\bar{x}}$ ∴ $\boxed{V' = a^2 V}$

and $\sum y_i = a \sum x_i$

$$\sum y_i^2 = a^2 \sum x^2$$

♦ Standard Deviation, $\sigma = \sqrt{\dfrac{x_1^2 + x_2^2 + \ldots + x_n^2}{n} - (\bar{x})^2}$ and

$$\bar{x} = \dfrac{x_1 + x_2 + \ldots + x_n}{n}$$

♦ Added observations = a, b
Removed observation = C
Old Number of observations = N
New Number of observations = N′ = N + n
n = No. of added observations − No. of removed observation

Old Mean, $\bar{x} = \dfrac{\sum x_i}{N}$

New Mean, $\bar{y} = \dfrac{\sum y_i}{N'} = \dfrac{N\bar{x} - C + a + b}{N'}$

Tips/Tricks/Techniques ONE-LINERS
(Exam Special)

- **Geometric mean**

  (a) If $x_1, x_2, x_3, \ldots\ldots, x_n$ are n values of a variate x, none of them being zero, then the geometric mean G is defined as
  $$G = (x_1 x_2 x_3 \ldots x_n)^{1/n}$$

  (b) Let $x_1, x_2, \ldots\ldots, x_n$ be n observation and $f_1, f_2, \ldots\ldots, f_n$ be their corresponding frequency then their Geometric Mean is

  $$G = \left(x_1^{f_1} x_2^{f_2} \ldots\ldots x_n^{f_n} \right)^{1/N}, \quad \text{where } N = \sum_{i=1}^{n} f_i$$

- Relationship between A.M., G.M., and H.M.

  A.M. $\geq$ G.M. $\geq$ H.M.

  Equality sign holds only when all the observations are same.

- **Relationship between mean, mode and median**

  (a) **In symmetrical distribution**

  Mean = Mode = Median

  (b) **In skew (moderately symmetrical) distribution**

  Mode = 3 median − 2 mean

- In a statistical data, the sum of the deviation of items from A.M. is always zero.

  i.e. $\displaystyle\sum_{i=1}^{n} (x_i - \bar{x}) = 0$

- In a statistical data, the sum of squares of the deviation of items is least if it is

  measured from A.M. *i.e.* $\displaystyle\sum_{i=1}^{n} (x_1 - \bar{x})^2$ is least.

- If arithmetic mean of $x_1, x_2, x_3, \ldots, x_n$ be $\bar{x}$, then arithmetic mean of $x_1 \pm a, x_2 \pm a, x_3 \pm a, \ldots, x_n \pm a$ will be $\bar{x} \pm a$.

- If $\bar{x}$ is the mean of $x_1, x_2, \ldots\ldots, x_n$, The mean of $ax_1, ax_2, \ldots\ldots, ax_n$ is $a\bar{x}$, where a is any number different from zero.

- If mean of $x_1, x_2, x_3, \ldots\ldots, x_n$ be $\bar{x}$, then mean of $\dfrac{x_1}{a}, \dfrac{x_2}{a}, \dfrac{x_3}{a}, \ldots\ldots, \dfrac{x_n}{a}$ will be $\dfrac{\bar{x}}{a}$.

- The sum of the absolute value of deviations of the items from median is minimum.

- It is a positional average and it is not influenced by the position of the items.

- Mode is not effected by presence of extremely large or small items.

- If all values of the variate in a distribution are added (subtracted) by the same quantity (say λ), then the variance of the distribution remains unchanged. Hence $\text{Var}(X + \lambda) = \text{Var}(X)$

- If all values of the variate in a distribution are multiplied by a constant number k, then the variance of the distribution is multiplied by k^2. Hence $\text{Var}(kX) = k^2 \text{var}(X)$

- From above results (i) and (ii) it is obvious that
$\text{Var}(aX + b) = a^2 \text{Var}(X)$

$$\text{M.D.} = \frac{4}{5}(\text{S.D.})$$

- If AM's of two series containing n_1, n_2 values are $\bar{x}_1, \bar{x}_2$ and their variance's are σ_1^2, σ_2^2 respectively and combined mean is $\bar{x}$ then the variance of their combined series is given by

$$\sigma^2 = \frac{n_1\sigma_1^2 + n_2\sigma_2^2}{(n_1 + n_2)} + \frac{n_1 n_2}{(n_1 + n_2)^2}(\bar{x}_1 - \bar{x}_2)^2$$

- The square of S.D., i.e., σ^2 is called the VARIANCE.

- The ratio of S.D. (σ) and the A.M. (A) is called the **coefficient of standard deviation** $\left(\dfrac{\sigma}{A}\right)$.

- The percentage form of coefficient of S.D., i.e. $\left(\dfrac{\sigma}{A}\right) \times 100$ is called **Coefficient of Variance.**

- The distribution for which the coefficient of variance is less is called more consistent.

- The RMS deviation is the least when measured from A.M.

- The sum of the squares of the deviation of the values of the variables is the least when measured from A.M.

- $$\sigma^2 + A^2 = \frac{\sum fx^2}{\sum f}.$$

- For discrete distribution $f = 1$, thus $\sigma^2 + A^2 = \dfrac{\sum x^2}{n}$.

- Above formula is a short-cut for finding σ.

$$\text{Variance} = \sigma^2 = \frac{\sum fx^2}{n} - A^2$$

- The mean deviation about the mean is less than or equal to the S.D., i.e., $\text{M.D.} \le \sigma$.

16. Probability-I

- An experiment is called random experiment if it satisfies the following two conditions:
  (i) It has more than one possible outcome.
  (ii) It is not possible to predict the outcome in advance.

Outcomes and sample space

- A possible result of a random experiment is called its *outcome*.
- The set of all possible outcomes of a random experiment is called the *sample space* associated with the experiment.
- Sample space is denoted by the symbol S.
- Each element of the sample space is called a *sample point*.
- Each outcome of the random experiment is also called *sample point*.

Any subset E of a sample space S is called *an event.*

Occurrence of an event

- The event E of a sample space S is said to have occurred if the outcome ω of the experiment is such that $\omega \in$ E.
- If the outcome ω is such that $\omega \notin$ E, we say that the event E has not occurred.
- **Types of events:** Events can be classified into various types on the basis of the elements they have.

1. **Impossible and Sure Events**

- The empty set ϕ and the sample space S describe events ϕ is called an impossible event and S. The whole sample space is called the sure event.
- We say that the empty set only correspond to the event E.

2. **Simple Event**

- If an event E has only one sample point of a sample space, it is called a **simple** (or **elementary**) **event**.
- In a sample space containing n distinct elements, there are exactly n simple events.

For example in the experiment of tossing two coins, a sample space is
$$S = \{HH, HT, TH, TT\}$$

♦ There are four simple events corresponding to this sample space. These are
$$E_1 = \{HH\}, E_2 = \{HT\}, E_3 = \{TH\} \text{ and } E_4 = \{TT\}.$$

3. **Compound Event :** If an event has more than one sample point, it is called a **Compound event**.

   Algebra of events : Let A, B, C be events associated with an experiment whose sample space is S.

1. **Complementary Event :** For every event A, there corresponds another event A' called the complementary event to A. It is also called the event **'not A'**.

2. **The Event 'A or B' :** Union of two sets A and B denoted by $A \cup B$ contains all those elements which are either in A or in B or in both.

♦ Event 'A or B' $= A \cup B$
$$= \{\omega : \omega \in A \text{ or } \omega \in B\}$$

3. **The Event 'A and B' :** Intersection of two sets $A \cap B$ is the set of those elements which are common to both A and B. i.e., which belong to both 'A and B'.

♦ If A and B are two events, then the set $A \cap B$ denotes the event 'A and B'. Thus, $A \cap B = \{\omega : \omega \in A \text{ and } \omega \in B\}$

4. **The Event 'A but not B' :** We know that A–B is the set of all those elements which are in A but not in B.

   Therefore, $A - B = A \cap B'$

♦ **Mutually exclusive events :** Two events A and B are called **mutually exclusive** events if the occurrence of any one of them excludes the occurrence of the other event.

♦ In this case the sets A and B are disjoint.

♦ Simple events of a sample space are always mutually exclusive.

♦ **Exhaustive events :** In general, if $E_1, E_2, ..., E_n$ are n events of a sample space S and if

$$E_1 \cup E_2 \cup E_3 \cup ..._2 \cup E_n = \bigcup_{i=1}^{n} E_i = S$$

then $E_1, E_2, ..., E_n$ are called **exhaustive events**.

♦ If $E_i \cap E_j = \phi$ for $i \neq j$ i.e., events E_i and E_j are pairwise disjoint and $\bigcup_{i=1}^{n} E_i = S$, then events $E_1, E_2, ..., E_n$ are called **mutually exclusive and exhaustive events**.

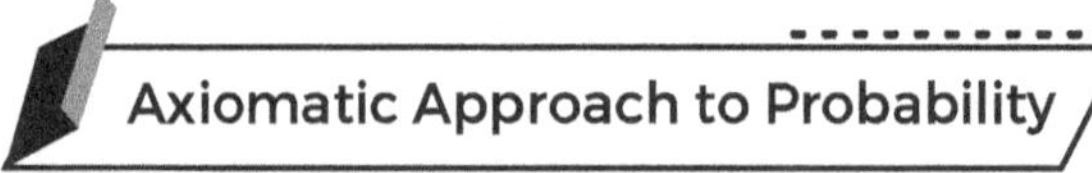

♦ Let S be a sample space containing outcomes $\omega_1, \omega_2, ..., \omega_n$, i.e., $S = \{\omega_1, \omega_2, ..., \omega_n\}$

- It follows from the axiomatic definition of probability that
  (i) $0 \leq P(\omega_i) \leq 1$ for each $\omega_i \in S$
  (ii) $P(\omega_1) + P(\omega_2) + ... + P(\omega_n) = 1$
  (iii) For any event A, $P(A) = \Sigma P(\omega_i)$, $\omega_i \in A$.
- It may be noted that the singleton $\{\omega_i\}$ is called elementary event and for notational convenience, we write $P(\omega_i)$ for $P(\{\omega_i\})$.
- **Probability of an event**
- **Probabilities of equally likely outcomes :** Let a sample space of an experiment be
$$S = \{\omega_1, \omega_2,..., \omega_n\}.$$
- E be an event, such that $n(S) = n$ and $n(E) = m$. If each out come is equally likely, then it follows that

$$P(E) = \frac{m}{n} = \frac{\text{Number of outcomes favourable to E}}{\text{Total possible outcomes}}$$

- $P(A \cup B) = P(A) + P(B) - P(A \cap B)$
- $A \cup B = A \cup (B - A)$, where A and B – A are mutually exclusive.
- If A and B are disjoint sets, i.e., they are mutually exclusive events, then
  $A \cap B = \phi$
  Therefore $P(A \cap B) = P(\phi) = 0$
- Thus, for mutually exclusive events A and B, we have
  $$P(A \cup B) = P(A) - P(B)$$
- **Probability of event 'not A' :** We know that A¢ and A are mutually exclusive and exhaustive events i.e.,
- $A \cap A' = \phi$ and $A \cup A' = S$
  or $P(A \cup A') = P(S)$
- Now $P(A) + P(A') = 1$
  or $P(A') = P(\text{not A}) = 1 - P(A)$

Past Years ONE-LINERS
JEE Main/Board

- From additional theorem of probability
  $[P(\text{Exactly A}) = P(A) - P(A \cap B)]$
- To get number of subsets $= 2^n$
- From additional theorem of probability
  P(Exactly one of A or B occurs)
  $= P(A) + P(B) - 2P(A \cap B)$
- Here, number of mass of n balls placed in 3 boxes $= 3^n$

Tips/Tricks/Techniques ONE-LINERS
(Exam Special)

- -

♦ **ODDS against and odds in favour of an event**

Let there be $(m + n)$ equally likely, mutually exclusive and exhaustive cases out of which an event A can occur in m cases and does not occur in n cases. Then by definition of probability of occurrences of event A,

$$P(A) = \frac{m}{m+n}$$

The probability of non- occurrence of event A, $P(A') = \dfrac{n}{m+n}$

$\therefore \quad P(A) : P(A') = m : n$

Odd in favour of occurrences of the event A are defined by $m : n$ *i.e.* $P(A) : P(A')$; and the odds against the occurrence of the event A are defined by $n : m$ *i.e.* $P(A') : P(A)$.

♦ **Finite probability spaces**

Let S be a finite sample space; say, $S = \{a_1, a_2, ...a_n\}$. A finite probability space is obtained by assigning to each point $a_i \in S$ a real number p_i, called the probability of a_i, satisfying the following properties:

(a)   Each p_i is non negative, $p_i \geq 0$

(b)   The sum of the p_i is one, $p_1 + p_2 + ...+p_n = 1$.

The probability of an event 'A' given by $P(A)$ is then defined to be the sum of the probabilities of the points in A.

♦ **Special addition rule :**

If A and B are mutually exclusive, then $P(A \cap B) = 0$, so that $P(A \cup B) = P(A) + P(B)$

If $A_1, A_2, A_3,........, A_n$ are n mutually exclusive events, then $P(A_1 \cup A_2 \cup .... \cup A_n) = P(A_1) + P(A_2) + ... + P(A_n)$.

♦ **For two events A and B**

(a) $P(\text{at least one out of them}) = P(A) + P(B) - P(A \cap B)$

(b) $P(\text{exactly one out of them}) = P(A) + P(B) - 2P(A \cap B)$

(c) $P(\text{neither A nor B}) = P(A' \cap B') = 1 - P(A \cup B)$

(d) $P(\text{not A or not B}) = P(A' \cup B') = 1 - P(A \cap B)$

(e) $P(\text{A but not B}) = P(A \cup B') = P(A) - P(A \cap B)$

♦ **For three events A, B and C**

(a) $P(\text{at least one out of them})$

$$= P(A) + P(B) + P(C) - P(A \cap B) - P(B \cap C) - P(C \cap A) + P(A \cap B \cap C)$$

(b) P (at least two out of them)

$$= P(B \cap C) + P(C \cap A) + P(A \cap B) - 2P(A \cap B \cap C)$$

(c) P (exactly two out of them) =

$$P(B \cap C) + P(C \cap A) + P(A \cap B) - 3P(A \cap B \cap C)$$

(d) P (exactly one out of them)

$$= P(A) + P(B) + P(C) - 2P(B \cap C) - 2P(C \cap A)$$
$$-2P(A \cap B) + 3P(A \cap B \cap C)$$

Types of Relations

♦ We know that a relation in a set A is a subset of A × A. Thus, the empty set ϕ and A × A are two extreme relations.

♦ **Empty (or) void relation:** A relation R in a set A is called **empty relation**, if no element of A is related to any element of A, i.e., $R = \phi \subset A \times A$.

♦ **Universal Relation:** A relation R in a set A is called **universal relation,** if each element of A is related to every element of A, i.e., $R = A \times A$.

♦ **Note:** Both the empty relation and the universal relation are sometimes called trivial relations.

♦ **Reflexive Relation:** A relation R in a set A is called **reflexive,** if $(a, a) \in R$, for every $a \in A$.

♦ **Symmetric Relation:** A relation R in a set A is called **symmetric,** if $(a_1, a_2) \in R$ implies that $(a_2, a_1) \in R$, for all $a_1, a_2 \in A$.

♦ **Transivive Relation:** A relation R in a set A is called **transitive,** if $(a_1, a_2) \in R$ and $(a_2, a_3) \in R$ implies that $(a_1, a_3) \in R$, for all $a_1, a_2, a_3 \in A$.

♦ **Equivalence Relation:** A relation R in a set A is said to be an equivalence relation if R is reflexive, symmetric and transitive.

♦ **Equivalence Class:** *Equivalence class* [a] containing $a \in X$ for an equivalence relation R in X is the subset of X containing all elements b related to a.

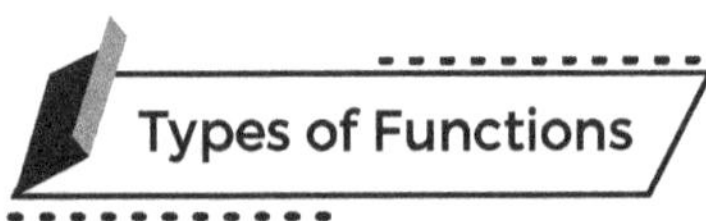

Types of Functions

♦ **One-one function (Injective Function):** A function $f : X \to Y$ is defined to be **one-one (or injective),** if the images of distinct elements of X under f are distinct, i.e., for every $x_1, x_2 \in X, f(x_1) = f(x_2)$ implies $x_1 = x_2$.

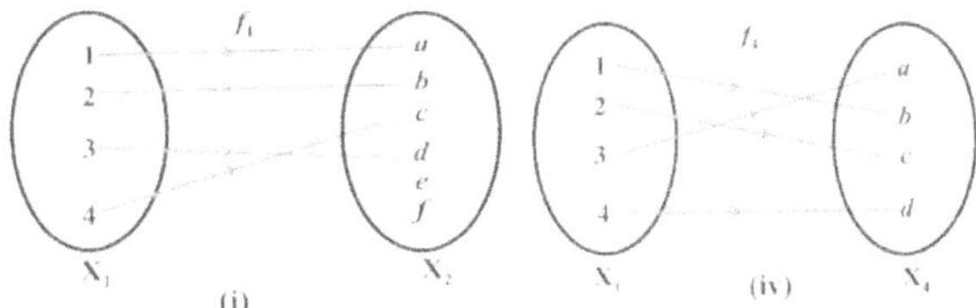

- **Onto Function (Surjective Function):** A function $f: X \to Y$ is said to be **onto (or surjective)**, if every element of Y is the image of some element of X under f, i.e., for every $y \in Y$, there exists an element x in X such that $f(x) = y$.

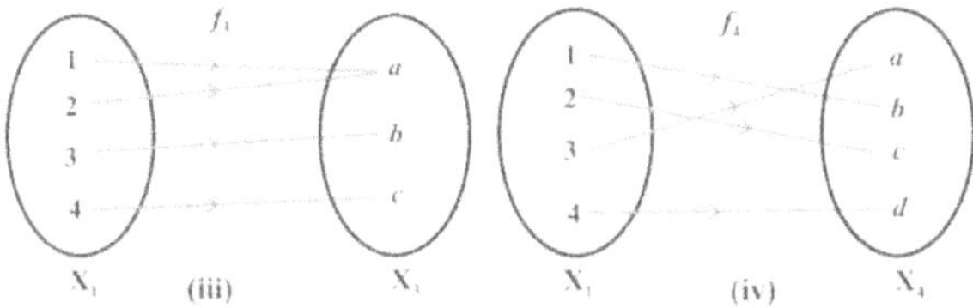

- **Many-one Function:** A function $f: X \to Y$ is defined to be **many-one,** if the images of two or more elements have the same image, i.e. for every $x_1, x_2 \in x$, $f(x_1) = f(x_2)$ implies $x_1 \neq x_2$.

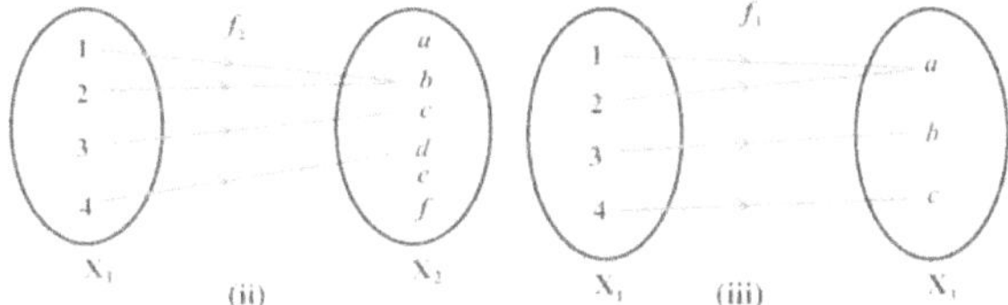

- **Bijective Function:** A function $f: X \to Y$ is said to be **one-one and onto (or bijective),** if f is both one-one and onto.

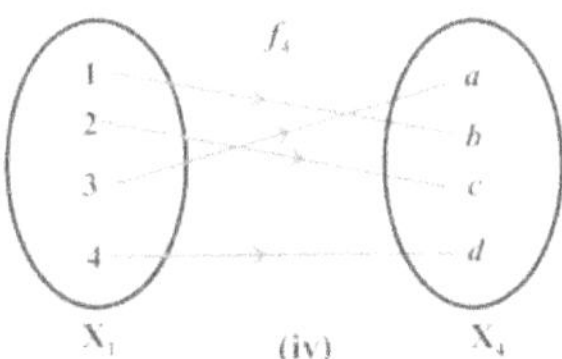

- **Remark** $f: X \to Y$ is onto if and only if Range of $f = Y$.

Composition of Functions and Invertible Function

- **Composition of Functions:** Let $f: A \to B$ and $g: B \to C$ be two functions. Then the composition of f and g, denoted by gof, is defined as the function $gof: A \to C$ given by $gof(x) = g(f(x)), \forall x \in A$.

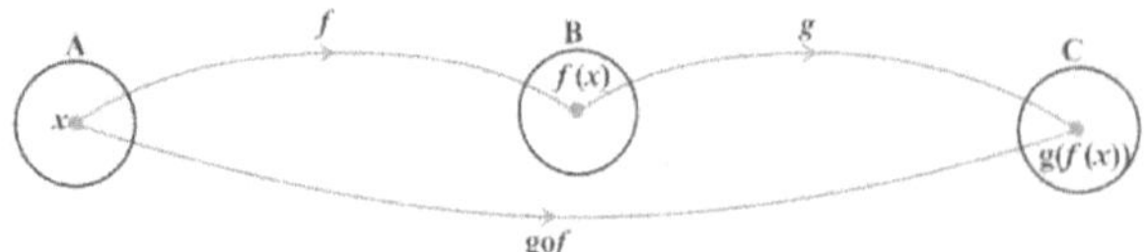

- **Inverse of a Function:** A function $f : X \to Y$ is defined to be **invertible,** if there exists a function $g : Y \to X$ such that $gof = I_X$ and $fog = I_Y$. The function g is called the **inverse of f** and is denoted by f^{-1}.

- Thus, if f is invertible, then f must be one-one and onto and conversely, if f is one-one and onto, then f must be invertible.

- This fact significantly helps for proving a function f to be invertible by showing that f is one-one and onto, specially when the actual inverse of f is not to be determined.

- **Theorem 1:**

  If $f : X \to Y$, $g : Y \to Z$ and $h : Z \to S$ are functions, then $ho(gof) = (hog) \, o f$.

- **Theorem 2:**

  Let $f : X \to Y$ and $g : Y \to Z$ be two invertible functions. Then gof is also invertible with $(gof)^{-1} = f^{-1}og^{-1}$.

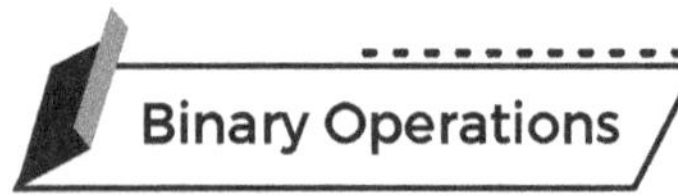

- It is to be noted that only two numbers can be added or multiplied at a time. When we need to add three numbers, we first add two numbers and the result is then added to the third number.

- Thus, addition, multiplication, subtraction and division are examples of **binary operation,** as 'binary' means two.

- If we want to have a general definition which can cover all these four operations, then the set of numbers is to be replaced by an arbitrary set X and then general binary operation is nothing but association of any pair of elements a, b from X to another element of X.

- **Binary Operation:** A binary operation * on a set A is a function * : A × A → A. We denote * (a, b) by a * b.

- **Identity of Element:** Identity element for binary operation * : X × X → X, if $a * e = a = e * a \, \forall \, a \in X$.

- An element $a \in X$ is **invertible** for binary operation * : X × X → X, if there exists $b \in X$ such that $a * b = e = b * a$ where, e is the identity for the binary operation *. The element b is called **inverse** of a and is denoted by a^{-1}.

- An operation * on X is **commutative** if $a * b = b * a \, \forall \, a, b$ in X.

- An operation * on X is **associative** if $(a * b) * c = a * (b * c) \, \forall \, a, b, c$ in X.

Past Years ONE-LINERS
JEE Main/Board

- Function, $f(x) = y \Rightarrow x = f^{-1}(y)$

  $ax^2 + bx + c = 0$

  $$\Rightarrow \alpha, \beta = = \frac{b \pm \sqrt{D}}{2a} \text{ where,}$$

  $D = b^2 - 4ac$

- $g(x) = ax + b, \; gof(x) = g(f(x)) = a\,f(x) + b \;...\;(1)$

  & given that $gof(x) = x \;...\;(2)$. Then

  From eq^n (1) & eq^n (2),

  $a\,f(x) + b = x$

  $$f(x) = \frac{x - b}{a}$$

- $f(-x) = = f(x) \rightarrow$ Even Function, $f(-x) = -f(x) \rightarrow$ Odd Function,

  $f'(x) > 0 \rightarrow$ Increasing Function,

  $f'(x) < 0 \rightarrow$ Decreasing Function,

  $f(x) = y \rightarrow$ Surjective Function (i.e. for every $y \in 4$, there exists an element n in x)

- Let $f_1(x) = ax, \; f_2(x) = x^2 + b, \; f_3(x) = dx^3$

  $(f_2 OJOf_1)(x) = f_3(x)$

  $f_2 OJ(f_1(x)) = f_3(x) \Rightarrow f_2[J(f_1(x))] = f_3(x)$

  $f_2[J(ax)] = f_3(x) = dx^3$

  $\therefore f_2[J(x)] = d(ax)^3$ Replacing $ax \rightarrow x$,

  $[J(x)]^2 + b = da^3x^3 \Rightarrow$ Gives desired Answer

- For a given function $f(x)$,

  $f'(x) = 0 \Rightarrow x = a, b \;.....$

  If $f'(x)$ does not change its sign in the intervals, then $f(x)$ is injective.

  If there is existance of $y \in 4$ for every element in $x \in X$. Then $f(x)$ is known as surjective.

Tips/Tricks/Techniques ONE-LINERS
(Exam Special)

- **Identity relation :** Let X be a set. Then the relation $I_X = \{(x, x) : x \in X\}$ is called the identity relation on X i.e. a relation I_X on X is identity relation if every element of X is related to itself only.

- **Anti-symmetric relation :** A relation R on set A is said to be an anti symmetric relation iff (a, b) $\in$ R and (b, a) $\in$ R
  $\Rightarrow a = b$ for all a, b $\in$ A

- **Inverse of a relation :** Let R be a relation from a set A to B. Then the inverse of R, denoted by R^{-1} , is a relation from B to A and is defined by
  $R^{-1} = \{(b, a) : (a, b) \in R\}$, Clearly, (a, b) $\in$ R $\Leftrightarrow$ (b, a) $\in R^{-1}$
  Also, Dom of R = Range of R^{-1} and Range of R = Dom of R^{-1}

- **One-one into function :** A function is said to be one-one into, if f is one-one but not onto

- **Many one-onto function:** A function f is said to be many one- onto, if f is onto but not one-one.

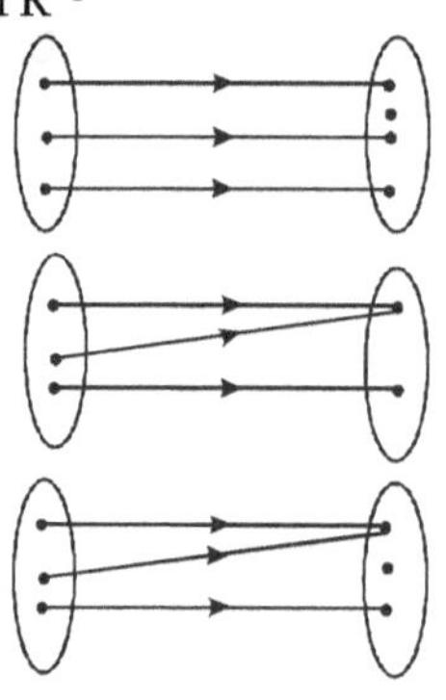

- **Many one-into function:** A function is said to be many one-into if it is neither one-one nor onto.

- **Composite relation:**
  Let R be a relation from set A to the set B and S be another relation from set B to the set C. Then we define a relation SoR (Read as "R composite S") from A to C such that
  (a, c) $\in$ SoR $\Leftrightarrow$ $\exists$ b$\in$B such that (a, b) $\in$ R and (b,c) $\in$S
  [The symbol $\exists$ is read as " there exists"]
  Clearly, aRb and bSc $\Rightarrow$ a SoRc

- **Properties of composite functions :**
  - ❖ If both f and g are one- one, then gof is also one -one.
  - ❖ If both f and g are onto, then gof is also onto.
  - ❖ If gof is one-one, then f is one-one but g may not be one-one.
  - ❖ If gof is onto, then g is onto but f may not be onto.
  - ❖ If f and g are bijective, then gof is also bijective.
  - ❖ It may happen that gof exists and fog does not exist. Even if both gof and fog exist, they may not be equal.

- **Properties of inverse function**
  - ❖ Inverse of a bijective is also a bijective function.
  - ❖ Inverse of a bijective function is unique.

- ❖ $(f^{-1})^{-1} = f$
- ❖ If f and g are two bijective functions such that (gof) exists then $(gof)^{-1} = f^{-1}og^{-1}$
- ❖ Inverse of an even function is not defined.
- ❖ In general fog (x) and gof (x) are not equal. But if f and g are inverse of each other, then gof = fog.

  fog (x) and gof (x) can be equal even if f and g are not inverses of each other.
- ❖ If f (x) and g (x) are inverse function of each other, then

$$f'(x) = \frac{1}{g'(x)}$$

- ◆ All identity relations are reflexive but all reflexive relations are not identity.
- ◆ Indentity relation on a non-void set A is always reflexive on A. However, the converse need not be true.
- ◆ Universal relation on a non-void set A is reflexive
- ◆ In null set ϕ, every relation is reflexive.
- ◆ Let X be a non-void set, then a relation R on P(X), the power set of X such that $(A, B) \in R \Leftrightarrow A \subseteq B$ is

  reflexive for $A \subseteq A \ \forall \ A$ [every set is subset by itself]
- ◆ Identity relation and universal relation on a non-void set are symmetric.
- ◆ In the null set every relation is symmetric.
- ◆ The relation R on P(X) for a non-empty set X, defined by $ARB \Leftrightarrow A \subseteq B$ is not symmetric.
- ◆ A reflexive relation on the set A is not necessarily symmetric.
- ◆ A relation R on a set A is symmetric if f $R = R^{-1}$.
- ◆ Identity and Universal relations on a non-empty set are transitive.
- ◆ Every relation defined on the null set ϕ is transitive
- ◆ Identity relation on a non-empty set is antisymmetric
- ◆ Universal relation on a set A containing at least two distinct elements connot be anti-symmetric.
- ◆ If f is both injective and surjective, then it is called a bijective mapping. The bijective functions are also named as invertible, or non singular functions.
- ◆ If f and g both are onto, then gof or fog may or may not be onto.
- ◆ If f and g are two bijections such that gof is defined, then gof is also a bijection only when co-domain of f is equal to the domain of g.
- ◆ Every polynomial function $f : R \rightarrow R$ of degree odd is **ONTO.**
- ◆ If A and B are two finite sets having m and n elements respectively, then
  - ❖ Total number of functions from the set A to the set B = n^m
  - ❖ The number of one-one (injective) functions from

$$A \text{ to } B = \begin{cases} {}^nP_m = \dfrac{n!}{(n-m)!} & \text{If } n \geq m \\ \\ 0, & \text{If } n < m \end{cases}$$

  - ❖ If n = m, then every one-one function is a bijective function, thus, the number of bijective functions from A to B, provided n = m is n! = m!
  - ❖ The number of onto (surjective) functions from A to B =

$$\sum_{r=1}^{n} (-1)^r \ {}^nC_r (n-r)^m, \text{ where } 1 \leq n \leq m$$

18 Inverse Trigonometric Functions

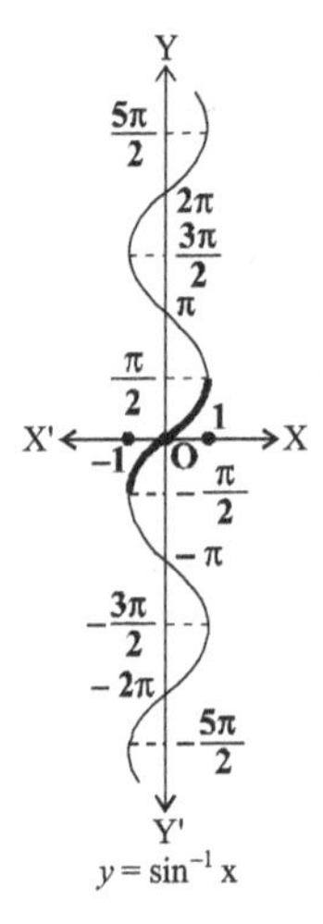

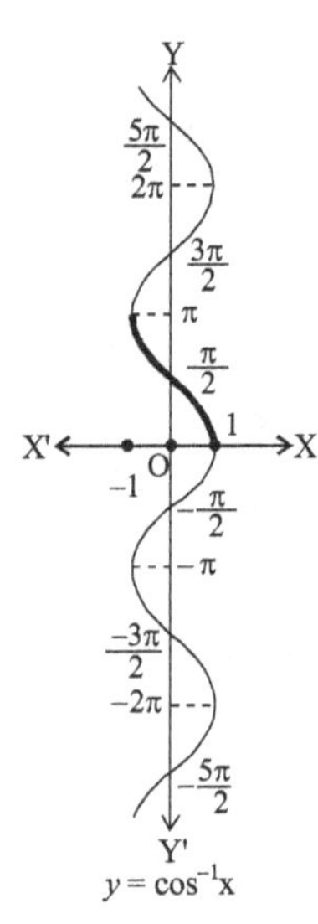

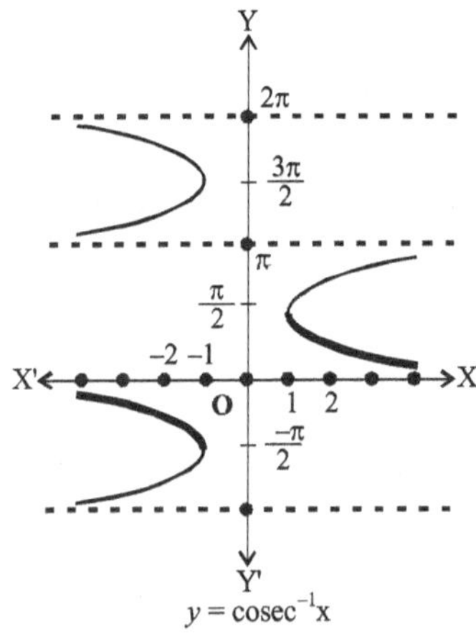

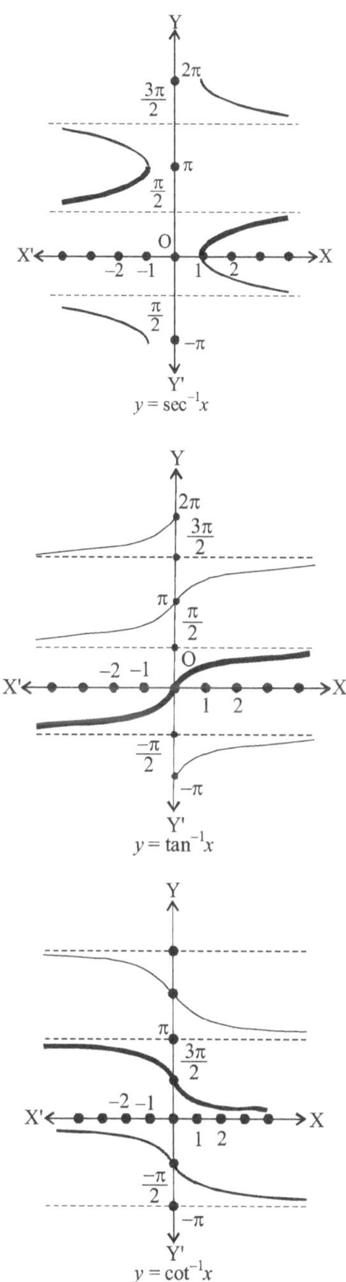

The following table gives the inverse trigonometric function (principal value branches) along with their domains and ranges.

$\sin^{-1}$	:	$[-1, 1]$	$\rightarrow$	$\left[-\dfrac{\pi}{2}, \dfrac{\pi}{2}\right]$
$\cos^{-1}$	:	$[-1, 1]$	$\rightarrow$	$[0, \pi]$
$\operatorname{cosec}^{-1}$	:	$\mathbf{R} - (-1, 1)$	$\rightarrow$	$\left[-\dfrac{\pi}{2}, \dfrac{\pi}{2}\right] - \{0\}$
$\sec^{-1}$	:	$\mathbf{R} - (-1, 1)$	$\rightarrow$	$[0, \pi] - \{\dfrac{\pi}{2}\}$
$\tan^{-1}$	:	$\mathbf{R}$	$\rightarrow$	$\left(\dfrac{-\pi}{2}, \dfrac{\pi}{2}\right)$
$\cot^{-1}$	:	$\mathbf{R}$	$\rightarrow$	$(0, \pi)$

♦ **Note:**

❖ $\sin^{-1}x$ should not be confused with $(\sin x)^{-1}$. In fact $(\sin x)^{-1} = \dfrac{1}{\sin x}$ and similarly for other trigonometric functions.

❖ Whenever no branch of an inverse trigonometric functions is mentioned, we mean the principal value branch of that function.

❖ The value of an inverse trigonometric functions which lies in the range of principal branch is called the *principal value* of that inverse trigonometric functions.

Properties of Inverse Trigonometric Functions

♦ ❖ $\sin^{-1} \dfrac{1}{x} = \operatorname{cosec}^{-1} x,\ x \geq 1$ or $x \leq -1$

❖ $\cos^{-1} \dfrac{1}{x} = \sec^{-1} x,\ x \geq 1$ or $x \leq -1$

❖ $\tan^{-1} \dfrac{1}{x} = \cot^{-1} x,\ x > 0$

♦ ❖ $\sin^{-1} (-x) = -\sin^{-1} x,\ x \in [-1, 1]$

(ii) $\tan^{-1} (-x) = -\tan^{-1} x,\ x \in \mathbf{R}$

(iii) $\operatorname{cosec}^{-1} (-x) = -\operatorname{cosec}^{-1} x,\ |x| \geq 1$

♦ ❖ $\cos^{-1} (-x) = \pi - \cos^{-1} x,\ x \in [-1, 1]$

❖ $\sec^{-1} (-x) = \pi - \sec^{-1} x,\ |x| \geq 1$

❖ $\cot^{-1}(-x) = \pi - \cot^{-1}x,\ x \in \mathbf{R}$

❖ $\sin^{-1}x + \cos^{-1}x = \dfrac{\pi}{2},\ x \in [-1, 1]$

❖ $\tan^{-1}x + \cot^{-1}x, = \dfrac{\pi}{2}, x \in \mathbf{R}$

❖ $\operatorname{cosec}^{-1}x + \sec^{-1}x = \dfrac{\pi}{2},\ |x| \geq 1$

❖ $\tan^{-1}x + \tan^{-1}y = \tan^{-1}\dfrac{x+y}{1-xy}, xy < 1$

❖ $\tan^{-1}x - \tan^{-1}y = \tan^{-1}\dfrac{x-y}{1+xy}, xy > -1$

❖ $\tan^{-1}x + \tan^{-1}y = \pi + \tan^{-1}\left(\dfrac{x+y}{1-xy}\right),\ xy > 1; x, y > 0$

❖ $2\tan^{-1}x = \sin^{-1}\dfrac{2x}{1+x^2}, |x| \leq 1$

❖ $2\tan^{-1}x = \cos^{-1}\dfrac{1-x^2}{1+x^2}, x \geq 0$

❖ $2\tan^{-1}x = \tan^{-1}\dfrac{2x}{1-x^2}, -1 < x < 1$

Past Years ONE-LINERS
JEE Main/Board

♦ $\dfrac{x}{a} = \dfrac{y}{b} = \dfrac{z}{c} = k \Rightarrow x = ak, y = bk, z = ck$

$\cos 2x = \dfrac{1-\tan^2 x}{1+\tan^2 x},\ \sin^{-1}x + \cos^{-1}x = \dfrac{\pi}{2}$

♦ $\sin^{-1}x + \cos^{-1}x = \dfrac{\pi}{2}$ and

$\sin^2\theta + \cos^2\theta = 1 \Rightarrow \cos\theta = \sqrt{1-\sin^2\theta}$

- $$\tan^{-1}\left(\frac{x+y}{1-xy}\right) = \tan^{-1}x + \tan^{-1}y \text{ and } \frac{d}{dx}\tan^{-1}\frac{x}{a}$$

$$= \frac{1}{1+\dfrac{x^2}{a^2}} \times \frac{1}{a} = \frac{a}{x^2+a^2}$$

- $$\tan^{-1}x + \tan^{-1}y = \tan^{-1}\left(\frac{x+y}{1-xy}\right)$$

$$\&\ 2\tan^{-1}x = \tan^{-1}\left(\frac{2x}{1-x^2}\right)$$

$$\&\ 3\tan^{-1}x = \tan^{-1}\left(\frac{3x-x^3}{1-3x^2}\right)$$

Tips/Tricks/Techniques ONE-LINERS
(Exam Special)

- $\tan^{-1} x + \tan^{-1} y$

$$= \begin{cases} \pi + \tan^{-1}\left(\dfrac{x+y}{1-xy}\right) &, \quad \text{if } x>0, y>0 \text{ and } xy>1 \\[3mm] -\pi + \tan^{-1}\left(\dfrac{x+y}{1-xy}\right) &, \quad \text{if } x<0, y<0 \text{ and } xy>1 \end{cases}$$

- $\tan^{-1} x - \tan^{-1} y$

$$= \begin{cases} \pi + \tan^{-1}\left(\dfrac{x-y}{1+xy}\right) &, \quad \text{if } x>0, y<0 \text{ and } xy<-1 \\[3mm] -\pi + \tan^{-1}\left(\dfrac{x-y}{1+xy}\right) &, \quad \text{if } x<0, y>0 \text{ and } xy<-1 \end{cases}$$

- $\sin^{-1} x + \sin^{-1} y$

$$= \begin{cases} \pi - \sin^{-1}\{x\sqrt{1-y^2}+y\sqrt{1-x^2}\}, & \text{if } 0<x,\ y\le 1 \text{ and } x^2+y^2>1 \\[3mm] -\pi - \sin^{-1}\{x\sqrt{1-y^2}+y\sqrt{1-x^2}\}, & \text{if } -1\le x,\ y<0 \text{ and } x^2+y^2>1 \end{cases}$$

- $\sin^{-1} x - \sin^{-1} y$

$$= \begin{cases} \pi - \sin^{-1}\{x\sqrt{1-y^2} - y\sqrt{1-x^2}\}, & \text{if } 0 < x \le 1, -1 \le y \le 0 \text{ and } x^2 + y^2 > 1 \\ -\pi - \sin^{-1}\{x\sqrt{1-y^2} - y\sqrt{1-x^2}\}, & \text{if } -1 \le x < 0, 0 < y \le 1 \text{ and } x^2 + y^2 > 1 \end{cases}$$

- $\cos^{-1} x + \cos^{-1} y$

$$= \left\{ 2\pi - \cos^{-1}\{xy - \sqrt{1-x^2}\sqrt{1-y^2}\}, \quad \text{if } -1 \le x, y \le 1 \text{ and } x + y \le 0 \right.$$

- $\cos^{-1} x - \cos^{-1} y$

$$= \left\{ -\cos^{-1}\{xy + \sqrt{1-x^2}\sqrt{1-y^2}\}, \quad \text{if } -1 \le y \le 0, 0 < x \le 1 \text{ and } x \ge y \right.$$

- $2\sin^{-1}x = \begin{cases} \pi - \sin^{-1}(2x\sqrt{1-x^2}) \ , & \text{if } \dfrac{1}{\sqrt{2}} \le x \le 1 \\[2ex] -\pi - \sin^{-1}(2x\sqrt{1-x^2}) \ , & \text{if } -1 \le x \le -\dfrac{1}{\sqrt{2}} \end{cases}$

- $3\sin^{-1} x = \begin{cases} \pi - \sin^{-1}(3x - 4x^3), & \text{if } \dfrac{1}{2} < x \le 1 \\[2ex] -\pi - \sin^{-1}(3x - 4x^3), & \text{if } -1 \le x < -\dfrac{1}{2} \end{cases}$

- $2\cos^{-1} x = \left\{ 2\pi - \cos^{-1}(2x^2 - 1), \quad \text{if } -1 \le x \le 0 \right.$

- $3\cos^{-1} x = \begin{cases} 2\pi - \cos^{-1}(4x^3 - 3x) \ , & \text{if } -\dfrac{1}{2} \le x \le \dfrac{1}{2} \\[2ex] 2\pi + \cos^{-1}(4x^3 - 3x) \ , & \text{if } -1 \le x - \dfrac{1}{2} \end{cases}$

- $2\tan^{-1} x = \begin{cases} \pi + \tan^{-1}\left(\dfrac{2x}{1-x^2}\right) \ , & \text{if } x > 1 \\[2ex] -\pi + \tan^{-1}\left(\dfrac{2x}{1-x^2}\right), & \text{if } x < -1 \end{cases}$

- $3\tan^{-1} x = \begin{cases} \pi + \tan^{-1}\left(\dfrac{3x - x^3}{1-3x^2}\right) \ , & \text{if } x > \dfrac{1}{\sqrt{3}} \\[2ex] -\pi + \tan^{-1}\left(\dfrac{3x - x^3}{1-3x^2}\right), & \text{if } x < -\dfrac{1}{\sqrt{3}} \end{cases}$

- $2\tan^{-1} x = \begin{cases} \pi - \sin^{-1}\left(\dfrac{2x}{1+x^2}\right) \ , & \text{if } x > 1 \\[2ex] -\pi - \sin^{-1}\left(\dfrac{2x}{1+x^2}\right), & \text{if } x < -1 \end{cases}$

- $2\tan^{-1}x = \left\{ -\cos^{-1}\left(\dfrac{1-x^2}{1+x^2}\right), \quad \text{if} -\infty < x \le 0 \right.$

- If $\tan^{-1}x + \tan^{-1}y + \tan^{-1}z = \dfrac{\pi}{2}$ then $xy + yz + zx = 1$

- If $\sin^{-1}x + \sin^{-1}y + \sin^{-1}z = \dfrac{\pi}{2}$ then $x^2 + y^2 + z^2 + 2xyz = 1$

- $\sin^{-1}x \ne \dfrac{1}{\sin x}$, $\sin^{-1}x \ne (\sin x)^{-1}$ but $(\sin x)^{-1} = \dfrac{1}{\sin x}$

- If for any other inverse trigonometric function, the numerical value of y is smallest in two branch, then we consider those branch as principal value branch in which there is no negative value.

- I quadrant is common to all the inverse functions.

- III quadrant is not used in inverse function.

- IV quadrant is used in the clockwise direction.

- If no branch of a inverse trigonometric function is mentioned, then the principal value branch is taken for the inverse trigonometric function.

19

Matrices

Matrix

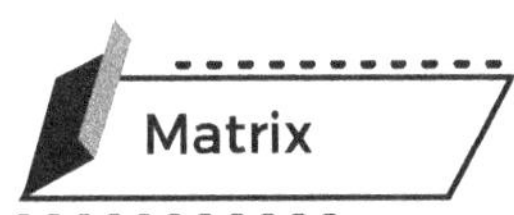

- A matrix is an ordered rectangular array of numbers or functions. The numbers or functions are called the elements or the entries of the matrix.
- We denote matrices by capital letters. The following are some examples of matrices:

$$A = \begin{bmatrix} -2 & 5 \\ 0 & \sqrt{5} \\ 3 & 6 \end{bmatrix} \text{ and } B = \begin{bmatrix} 2+i & 3 & \dfrac{1}{2} \\ 3.5 & -1 & 2 \\ \sqrt{3} & 5 & \dfrac{5}{7} \end{bmatrix},$$

- In the above examples, the horizontal lines of elements are said to constitute, **rows** of the matrix and the vertical lines of elements are said to **constitute**, columns of the matrix.
- Thus A has 3 rows and 2 columns while, B has 3 rows and 3 columns.

Order of a matrix:

- A matrix having m rows and n columns is called a matrix of order $m \times n$ or simply $m \times n$ matrix (read as an m by n matrix).
- In general, an $m \times n$ matrix has the following rectangular array:

$$\begin{bmatrix} a_{11} & a_{12} & a_{13} \cdots a_{1j} \cdots a_{1n} \\ a_{21} & a_{22} & a_{23} \cdots a_{2j} \cdots a_{2n} \\ a_{i1} & a_{i2} & a_{i3} \cdots a_{ij} \cdots a_{in} \\ a_{m1} & a_{m2} & a_{m3} \cdots a_{mj} \cdots a_{mn} \end{bmatrix}_{m \times n}$$

or $A = [a_{ij}]_{m \times n},\ 1 \le i \le m,\ 1 \le j \le n\ i, j \in N$

- **Note :**
    - We shall follow the notation, namely $A = [a_{ij}]_{m \times n}$ to indicate that A is a matrix of order $m \times n$.
    - We shall consider only those matrices whose elements are real numbers or functions taking real values.

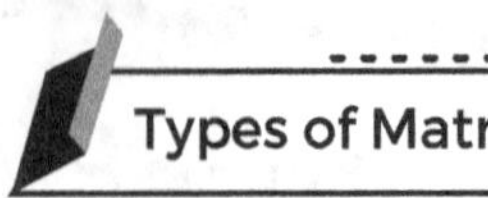

Types of Matrices

Column matrix :
- A matrix is said to be a *column matrix* if it has only one column.
- In general, $A = [a_{ij}]_{m \times 1}$ is a column matrix of order m × 1.

Row matrix :
- A matrix is said to be a *row matrix* if it has only one row.
- In general, $B = [b_{ij}]_{1 \times n}$ is a row matrix of order 1 × n.

Square matrix :
- A matrix in which the number of rows are equal to the number of columns, is said to be a *square matrix*. Thus an m × n matrix is said to be a *square matrix*, if m = n and is known as a square matrix of order 'n'.
- In general, $A = [a_{ij}]_{m \times m}$ is a square matrix of order m.
- **Note :**
  - ❖ If $A = [a_{ij}]$ is a square matrix of order n, then elements (entries) a_{11}, a_{22}, ..., a_{nn} are said to constitute the *diagonal*, of the matrix A. Thus, if A =
  $$\begin{bmatrix} 1 & -3 & 1 \\ 2 & 4 & -1 \\ 3 & 5 & 6 \end{bmatrix}.$$
  - ❖ Then the elements of the diagonal of A are 1, 4, 6.

Diagonal matrix :
- A square matrix $B = [b_{ij}]_{m \times m}$ is said to be a *diagonal matrix* if all its non diagonal elements are zero, that is a matrix $B = [b_{ij}]_{m \times m}$ is said to be a diagonal matrix if $b_{ij} = 0$, when i ≠ j.

Scalar matrix :
- A diagonal matrix is said to be a *scalar matrix* if its diagonal elements are equal, that is, a square matrix.

  $B = [b_{ij}]_{n \times n}$ is said to be a scalar matrix if
  $b_{ij} = 0,$　when i ≠ j
  $b_{ij} = k,$　when i = j, for some constant k.

Identity matrix :
- A square matrix in which elements in the diagonal are all 1 and rest are all zero is called an *identity matrix*.
- In other words, the square matrix $A = [a_{ij}]_{n \times n}$ is an identity matrix, if $a_{ij} =$

$$\begin{cases} 1 & \text{if } i = j \\ 0 & \text{if } i \neq j \end{cases}$$

- We denote the identity matrix of order n by I_n. When order is clear from the context, we simply write it as I.
- Observe that a scalar matrix is an identity matrix when k = 1. But every identity matrix is clearly a scalar matrix.

Zero matrix :
- A matrix is said to be *zero matrix* or *null matrix* if all its elements are zero.
- We denote zero matrix by O. Its order will be clear from the context.

Equality of matrices :
- Two matrices $A = [a_{ij}]$ and $B = [b_{ij}]$ are said to be *equal* if
  - ❖ They are of the same order
  - ❖ Each element of A is equal to the corresponding element of B, that is $a_{ij} = b_{ij}$ for all i and j.

- For example, $\begin{bmatrix} 2 & 3 \\ 0 & 1 \end{bmatrix}$ and $\begin{bmatrix} 2 & 3 \\ 0 & 1 \end{bmatrix}$ are equal matrices but $\begin{bmatrix} 3 & 2 \\ 0 & 1 \end{bmatrix}$ and $\begin{bmatrix} 2 & 3 \\ 0 & 1 \end{bmatrix}$

  are not equal matrices. Symbolically, if two matrices A and B are equal, we write $A = B$.

Operations on Matrices

Addition of matrices :
- *The Addition of two matrices* is a matrix obtained by adding the corresponding elements of the given matrices. Furthermore, the two matrices have to be of the same order.

- Thus, if $A = \begin{bmatrix} a_{11} & a_{12} & a_{13} \\ a_{21} & a_{22} & a_{23} \end{bmatrix}$ is a 2×3 matrix and

  $B = \begin{bmatrix} b_{11} & b_{12} & b_{13} \\ b_{21} & b_{22} & b_{23} \end{bmatrix}$ is another 2×3 matrix. Then, we define $A + B =$

  $\begin{bmatrix} a_{11} + b_{11} & a_{12} + b_{12} & a_{13} + b_{13} \\ a_{21} + b_{21} & a_{22} + b_{22} & a_{23} + b_{23} \end{bmatrix}$

Multiplication of a matrix by a scalar :
- In general, we may define *multiplication of a matrix* by a scalar as follows: if $A = [a_{ij}]_{m \times n}$ is a matrix and k is a scalar, then kA is another matrix which is obtained by multiplying each element of A by the scalar k.
- In other words, $kA = k[a_{ij}]_{m \times n} = [k\,(a_{ij})]_{m \times n}$, that is, $(i, j)^{th}$ element of kA is ka_{ij} for all possible values of i and j.
- **Negative of a matrix:** The negative of a matrix is denoted by $-A$. We define $-A = (-1)\,A$.
- **Difference of matrices:** If $A = [a_{ij}]$, $B = [b_{ij}]$ are two matrices of the same order, say $m \times n$, then difference $A - B$ is defined as a matrix $D = [d_{ij}]$, where $d_{ij} = a_{ij} - b_{ij}$, for all value of i and j. In other words, $D = A - B = A + (-1)\,B$, that is sum of the matrix A and the matrix $- B$.

Properties of matrix addition :
- **Commutative Law:** If $A = [a_{ij}]$, $B = [b_{ij}]$ are matrices of the same order, say $m \times n$, then $A + B = B + A$.

- **Associative Law:** For any three matrices $A = [a_{ij}]$, $B = [b_{ij}]$, $C = [c_{ij}]$ of the same order, say $m \times n$, $(A + B) + C = A + (B + C)$.
- **Existence of additive identity:** Let $A = [a_{ij}]$ be an $m \times n$ matrix and O be an $m \times n$ zero matrix, then $A + O = O + A = A$. In other words, O is the additive identity for matrix addition.
- **The existence of additive inverse:** Let $A = [a_{ij}]_{m \times n}$ be any matrix, then we have another matrix as $- A = [- a_{ij}]_{m \times n}$ such that $A + (- A) = (- A) + A = O$. So $- A$ is the additive inverse of A or negative of A.

Properties of scalar multiplication of a matrix :

- If $A = [a_{ij}]$ and $B = [b_{ij}]$ be two matrices of the same order, say $m \times n$, and k and l are scalars, then
  - ❖ $k(A + B) = k A + kB$,
  - ❖ $(k + I)A = k A + I A$

Multiplication of matrices :

- The product of two matrices A and B is defined if the number of columns of A is equal to the number of rows of B. Let $A = [a_{ij}]$ be an $m \times n$ matrix and $B = [b_{jk}]$ be an $n \times p$ matrix. Then the product of the matrices A and B is the matrix C of order $m \times p$.
- if $A = [a_{ij}]_{m \times n}$, $B = [b_{jk}]_{n \times p}$, then the ith row of A is $[a_{i1} \ a_{i2} \ ... \ a_{in}]$ and the kth

  column of B is $\begin{bmatrix} b_{1k} \\ b_{2k} \\ \vdots \\ b_{nk} \end{bmatrix}$, then $c_{ik} = a_{i1} \ b_{1k} + a_{i2} \ b_{2k} + a_{i3} \ b_{3k} + ... + a_{in} \ b_{nk}$

  $$= \sum_{j=1}^{n} a_{ij} \ b_{jk}.$$

  The matrix $C = [c_{ik}]_{m \times p}$ is the product of A and B.
- **Note :**
  - ❖ If AB is defined, then BA need not be defined.
  - ❖ If A, B are, respectively $m \times n$, $k \times l$ matrices, then both AB and BA are defined *if and only if* $n = k$ and $l = m$. In particular, if both A and B are square matrices of the same order, then both AB and BA are defined.

Properties of multiplication of matrices :

- **The associative law :** For any three matrices A, B and C. We have $(AB) C = A (BC)$, whenever both sides of the equality are defined.
- **The distributive law :** For three matrices A, B and C.
  - ❖ $A (B + C) = AB + AC$
  - ❖ $(A + B) C = AC + BC$, whenever both sides of equality are defined.
- **The existence of multiplicative identity :** For every square matrix A, there exist an identity matrix of same order such that $IA = AI = A$.

Transpose of a Matrix

Transpose of a Matrix :

♦ If $A = [a_{ij}]$ be an $m \times n$ matrix, then the matrix obtained by interchanging the rows and columns of A is called *the transpose of A*.

♦ Transpose of the matrix A is denoted by A' or (A^T). In other words, if $A = [a_{ij}]_{m \times n}$, then $A' = [a_{ji}]_{n \times m}$.

Properties of transpose of the matrices :

♦ For any matrices A and B of suitable orders, we have

❖ $(A')' = A$,

❖ $(kA)' = kA'$ (where k is any constant)

❖ $(A + B)' = A' + B'$

❖ $(A B)' = B' A'$

Symmetric and Skew Symmetric Matrices

♦ **Symmetric Matrix :** A square matrix $A = [a_{ij}]$ is said to be *symmetric* if $A' = A$, that is, $[a_{ij}] = [a_{ji}]$ for all possible values of i and j.

♦ **Skew Symmetric Matrix :** A square matrix $A = [a_{ij}]$ is said to be *skew symmetric matrix* if $A' = -A$, that is $a_{ji} = -a_{ij}$ for all possible values of i and j.

   Now, if we put $i = j$, we have $a_{ii} = -a_{ii}$. Therefore $2a_{ii} = 0$ or $a_{ii} = 0$ for all i's.

♦ This means that all the diagonal elements of a skew symmetric matrix are zero.

♦ **Theorem 1 :** For any square matrix A with real number entries, $A + A'$ is a symmetric matrix and $A - A'$ is a skew symmetric matrix.

♦ **Theorem 2 :** Any square matrix can be expressed as the sum of a symmetric and a skew symmetric matrix.

$$A = \frac{1}{2}(A + A') + \frac{1}{2}(A - A')$$

♦ It follows that $\frac{1}{2}(A + A')$ is symmetric matrix and $\frac{1}{2}(A - A')$ is skew symmetric matrix.

Elementary Operation (Transformation) of a Matrix

♦ There are six operations (transformations) on a matrix, three of which are due to rows and three due to columns, which are known as elementary operations or transformations.

- The interchange of any two rows or two columns. Symbolically the interchange of ith and j^{th} rows is denoted by $R_i \leftrightarrow R_j$ and interchange of ith and j^{th} column is denoted by $C_i \leftrightarrow C_j$.

- The multiplication of the elements of any row or column by a non zero number. Symbolically, the multiplication of each element of the ith row by k, where $k \neq 0$ is denoted by $R_i \rightarrow k R_i$ and the corresponding column operation is denoted by $C_i \rightarrow kC_i$.

- The addition to the elements of any row or column, the corresponding elements of any other row or column multiplied by any non zero number. Symbolically, the addition to the elements of ith row, the corresponding elements of jth row multiplied by k is denoted by $R_i \rightarrow R_i + kR_j$ and the corresponding column operation is denoted by $C_i \rightarrow C_i + kC_j$.

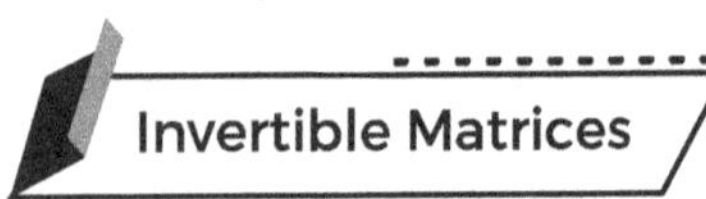

Invertible Matrices

- **Inverse of a Matrix :** If A is a square matrix of order m, and if there exists another square matrix B of the same order m, such that AB = BA = I, then B is called the *inverse matrix* of A and it is denoted by A^{-1}. In that case A is said to be invertible.

- **Note :**
  - ❖ A rectangular matrix does not possess inverse matrix, since for products BA and AB to be defined and to be equal, it is necessary that matrices A and B should be square matrices of the same order.
  - ❖ If B is the inverse of A, then A is also the inverse of B.

- **Uniqueness of inverse :** Inverse of a square matrix, if it exists, is unique.

- If A and B are invertible matrices of the same order, then $(AB)^{-1} = B^{-1} A^{-1}$.

Inverse of a matrix by elementary operations :

- If A is a matrix such that A^{-1} exists, then to find A^{-1} using elementary row operations, write A = IA and apply a sequence of row operation on A = IA till we get, I = BA. The matrix B will be the inverse of A.

- Similarly, if we wish to find A^{-1} using column operations, then, write A = AI and apply a sequence of column operations on A = AI till we get, I = AB. The matrix B will be the inverse of A.

- **Note :** In case, after applying one or more elementary row (column) operations on A = IA (A = AI), if we obtain all zeros in one or more rows of the matrix A on L.H.S., then A^{-1} does not exist.

Past Years ONE-LINERS
JEE Main/Board

- Let A be a matrix of order 3×3,
  $A^2 = AA$, $A^3 = A^2A$ & So on,
  Thus, $A^n = (1 + C)^n = 1 + nC + n_{C_2} C^2$
  (i.e., Neglecting higher order terms)

- Roots of equation $x^2 + x + 1 = 0$: ω and ω^2
  $1 + \omega + \omega^2 = 0$, $\qquad A^n = A^{n-1} A$

  $$I = \begin{bmatrix} 1 & 0 & 0 \\ 0 & 1 & 0 \\ 0 & 0 & 1 \end{bmatrix}$$

- Sum of first n natural numbers,

  $$S_n = 1 + 2 + 3 + ... + n = \frac{n(n+1)}{2}$$

  If two matrices A and B are equal

  $$A = B$$

  $$\begin{bmatrix} a_{11} & a_{12} \\ a_{21} & a_{22} \end{bmatrix} = \begin{bmatrix} b_{11} & b_{12} \\ b_{21} & b_{22} \end{bmatrix}$$

  $\therefore \quad a_{11} = b_{11}, a_{12} = b_{12}, a_{21} = b_{21}, a_{22} = b_{22}$

- Let two matrices A and B,

  $$A = \begin{bmatrix} a_{11} & a_{12} \\ a_{21} & a_{22} \end{bmatrix} B = \begin{bmatrix} b_{11} & b_{12} \\ b_{21} & b_{22} \end{bmatrix}, KB = \begin{bmatrix} kb_{11} & kb_{12} \\ kb_{21} & kb_{22} \end{bmatrix}$$

  $$A + KB \begin{bmatrix} a_{11} + kb_{11} & a_{12} + kb_{12} \\ a_{21} + kb_{21} & a_{22} + kb_{22} \end{bmatrix}$$

- According to the property of matrix,
  $A \,(\text{adj } A) = AA^T$
  Multiplying A^{-1} both the sides,
  $A^{-1} A \,(\text{adj } A) = A^{-1} AA^T \qquad$ (i.e., $A^{-1} A = I$ and $AI = A$)
  $\therefore \quad I \,(\text{adj } A) = IA^T$
  Thus, adj $A = A^T$

- Let A be a matrix, $A = \begin{bmatrix} a_{11} & a_{12} \\ a_{21} & a_{22} \end{bmatrix}$

  Then $A^T = \begin{bmatrix} a_{11} & a_{12} \\ a_{12} & a_{22} \end{bmatrix}$ and $I = \begin{bmatrix} 1 & 0 \\ 0 & 1 \end{bmatrix}$

$$AA^T = \begin{bmatrix} a_{11} & a_{12} \\ a_{21} & a_{22} \end{bmatrix}\begin{bmatrix} a_{11} & a_{21} \\ a_{12} & a_{22} \end{bmatrix} = I$$

$$\Rightarrow \begin{bmatrix} a_{11}^2 + a_{12}^2 & a_{11}a_{21} + a_{12}a_{22} \\ a_{21}a_{11} + a_{22}a_{12} & a_{21}^2 + a_{22}^2 \end{bmatrix} = \begin{bmatrix} 1 & 0 \\ 0 & 1 \end{bmatrix}$$

Tips/Tricks/Techniques ONE-LINERS
(Exam Special)

- -

♦ **Singleton matrix :** If in a matrix there is only one element then it is called singleton matrix. Thus

$A = [a_{ij}]_{m \times n}$ is a singleton matrix if $m = n = 1$

♦ **Trace of a matrix :** The sum of diagonal elements of a square matrix A is called the trace of matrix A which is denoted by tr A.

$$\text{tr } A = \sum_{i=1}^{n} a_{ii} = a_{11} + a_{22} + ... a_{nn}$$

♦ **Triangular matrix :** A Square Matrix $[a_{ij}]$ is said to be triangular matrix if each element above or below the principal diagonal is zero it is of two types –

❖ **Upper triangular matrix :** A square matrix $[a_{ij}]$ is called the upper triangular matrix, if $a_{ij} = 0$ when $i > j$.

❖ **Lower triangular matrix :** A square matrix $[a_{ij}]$ is called the lower triangular matrix, if $a_{ij} = 0$ when $i < j$

♦ **Positive integral powers of a matrix :** The positive integral powers of a matrix A are defined only when A is a square matrix. Also

$A^2 = A. A, A^3 = A.A.A = A^2 A$

For any positive integers m, n

❖ $A^m A^n = A^{m+n}$

❖ $(A^m)^n = A^{mn} = (A^n)^m$

❖ $I^n = I, I^m = I$

❖ $A^\circ = I_n$ where A is a square matrices of order n.

♦ **Nilpotent matrix :** A square matrix A is said to be nilpotent matrix if there exists a positive integer m such that $A^m = 0$. If m is the least positive integer such that $A^m = 0$, then m is called the index of the nilpotent matrix A.

♦ **Idempotent matrix :** A square matrix A is called an idempotent matrix if $A^2 = A$.

♦ **Involutory matrix :** A square matrix A is said to be involutory matrix if $A^2 = I$.

Properties of transpose :

♦ $I^T = I$

♦ $\text{tr } (A) = \text{tr } (A)^T$

♦ $(A_1 A_2 A_3 ..... A_{n-1} A_n)^T = A_n^T A_{n-1}^T ..... A_3^T A_2^T A_1^T$

Properties of symmetric and skew-symmetric matrices :

♦ If A is a square matrix, then $A + A^T$, AA^T, A^TA are symmetric matrices while A $- A^T$ is Skew - Symmetric Matrix.

♦ If A is a Symmetric Matrix, then $-A$, kA, A^T, A^n, A^{-1}, $B^T AB$ are also symmetric matrices where $n \in N$, $k \in R$ and B is a square matrix of order that of A

♦ If A is a skew symmetric matrix, then
  ❖ A^{2n} is a symmetric matrix for $n \in N$
  ❖ A^{2n+1} is a skew-symmetric matrices for $n \in N$
  ❖ kA is also skew -symmetric matrix where $k \in R$
  ❖ $B^T AB$ is also skew - symmetric matrix where B is a square matrix of order that of A.

♦ If A, B are two symmetric matrices, then –
  ❖ $A \pm B$, $AB + BA$ are also symmetric matrices.
  ❖ $AB - BA$ is a skew-symmetric matrix
  ❖ AB is a symmetric matrix when $AB = BA$.

♦ If A, B are two skew-symmetric matrices, then
  ❖ $A \pm B$, $AB - BA$ are skew-symmetric matrices
  ❖ $AB + BA$ is a symmetric matrix

♦ If A is a skew-symmetric matrix and C is a column matrix, then $C^T AC$ is a zero matrix.

♦ If $m \neq n$, then matrix is called a Rectangular Matrix.

♦ The elements of a square matrix A for which $i = j$ i.e. a_{11}, a_{22}, a_{33}, ..., a_{nn} are called diagonal elements and the line joining these elements is called the principal diagonal or leading diagonal of matrix A.

♦ No element of principal diagonal in diagonal matrix is zero.

♦ Number of zero in a diagonal matrix is given by $n^2 - n$ where n is a order of the matrix.

♦ Minimum number of zero in a triangular matrix is given by $\dfrac{n(n-1)}{2}$, where n is order of matrix.

♦ The multiplication of two diagonal matrices is again a diagonal matrix.

♦ The multiplication of two triangular matrices is again a triangular matrix.

♦ The multiplication of two scalar matrices is also a scalar matrix.

♦ If A and B are two square matrices of the same order, then
  ❖ $(A + B)^2 = A^2 + B^2 + AB + BA$
  ❖ $(A - B)^2 = A^2 + B^2 - AB - BA$
  ❖ $(A - B)(A + B) = A^2 - B^2 + AB - BA$
  ❖ $(A + B)(A - B) = A^2 - B^2 - AB + BA$
  ❖ $A(-B) = (-A)B = -(AB)$

♦ All Principal diagonal elements of a skew-symmetric matrix are always zero because for any diagonal element
$a_{ii} = -a_{ii} \Rightarrow a_{ii} = 0$

♦ Trace of a skew symmetric matrix is always 0.

20

Determinants

Determinant

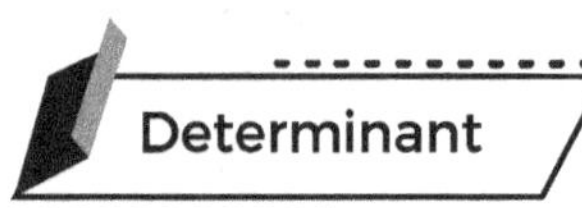

- To every square matrix A = $[a_{ij}]$ of order n, we can associate a number (real or complex) called **determinant** of the square matrix A, where $a_{ij} = (i, j)^{\text{th}}$ element of A.

- If A = $\begin{bmatrix} a & b \\ c & d \end{bmatrix}$, then determinant of A is written as $|A| = \begin{vmatrix} a & b \\ c & d \end{vmatrix} = \det(A)$

- **Note:**
    - ❖ For matrix A, $|A|$ is read as determinant of A and not modulus of A.
    - ❖ Only square matrices have determinants.

Determinant of a matrix of order one :

- Let A = $[a]$ be the matrix of order 1, then determinant of A is defined to be equal to a.

Determinant of a matrix of order two :

- Let A = $\begin{bmatrix} a_{11} & b_{12} \\ c_{21} & d_{22} \end{bmatrix}$ be a matrix of order 2×2,

    then the determinant of A is defined as:

$$\det(A) = |A| = \Delta = \begin{vmatrix} a_{11} & a_{12} \\ a_{21} & a_{22} \end{vmatrix} = a_{11}a_{22} - a_{21}a_{12}$$

Determinant of a matrix of order 3×3 :

- Determinant of a matrix of order three can be determined by expressing it in terms of second order determinants. This is known as expansion of a determinant along a row (or a column).

- There are six ways of expanding a determinant of order 3 corresponding to each of three rows (R_1, R_2 and R_3) and three columns (C_1, C_2 and C_3) giving the same value as shown below.

♦ Consider the determinant of square matrix $A = [a_{ij}]_{3 \times 3}$

$$|A| = \begin{vmatrix} a_{11} & a_{12} & a_{13} \\ a_{21} & a_{22} & a_{23} \\ a_{31} & a_{32} & a_{33} \end{vmatrix}$$

Expansion along first Row (R_1) :

$$|A| = a_{11}(a_{22}a_{33} - a_{32}a_{23}) - a_{12}(a_{21}a_{33} - a_{31}a_{23}) + a_{13}(a_{21}a_{32} - a_{31}a_{22})$$
$$= a_{11}a_{22}a_{33} - a_{11}a_{32}a_{23} - a_{12}a_{21}a_{33} + a_{12}a_{31}a_{23} + a_{13}a_{21}a_{32}$$
$$- a_{13}a_{31}a_{22} \qquad \qquad \qquad \dots (1)$$

Expansion along second Row (R_2) :

$$|A| = - a_{21}(a_{12}a_{33} - a_{32}a_{13}) + a_{22}(a_{11}a_{33} - a_{31}a_{13})$$
$$- a_{23}(a_{11}a_{32} - a_{31}a_{12})$$
$$= a_{11}a_{22}a_{33} - a_{11}a_{23}a_{32} - a_{12}a_{21}a_{33} + a_{12}a_{23}a_{31} + a_{13}a_{21}a_{32}$$
$$- a_{13}a_{31}a_{22} \qquad \qquad \qquad \dots (2)$$

Expansion along first Column (C_1) :

$$|A| = a_{11}(a_{22}a_{33} - a_{23}a_{32}) - a_{21}(a_{12}a_{33} - a_{13}a_{32}) + a_{31}(a_{12}a_{23} - a_{13}a_{22})$$
$$= a_{11}a_{22}a_{33} - a_{11}a_{23}a_{32} - a_{12}a_{21}a_{33} + a_{12}a_{23}a_{31} + a_{13}a_{21}a_{32} - a_{13}a_{31}a_{22}$$
$$\qquad \qquad \qquad \dots (3)$$

Clearly, values of $|A|$ in (1), (2) and (3) are equal.

Hence, expanding a determinant along any row or column gives same value.

♦ **Note:**

❖ For easier calculations, we shall expand the determinant along that row or column which contains maximum number of zeros.

❖ While expanding, instead of multiplying by $(-1)^{i+j}$, we can multiply by $+1$ or -1 according as $(i + j)$ is even or odd.

❖ In general, if $A = kB$ where A and B are square matrices of order n, then $|A| = k^n |B|$, where $n = 1, 2, 3$

Properties of Determinants

♦ **Property 1:** The value of the determinant remains unchanged if its rows and columns are interchanged.

♦ **Note:**

❖ If A is a square matrix, then det (A) = det (A′),
where A′ = transpose of A.

❖ If $R_i = i^{th}$ row and $C_i = i^{th}$ column, then for interchange of row and columns, we will symbolically write $C_i \leftrightarrow R_i$

- **Property 2:** If any two rows (or columns) of a determinant are interchanged, then sign of determinant changes.
- **Note:** We can denote the interchange of rows by $R_i \leftrightarrow R_j$ and interchange of columns by $C_i \leftrightarrow C_j$.
- **Property 3:** If any two rows (or columns) of a determinant are identical (all corresponding elements are same), then value of determinant is zero.
- **Property 4:** If each element of a row (or a column) of a determinant is multiplied by a constant k, then its value gets multiplied by k.
- **Note:**
  - ❖ By this property, we can take out any common factor from any one row or any one column of a given determinant.
  - ❖ If corresponding elements of any two rows (or columns) of a determinant are proportional (in the same ratio), then its value is zero.
- **Property 5:** If some or all elements of a row or column of a determinant are expressed as sum of two (or more) terms, then the determinant can be expressed as sum of two (or more) determinants.
- **Property 6:** If, to each element of any row or column of a determinant, the equimultiples of corresponding elements of other row (or column) are added, then value of determinant remains the same, i.e., the value of determinant remain same if we apply the operation $R_i \to R_i + kR_j$ or $C_i \to C_i + kC_j$.
- **Note:**
  - ❖ If Δ_1 is the determinant obtained by applying $R_i \to kR_i$ or $C_i \to kC_i$ to the determinant Δ, then $\Delta_1 = k\Delta$.
  - ❖ If more than one operation like $R_i \to R_i + kR_j$ is done in one step, care should be taken to see that a row that is affected in one operation should not be used in another operation. A similar remark applies to column operations.

Area of a Triangle

- Area of a triangle whose vertices are (x_1, y_1), (x_2, y_2) and (x_3, y_3), is given by the expression

$$\frac{1}{2} [x_1(y_2 - y_3) + x_2(y_3 - y_1) + x_3(y_1 - y_2)].$$

- Now this expression can be written in the form of a determinant as

$$\Delta = \frac{1}{2} \begin{vmatrix} x_1 & y_1 & 1 \\ x_2 & y_2 & 1 \\ x_3 & y_3 & 1 \end{vmatrix} \qquad \text{...(1)}$$

♦ **Note:**

❖ Since area is a positive quantity, we always take the absolute value of the determinant.

❖ If area is given, use both positive and negative values of the determinant for calculation.

❖ The area of the triangle formed by three collinear points is zero.

Minors and Cofactors

♦ **Minor of an element:** Minor of an element a_{ij} of a determinant is the determinant obtained by deleting its ith row and j^{th} column in which element a_{ij} lies. Minor of an element a_{ij} is denoted by M_{ij}.

♦ Minor of an element of a determinant of order $n(n \geq 2)$ is a determinant of order $n - 1$.

♦ **Cofactor of an element:** Cofactor of an element a_{ij}, denoted by A_{ij} is defined by $A_{ij} = (-1)^{i+j} M_{ij}$, where M_{ij} is minor of a_{ij}.

♦ **Note:** Δ = sum of the product of elements of any row (or column) with their corresponding cofactors.

♦ If elements of a row (or column) are multiplied with cofactors of any other row (or column), then their sum is zero.

Adjoint and Inverse of a Matrix

♦ To find inverse of a matrix A, i.e., A^{-1} we shall first define adjoint of a matrix.

Adjoint of a matrix :

♦ The adjoint of a square matrix $A = [a_{ij}]_{n \times n}$ is defined as the transpose of the matrix $[A_{ij}]_{n \times n}$, where A_{ij} is the cofactor of the element a_{ij}. Adjoint of the matrix A is denoted by *adj* A.

♦ Let $A = \begin{bmatrix} a_{11} & a_{12} & a_{13} \\ a_{21} & a_{22} & a_{23} \\ a_{31} & a_{32} & a_{33} \end{bmatrix} \begin{bmatrix} A_{11} & A_{12} & A_{13} \\ A_{21} & A_{22} & A_{23} \\ A_{31} & A_{32} & A_{33} \end{bmatrix}$

Then *adj* A = Transpose of

$$= \begin{bmatrix} A_{11} & A_{21} & A_{33} \\ A_{12} & A_{22} & A_{32} \\ A_{13} & A_{23} & A_{33} \end{bmatrix}$$

♦   **Note:** For a square matrix of order 2, given by

$$A = \begin{bmatrix} a_{11} & a_{12} \\ a_{21} & a_{22} \end{bmatrix}$$

The *adj* A can also be obtained by interchanging a_{11} and a_{22} and by changing signs of a_{12} and a_{21}, i.e.,

$$adj\ A = \begin{bmatrix} a_{11} & a_{12} \\ a_{21} & a_{22} \end{bmatrix} = \begin{bmatrix} a_{22} & -a_{12} \\ -a_{21} & a_{11} \end{bmatrix}$$

Change sign   Interchange

♦   **Theorem 1:** If A be any given square matrix of order n, then A(*adj* A) = (*adj* A) A = A I ,
where I is the identity matrix of order n

♦   **Singular Matrix:** A square matrix A is said to be singular if $|A| = 0$.

♦   **Non-singular Matrix:** A square matrix A is said to be non-singular if $|A| \neq 0$

♦   **Note:**
  ❖ If A and B are nonsingular matrices of the same order, then AB and BA are also nonsingular matrices of the same order.
  ❖ The determinant of the product of matrices is equal to product of their respective determinants, that is, $|AB| = |A|\ |B|$, where A and B are square matrices of the same order.
  ❖ In general, if A is *a* square matrix of order n, then $|adj(A)| = |A|^{n-1}$.

♦   **Invertible Matrix:** A square matrix A is **invertible** if and only if A is nonsingular matrix.

Let A be nonsingular. Then $|A| \neq 0$. A is invertible and $A^{-1} = \dfrac{1}{|A|} adj\ A$

Applications of Determinants and Matrices

♦   The main application of determinants and matrices for solving the system of linear equations in two or three variables and for checking the consistency of the system of linear equations.

♦   **Consistent system:** A system of equations is said to be **consistent** if its solution (one or more) exists.

♦   **Inconsistent system:** A system of equations is said to be **inconsistent** if its solution does not exist.

Solution of system of linear equations using inverse of a matrix:

♦ Let us express the system of linear equations as matrix equations and solve them using inverse of the coefficient matrix.

♦ Consider the system of equations
$$a_1 x + b_1 y + c_1 z = d_1$$
$$a_2 x + b_2 y + c_2 z = d_2$$
$$a_3 x + b_3 y + c_3 z = d_3$$

♦ Let $A = \begin{bmatrix} a_1 & b_1 & c_1 \\ a_2 & b_2 & c_2 \\ a_3 & b_3 & c_3 \end{bmatrix}, X = \begin{bmatrix} x \\ y \\ z \end{bmatrix}$ and $B = \begin{bmatrix} d_1 \\ d_2 \\ d_3 \end{bmatrix}$

Then, the system of equations can be written as, $AX = B$, i.e.,

$$\begin{bmatrix} a_1 & b_1 & c_1 \\ a_2 & b_2 & c_2 \\ a_3 & b_3 & c_3 \end{bmatrix} \begin{bmatrix} x \\ y \\ z \end{bmatrix} = \begin{bmatrix} d_1 \\ d_2 \\ d_3 \end{bmatrix}$$

♦ **Case I:** If A is a nonsingular matrix, then its inverse exists. Now $AX = B$
or $A^{-1}(AX) = A^{-1}B$ (premultiplying by A^{-1})
or $(A^{-1}A)X = A^{-1}B$ (by associative property)
or $IX = A^{-1}B$
or $X = A^{-1}B$

This matrix equation provides unique solution for the given system of equations as inverse of a matrix is unique. This method of solving system of equations is known as **Matrix Method.**

♦ **Case II:** If A is a singular matrix, then $|A| = 0$. In this case, we calculate $(adj\,A)\,B$.

❖ If $(\mathbf{adj}\,A)\,B \neq O$, (O being zero matrix), then solution does not exist and the system of equations is called **inconsistent.**

❖ If $(\mathbf{adj}\,A)\,B = O$, then system may be either **consistent** or **inconsistent** according as the system have either **infinitely many solutions** or **no solution.**

Past Years ONE-LINERS
JEE Main/Board

- $I_2 = \begin{bmatrix} 1 & 0 \\ 0 & 1 \end{bmatrix}, A = \begin{bmatrix} a & b \\ c & d \end{bmatrix}, |A| = ad - bc$

  $A^{-1} = \dfrac{1}{|A|} adj\, A$ and $adj\, A = \begin{bmatrix} d & -b \\ -c & a \end{bmatrix}$

  $I_2 \pm A = \begin{bmatrix} 1 & 0 \\ 0 & 1 \end{bmatrix} \pm \begin{bmatrix} a & b \\ c & d \end{bmatrix} = \begin{bmatrix} 1\pm a & \pm b \\ \pm c & 1\pm d \end{bmatrix}$

- Let the system of equation,

  $$a_1 x + b_1 y + c_1 z = d_1$$
  $$a_2 x + b_2 y + c_2 z = d_2,$$
  $$a_3 x + b_2 y + c_3 z = d_3$$

  $$A = \begin{bmatrix} a_1 & b_1 & c_1 \\ a_2 & b_2 & c_2 \\ a_3 & b_3 & c_3 \end{bmatrix}$$

  For non–zero solution, $|A| = 0$

- For a matrix A, $|A| \neq 0$

  $\therefore$ A is invertible

- $(A + Bx)(x + B) = \begin{vmatrix} x-1 & -2x \\ 2x & x^2 \end{vmatrix}$

  Here, we have two constants A and B. To find the values of A & B, Substitute any two values of x in the above determinant, Then we will get the value of A and B.

- Area of triangle, $\Delta = \dfrac{1}{2} \begin{bmatrix} x_1 & y_1 & 1 \\ x_2 & y_2 & 1 \\ x_3 & y_3 & 1 \end{bmatrix}$

  To calculate orthocentre O,

  $BO \perp AC, CO \perp AB, AO \perp BC$

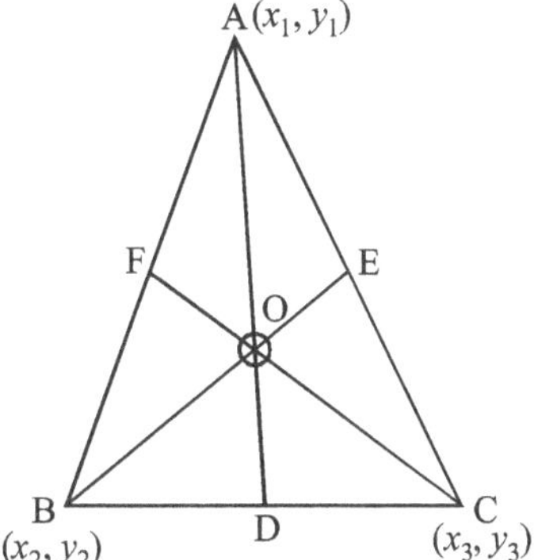

Slope of perpendicular lines, $m_1 \times m_2 = -1$

♦ For a system of Linear equations,

$$a_1x + b_1y + c_1z = d_1$$
$$a_2x + b_2y + c_2z = d_2$$
$$a_3x + b_3y + c_3z = d_3$$

$$A = \text{coefficient matrix} = \begin{bmatrix} a_1 & b_1 & c_1 \\ a_2 & b_2 & c_2 \\ a_3 & b_3 & c_3 \end{bmatrix}, B = \begin{bmatrix} d_1 \\ d_2 \\ d_3 \end{bmatrix}, X = \begin{bmatrix} x \\ y \\ z \end{bmatrix}$$

For non-trivial solution, matrix A should be singular matrix. (i.e. $\therefore |A| = 0$)

Tips/Tricks/Techniques ONE-LINERS
(Exam Special)

♦ **Solution of homogeneous system of linear equations by cramer's rule (or determinant method)**

Let us now consider a homogeneous system of equations given by

$$a_1x + b_1 y + c_1z = 0$$
$$a_2x + b_2 y + c_2z = 0$$
$$a_3 x + b_3 y + c_3z = 0$$

For this system of equations, we have

$$D_1 = \begin{vmatrix} 0 & b_1 & c_1 \\ 0 & b_2 & c_2 \\ 0 & b_3 & c_3 \end{vmatrix} = 0, D_2 = \begin{vmatrix} a_1 & 0 & c_1 \\ a_2 & 0 & c_2 \\ a_3 & 0 & c_3 \end{vmatrix} = 0 \text{ and,}$$

$$D_3 = \begin{vmatrix} a_1 & b_1 & 0 \\ a_2 & b_2 & 0 \\ a_3 & b_3 & 0 \end{vmatrix} = 0$$

If $D = \begin{vmatrix} a_1 & b_1 & c_1 \\ a_2 & b_2 & c_2 \\ a_3 & b_3 & c_3 \end{vmatrix} \neq 0$, then

$$x = \frac{D_1}{D} = 0, \ y = \frac{D_2}{D} = 0 \text{ and } z = \frac{D_3}{D} = 0.$$

Thus, if $D \neq 0$, then the homogeneous system of equations has unique solution $x = 0$, $y = 0$, $z = 0$. This solution is called the trivial solution.

If $D = 0$, then a homogeneous system of equations has infinitely many solutions. This solutions are called non-trivial or non-zero solutions.

♦ Three straight lines having equations $a_1x + b_1y + c_1 = 0$, $a_2x + b_2y + c_2 = 0$ and $a_3x + b_3y + c_3 = 0$ are concurrent if.

$$\begin{vmatrix} a_1 & b_1 & c_1 \\ a_2 & b_2 & c_2 \\ a_3 & b_3 & c_3 \end{vmatrix} = 0$$

♦ $|A|$ exists $\Leftrightarrow$ A is a square matrix

♦ $|AB| = |A||B|$

♦ $|A^T| = |A|$

♦ $|kA| = k^n|A|$, if A is a square matrix of order n.

♦ If A and B are square matrices of same order then
$|AB| = |BA|$

♦ If A is a skew symmetric matrix of odd order then $|A| = 0$

♦ If $A = \text{diag}(a_1, a_2, \ldots, a_n)$ then $|A| = a_1 a_2 \ldots a_n$

♦ $|A|^n = |A^n|$, $n \in N$.

♦ Every diagonal element of a skew symmetric determinant is always zero.

♦ The value of a skew symmetric determinant of even order is always a perfect square and that of odd order is always zero.

If A, B are square matrices of order n and I_n is corresponding unit matrix, then

♦ $A(\text{adj. } A) = |A| I_n = (\text{adj } A) A$

♦ $|\text{adj } A| = |A|^{n-1}$

- adj (adj A) = $| A |^{n-2}$ A

- $|\text{adj (adj A)}| = | A |^{(n-1)^2}$

- adj (A^T) = (adj A)^T

- adj (AB) = (adj B) (adj A)

- adj (A^m) = (adj A)^m, $m \in N$

- adj $(kA) = k^{n-1}$ (adj. A), $k \in R$

- adj $(I_n) = I_n$

- adj O = O

- A is symmetric $\Rightarrow$ adj A is also symmetric

- A is diagonal matrix $\Rightarrow$ adj A is also diagonal

- A is triangular matrix $\Rightarrow$ adj A is also triangular

- A is singular matrix $\Rightarrow |$ adj A $| = $ O

- **Let A and B are two invertible matrices of the same order, then**

  - $(A^k)^{-1} = (A^{-1})^k$, $k \in N$

  - $(A^{-1})^{-1} = A$

  - $| A^{-1} | = \dfrac{1}{| A |} = | A |^{-1}$

  - If A = diag $(a_1, a_2.....,a_n)$, then
    $$A^{-1} = \text{diag} (a_1^{-1}, a_2^{-1}, ...a_n^{-1})$$

  - A is symmetric matrix $\Rightarrow A^{-1}$ is symmetric matrix.

  - A is triangular matrix and $| A | \neq 0 \Rightarrow A^{-1}$ is a triangular matrix.

  - A is scalar matrix $\Rightarrow A^{-1}$ is scalar matrix

  - A is diagonal matrix $\Rightarrow A^{-1}$ is diagonal matrix

  - AB = AC $\Rightarrow$ B = C, iff $| A | \neq 0$.

21 Continuity and Differentiability

- Suppose f is a real function on a subset of the real numbers and let c be a point in the domain of f. Then f is continuous at c if $\lim\limits_{x \to c} f(x) = f(c)$
- More elaborately, if the left hand limit, right hand limit and the value of the function at $x = c$ exist and equal to each other, then f is said to be continuous at $x = c$.
- If f is not continuous at c, we say f is *discontinuous* at c and c is called a *point of discontinuity* of f.

Continuity of a function at a given point:

- A real function f is said to be continuous if it is continuous at every point in the domain of f.
- If f is defined only at one point, it is continuous there, i.e., if the domain of f is a singleton, f is a continuous function.

Algebra of continuous functions:

- Suppose f and g be two real functions continuous at a real number c. Then
  - ❖ $f + g$ is continuous at $x = c$.
  - ❖ $f - g$ is continuous at $x = c$.
  - ❖ $f \cdot g$ is continuous at $x = c$.
  - ❖ $\left(\dfrac{f}{g}\right)$ is continuous at x = c, (provided g(c) ≠ 0).
- If f is a constant function, then the function $(\lambda \cdot g)$ defined by $(\lambda \cdot g)(x) = \lambda \cdot g(x)$ is also continuous.
- If f is the constant function $f(x) = \lambda$, then the function $\dfrac{\lambda}{g}$ defined by $\dfrac{\lambda}{g}(x) = \dfrac{\lambda}{g(x)}$ is also continuous wherever $g(x) \neq 0$.

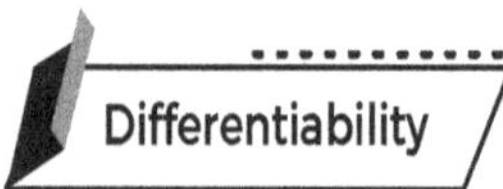

- Suppose f is a real function and c is a point in its domain. The derivative of f at c is defined by
$$\lim\limits_{h \to 0} \frac{f(c+h) - f(c)}{h}$$ provided this limit exists.

♦ Derivative of f at c is denoted by $f'(c)$ or $\dfrac{d}{dx}(f(x))\big|_c$

♦ The function defined by

$$f'(x) = \lim_{h \to 0} \frac{f(x+h) - f(x)}{h}$$

♦ The derivative of f is denoted by $f'(x)$ or $\dfrac{d}{dx}(f(x))$ or if $y = f(x)$ by $\dfrac{dy}{dx}$ or y'.

♦ The process of finding derivative of a function is called differentiation.

♦ The phrase *differentiate* $f(x)$ with respect to x to mean find $f'(x)$.

Algebra of derivatives:

    (i) $(u \pm v)' = u' \pm v'$

    (ii) $(uv)' = u'v + uv'$ (Leibnitz or product rule)

    (iii) $\left(\dfrac{u}{v}\right)' = \dfrac{u'v - uv'}{v^2}$, wherever $v \neq 0$ (Quotient rule).

$f(x)$	x^n	$\sin x$	$\cos x$	$\tan x$
$f'(x)$	nx^{n-1}	$\cos x$	$-\sin x$	$\sec^2 x$

♦ Whenever we defined derivative, we had put a caution provided the limit exists.

♦ If $\lim\limits_{h \to 0} \dfrac{f(c+h) - f(c)}{h}$ does not exist, we say that f is not differentiable at c.

♦ We say that a function f is differentiable at a point c in its domain if both

$$\lim_{h \to 0^-} \frac{f(c+h) - f(c)}{h}$$

and $\lim\limits_{h \to 0^+} \dfrac{f(c+h) - f(c)}{h}$ are finite and equal.

♦ A function is said to be differentiable in an interval $[a, b]$ if it is differentiable at every point of $[a, b]$.

♦ A function is said to be differentiable in an interval (a, b) if it is differentiable at every point of (a, b).

♦ If a function f is differentiable at a point c, then it is also continuous at that point.

♦ Every differentiable function is continuous.

Derivatives of composite functions:
- **Chain Rule :** Let f be a real valued function which is a composite of two functions u and v; i.e., $f = v \text{ o } u$. Suppose $t = u(x)$ and if both $\dfrac{dt}{dx}$ and $\dfrac{dv}{dt}$ exist,

  we have $\dfrac{df}{dx} = \dfrac{dv}{dt} \cdot \dfrac{dt}{dx}$

Derivatives of implicit functions:
- The following relationships between x and y:
  $x + \sin xy - y = 0$
- In this case, it is implicit that y is a function of x and we say that the relationship of the second type, gives function implicitly.

Derivatives of inverse trigonometric functions:

$f(x)$	$\cos^{-1} x$	$\cot^{-1} x$	$\sec^{-1} x$	$\text{cosec}^{-1} x$
$f'(x)$	$\dfrac{-1}{\sqrt{1-x^2}}$	$\dfrac{-1}{1+x^2}$	$\dfrac{1}{\|x\|\sqrt{x^2-1}}$	$\dfrac{-1}{\|x\|\sqrt{x^2-1}}$
Domain of f'	$(-1,1)$	R	$(-\infty,-1)\cup(1,\infty)$	$(-\infty,-1)\cup(1,\infty)$

Exponential and Logarithmic Functions

- The exponential function with positive base $b > 1$ is the function $y = f(x) = b^x$
- **Some of the salient features of the exponential functions:**
  - ❖ Domain of the exponential function is **R**, the set of all real numbers.
  - ❖ Range of the exponential function is the set of all positive real numbers.
  - ❖ The point $(0, 1)$ is always on the graph of the exponential function (this is a restatement of the fact that $b^0 = 1$ for any real $b > 1$).
  - ❖ Exponential function is ever increasing; i.e., as we move from left to right, the graph rises above.
  - ❖ For very large negative values of x, the exponential function is very close to 0. In other words, in the second quadrant, the graph approaches x-axis (but never meets it).
- Exponential function with base 10 is called the common exponential function.
- It was observed that the sum of the series

  $$1 + \frac{1}{1!} + \frac{1}{2!} + ...$$

  is a number between 2 and 3 and is denoted by e.
- Using this e as the base we obtain an extremely important exponential function $y = e^x$. This is called natural exponential function.
- Let $b > 1$ be a real number. Then we say logarithm of a to base b is x if $b^x = a$.

♦   Fixing a base $b > 1$, you may look at logarithm as a function from positive real numbers to all real numbers.

♦   This function, called the *logarithmic function*, is defined by
$$\log_b : \mathbf{R}^+ \to \mathbf{R}$$
$$x \to \log_b x = y \text{ if } b^y = x$$

♦   If the base $b = 10$, we say it is common logarithms and if $b = e$, then we say it is natural logarithms.

♦   Often natural logarithm is denoted by *ln*.

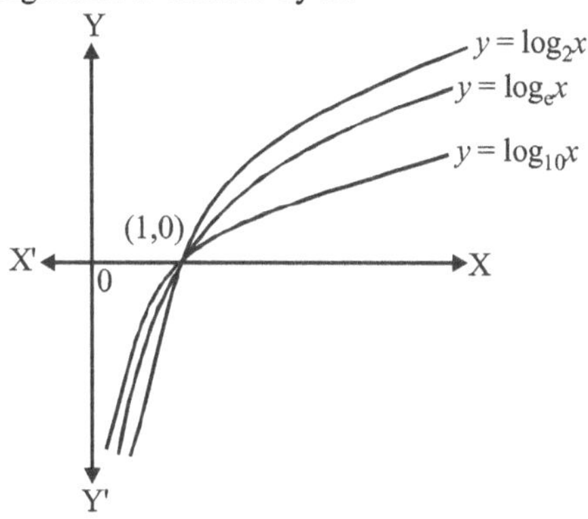

Observations:

♦   The logarithm function to any base $b > 1$ are listed below:

❖   We cannot make a meaningful definition of logarithm of non-positive numbers and hence the domain of log function is $\mathbf{R}^+$.

❖   The range of log function is the set of all real numbers.

❖   The point $(1, 0)$ is always on the graph of the log function.

❖   The log function is ever increasing, i.e., as we move from left to right the graph rises above.

❖   For x very near to zero, the value of log x can be made lesser than any given real number.

❖   Fig. gives the plot of $y = e^x$ and $y = ln\ x$. It is of interest to observe that the two curves are the mirror images of each other reflected in the line $y = x$.

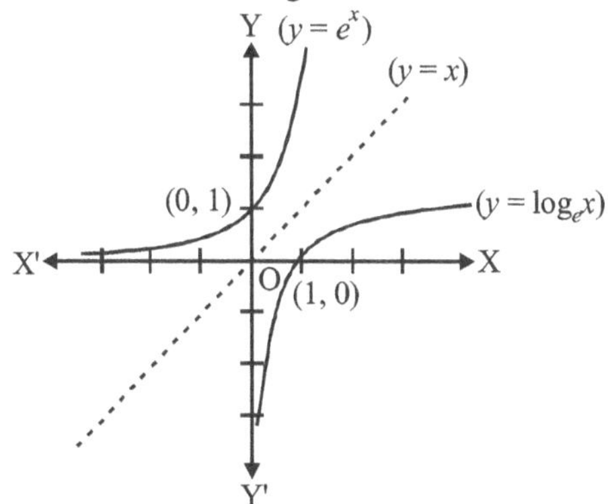

Properties of 'log' functions are given below:

- $\log_a p = \dfrac{\log_b p}{\log_b a}$

- $\log_b pq = \log_b p + \log_b q$

- $\log_b \dfrac{x}{y} = \log_b x - \log_b y$

- $\log_a m^n = n \log_a m$

The striking properties of the natural exponential function:

- The derivative of e^x w.r.t., x is e^x; i.e., $\dfrac{d}{dx}(e^x) = e^x$.

- The derivative of $\log x$ w.r.t., x is $\dfrac{1}{x}$; i.e., $\dfrac{d}{dx}(\log x) = \dfrac{1}{x}$.

Logarithmic Differentiation

- Now, you will learn to differentiate certain special class of functions given in the form
  $$y = f(x) = [u(x)]^{v(x)}$$
  By taking logarithm (to base e) the above may be rewritten as
  $$\log y = v(x) \log [u(x)]$$
  Using chain rule, we may differentiate this to get
  $$\frac{dy}{dx} = y\left[\frac{v(x)}{u(x)} \cdot u'(x) + v'(x) \cdot \log[u(x)] \right]$$

- The main point to be noted in this method is that $f(x)$ and $u(x)$ must always be positive as otherwise their logarithms are not defined.

Derivatives of Functions in Parametric Forms

- In order to find derivative of function in such form, we have by chain rule.
  $$\frac{dy}{dt} = \frac{dy}{dx} \cdot \frac{dx}{dt}$$
  $$\frac{dy}{dx} = \frac{g'(t)}{f'(t)} \left(\text{as} \frac{dy}{dt} = g'(t) \text{ and } \frac{dx}{dt} = f'(t) \right) \qquad [\text{provided } f'(t) \neq 0]$$

Second Order Derivative

- $y = f(x)$. Then $\dfrac{dy}{dx} = f'(x)$

♦   Again w.r.t. x. Then, the left hand side becomes $\dfrac{d}{dx}\left(\dfrac{dy}{dx}\right)$ which is called the

second order derivative of y w.r.t. x and is denoted by $\dfrac{d^2y}{dx^2}$.

♦   The second order derivative of $f(x)$ is denoted by $f''(x)$.
♦   It is also denoted by D^2y or y'' or y_2 if $y = f(x)$.

Mean Value Theorem

Rolle's Theorem:
♦   Let $f : [a, b] \to \mathbf{R}$ be continuous on $[a, b]$.
♦   Differentiable on (a, b), such that $f(a) = f(b)$.
♦   Then there exists some c in (a, b) such that $f'(c) = 0$, $a, b \in \mathbf{R}$.

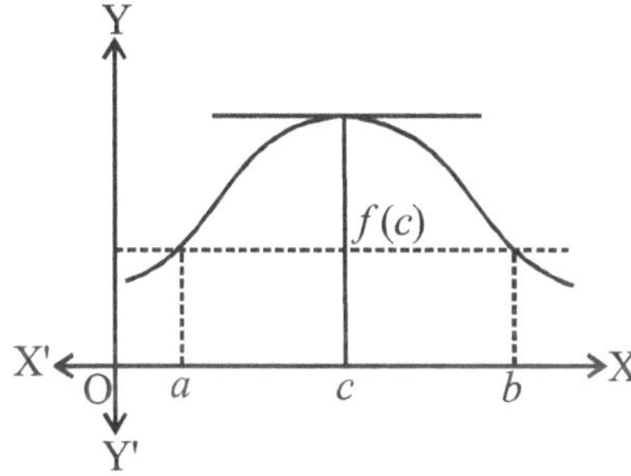

Mean Value Theorem:
♦   Let $f : [a, b] \to \mathbf{R}$ be a continuous function on $[a, b]$.
♦   Differentiable on (a, b). Then there exists some c in (a, b) such that

$$f'(c) = \dfrac{f(b) - f(a)}{b - a}$$

Past Years ONE-LINERS
JEE Main/Board

- Continuity of a composite function.
  Since $(g o f)\,(x)$ is continuous for all
  $\therefore\;\; f(x)$ should be continuous at $x = 0$

- Using of trigonometric identities e.g.

$$\cos(\sin x) - \cos x = 2 \sin\left(\frac{x+\sin x}{2}\right) \cdot \sin\left(\frac{x-\sin x}{2}\right)$$

$$\tan 2x - \sin 2x = \frac{\sin 2x\,(1-\cos 2x)}{\cos 2x}.$$

- Differentiating both side as $f(f(f(x))) + (f(x))^2 = g\,(x)$ then
  $g'(x) = f'\,(f(f(x)))\,f'\,(f(x))\,f'(x) + 2f(x)f'(x)$

- Using second derivative as $\dfrac{d(y)}{dx}$ and $\dfrac{d^2}{dx^2}(y)$

  e.g. $x^2 + y^2 + \sin y = 4$

  $$\frac{dy}{dx} = \frac{-2x}{2y + \cos y}$$

  $$\frac{d^2 y}{dx^2} = \frac{-2 - (2 - \sin y)\left(\dfrac{dy}{dx}\right)^2}{2y + \cos y}$$

Tips/Tricks/Techniques ONE-LINERS
(Exam Special)

- **Removable discontinuity :** A function f is said to have removable discontinuity at $x = a$ if $\lim\limits_{x \to a^-} f(x) = \lim\limits_{x \to a^+} f(x)$ but their common value is not equal to f (a). Such a discontinuity can be removed by assigning a suitable value to the function f at $x = a$.

♦ **Discontinuity of the first kind :** A function f is said to have a discontinuity of the first kind at x = a, if $\lim\limits_{x \to a^-} f(x)$ and $\lim\limits_{x \to a^+} f(x)$ both exist but are not equal. f, is said to have a discontinuity of the first kind from the left at x = a, if $\lim\limits_{x \to a^-} f(x)$ exists but not equal to f (a). Discontinuity of the first kind from the right is similarly defined.

♦ **Discontinuity of the second kind :** A function f is said to have a discontinuity of the second kind at x = a, if neither $\lim\limits_{x \to a^-} f(x)$ nor $\lim\limits_{x \to a^+} f(x)$ exists. f is said to have a discontinuity of the second kind from the left at x = a, if $\lim\limits_{x \to a^-} f(x)$ does not exist.

Similarly, if $\lim\limits_{x \to a^+} f(x)$ does not exist, then f is said to have discontinuity of the second kind from the right at x = a.

♦ **Some standard results on differentiability**

❖ Every polynomial function is differentiable at each x ∈ R.

❖ The exponential function a^x, a > 0 is differentiable at each x ∈ R.

❖ Every constant function is differentiable at each x ∈ R.

❖ The logarithmic function is differentiable at each point in its domain.

❖ Trigonometric and inverse-trigonometric functions are differentiable in their domains.

❖ The sum, difference, product and quotient of two differentiable functions is differentiable.

❖ The composition of differentiable functions is a differentiable function.

❖ If a function is not differentiable but is continuous at a point, it geometrically implies there is a sharp corner or a kink at that point.

❖ If f (x) and g(x) both are not differentiable at a point, then the sum function f (x) + g(x) and the product function f (x). g(x) can still be differentiable at that point.

- $\dfrac{d}{dx}(e^{ax}\sin bx) = e^{ax}(a\sin bx + b\cos bx)$

- $\dfrac{d}{dx}(e^{ax}\cos bx) = e^{ax}(a\cos b\,x - b\sin b\,x)$

- If $y = \sqrt{f(x) + \sqrt{f(x) + \sqrt{f(x)} + \ldots\ldots\infty}}$

  then $y = \sqrt{f(x)+y} \Rightarrow y^2 = f(x) + y$

  $2y\,\dfrac{dy}{dx} = f'(x) + \dfrac{dy}{dx}, \quad \therefore \dfrac{dy}{dx} = \dfrac{f'(x)}{2y-1}$

- If $y = f(x)^{f(x)^{f(x)^{\ldots\infty}}}$

  then $\dfrac{dy}{dx} = \dfrac{y^2 f'(x)}{f(x)[1 - y\log f(x)]}$

- If $y = f(x) + \cfrac{1}{f(x) + \cfrac{1}{f(x) + \cfrac{1}{f(x) + \ldots\ldots}}}$

  then $\dfrac{dy}{dx} = \dfrac{y f'(x)}{2y - f(x)}$

- $\dfrac{d^n}{dx^n}\sin(ax + b) = a^n \sin\left(\dfrac{n\pi}{2} + ax + b\right)$

- $\dfrac{d^n}{dx^n}(ax + b)^m = \dfrac{m!}{(m-n)!}\,a^n (ax+b)^{m-n}$, where $m < n$

- $\dfrac{d^n}{dx^n}(\log(ax+b)) = \dfrac{(-1)^{n-1}(n-1)!a^n}{(ax+b)^n}$

- $\dfrac{d^n}{dx^n}(e^{ax}) = a^n e^{ax}$

- $\dfrac{d^n(a^x)}{dx^n} = a^x (\log a)^n$

- $\dfrac{d^n}{dx^n}(e^{ax}\sin(bx+c)) = r^n e^{ax}\sin(bx+c+n\phi)$

- **Leibnitz's theorem:** G.W. Leibnitz, a German mathematician gave a method for evaluating the nth differential coefficient of the product of two functions. This method is known as Leibnitz's Theorem.

  Statement of the theorem: If u and v are two functions of x such that their nth derivative exist, then

  $$D^n(uv) = {}^nC_0\,(D^n u)v + {}^nC_1\,(D^{n-1}u)\,Dv + {}^nC_2(D^{n-2}u)\,D^2v$$
  $$+ \,.... + {}^nC_r\,(D^{n-r}u)\,D^r v + \,....... + {}^nC_n\,u\,(D^n v)$$

- If f and g are two continuous functions on their common domain D, then
  - ❖ α f is continuous on D, where α is any real number.

  - ❖ $\dfrac{1}{f}$ is continuous on $D_f - \{\, x : f(x) = 0 \}$,

    where D_f is the domain off.
- The composition of two continuous functions is a continuous function.
- If f is continuous on its domain D_f, then $|\,f\,|$ is also continuous on D_f.
- The product of one continuous and one discontinuous function may or may not be continuous.

  Examples :
  - ❖ $f(x) = x$ is continuous and g (x) = cos 1/x is discontinuous, whereas their product x cos 1/x is continuous
  - ❖ $f(x) = C$ is continuous and g(x) = sin 1/x is discontinuous, whereas their product C sin 1/x is discontinuous

- **Relation between continuity and differentiability:**
  - ❖ If a function f (x) is differentiable at a point (x = a) then it is continuous at (x = a).
  - ❖ If f (x) is continuous at a point x = a, there is no guarantee that f (x) is differentiable there.
  - ❖ If f (x) is not differentiable at x = a then it may or may not be continuous at x = a.
  - ❖ If f (x) is not continuous at x = a, then it is not differentiable at x = a.
  - ❖ If left hand derivative and right hand derivative of f (x) at (x = a) are finite (they may or may not be equal) then f (x) is continuous at x = a.

♦ The chain rule can also be restated as follows

If $z = f(y)$ and $y = g(x)$, then $\dfrac{dz}{dx} = \dfrac{dz}{dy} \cdot \dfrac{dy}{dx}$

Derivative of z w.r.t. x = (Derivative of z w.r.t. y)

$\times$ (Derivative of y w.r.t. x)

This chain rule can be extended further

Derivative of z w.r.t. x = (Derivative of z w.r.t. u)

$\times$ (Derivative of u w.r.t v) $\times$ (Derivative of v w.r.t x)

♦ If $y = f(x)$, then the value of the nth derivative at $x = a$ is usually denoted by

$\left(\dfrac{d^n y}{dx^n}\right)_{x=a}$ or $(y^n)_{x=a}$ or $(y_n)_{x=a}$ or $f^n(a)$

♦ On Rolle's theorem generally two types of problems are formulated.

❖ To check the applicability of Rolle's theorem to a given function on a given interval.

❖ To verify Rolle's theorem for a given function on a given interval.

22

Application of Derivatives

Rate of Change of Quantities

- whenever one quantity y varies with another quantity x, satisfying some rule $y = f(x)$, then $\dfrac{dy}{dx}$ (or $f'(x)$) represents the rate of change of y with respect to x.

- $\dfrac{dy}{dx}\Big]_{x=x_0}$ (or $f'(x_0)$) represents the rate of change of y with respect to x at $x = x_0$.

- If two variables x and y are varying with respect to another variable t, i.e., if $x = f(t)$ and $y = g(t)$, then by Chain Rule.

$$\frac{dy}{dx} = \frac{dy}{dt} \Big/ \frac{dy}{dx}, \text{ if } \frac{dx}{dt} \neq 0$$

- $\dfrac{dy}{dx}$ is positive if y increases as x increases and is negative if y decreases as x increases.

Increasing and Decreasing Functions

- Let I be an interval contained in the domain of a real valued function f. Then f is said to be
  - increasing on I if $x_1 < x_2$ in I $\Rightarrow f(x_1) < f(x_2)$ for all $x_1, x_2 \in I$.
  - decreasing on I, if x_1, x_2 in I $\Rightarrow f(x_1) < f(x_2)$ for all $x_1, x_2 \in I$.
  - constant on I, if $f(x) = c$ for all $x \in I$, where c is a constant.
  - decreasing on I if $x_1 < x_2$ in I $\Rightarrow f(x_1) \geq f(x_2)$ for all $x_1, x_2 \in I$.
  - strictly decreasing on I if $x_1 < x_2$ in I $\Rightarrow f(x_1) > f(x_2)$ for all $x_1, x_2 \in I$.

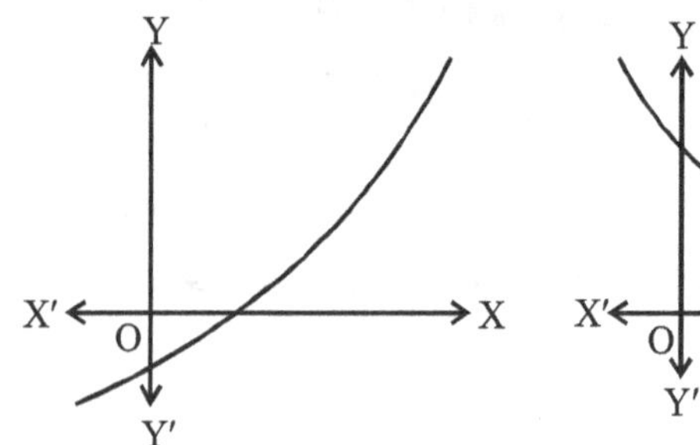

Strictly Increasing function

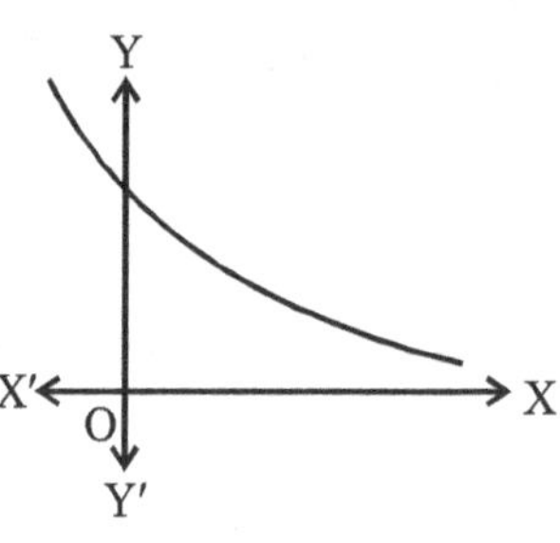

Strictly Decreasing function

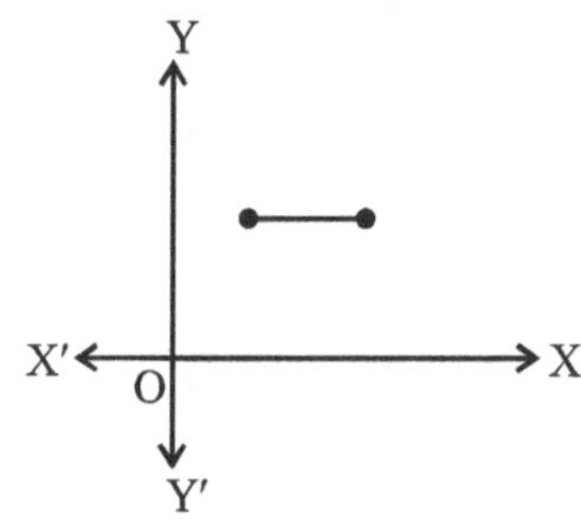

Neither Increasing nor
Decreasing function

A function is increasing or decreasing at a point:
♦ Let x_0 be a point in the domain of definition of a real valued function f.
First derivative test for increasing and decreasing functions:
♦ Let f be continuous on $[a, b]$ and differentiable on the open interval (a,b). Then
  ❖ f is increasing in $[a,b]$ if $f'(x) > 0$ for each $x \in (a, b)$
  ❖ f is decreasing in $[a,b]$ if $f'(x) < 0$ for each $x \in (a, b)$
  ❖ f is a constant function in $[a,b]$ if $f'(x) = 0$ for each $x \in (a, b)$

Remarks:
♦ If $f'(x) > 0$ for x in an interval excluding the end points and f is continuous in the interval, then f is increasing.
♦ If $f'(x) < 0$ for x in an interval excluding the end points and f is continuous in the interval, then f is decreasing.

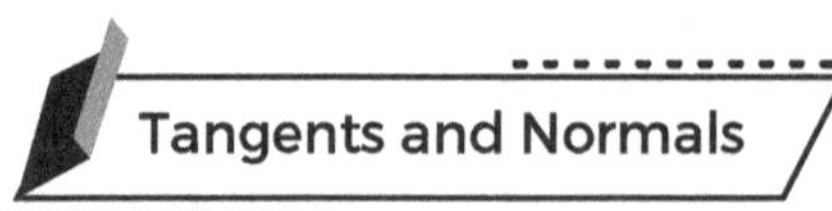

♦ Use differentiation to find the equation of the tangent line and the normal line to a curve at a given point.

♦ The equation of a straight line passing through a given point (x_0, y_0) having finite slope m is given by
$$y - y_0 = m(x - x_0)$$

♦ The slope of the tangent to the curve $y = f(x)$ at the point (x_0, y_0) is given by
$$\frac{dy}{dx}\bigg]_{(x_0 = y_0)} \quad (= f'(x_0)).$$

♦ Hence, the equation of the tangent at (x_0, y_0) to the curve $y = f(x)$ is given by
$$y - y_0 = f'(x_0)(x - x_0)$$

♦ The slope of the normal to the curve $y = f(x)$ at (x_0, y_0) is $\dfrac{-1}{f'(x_0)}$, if $f'(x_0) \neq 0$.

♦ The equation of the normal to the curve $y = f(x)$ at (x_0, y_0) is given by
$$y - y_0 = \frac{-1}{f'(x_0)}(x - x_0)$$
i.e. $(y - y_0)f'(x_0) + (x - x_0) = 0$

♦ If a tangent line to the curve $y = f(x)$ makes an angle θ with x-axis in the positive direction, then $\dfrac{dy}{dx} =$ slope of the tangent $= \tan\theta$.

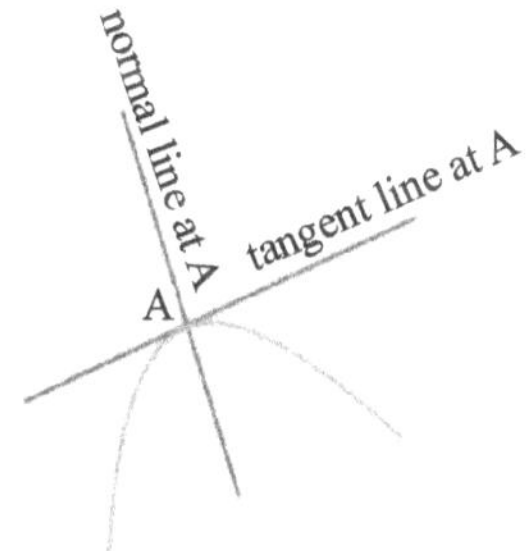

Particular cases:
♦ If slope of the tangent line is zero, the equation of the tangent at the point (x_0, y_0) is given by $y = y_0$.

♦ If $\theta \to \dfrac{\pi}{2}$, then $\tan\theta \to \infty$, which means the tangent line is perpendicular to the x-axis, the equation of the tangent at (x_0, y_0) is given by $x = x_0$.

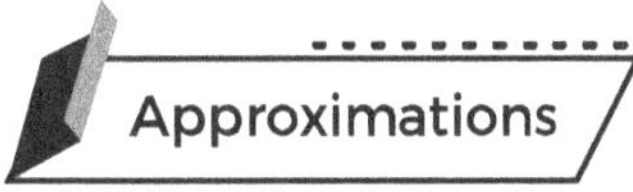

Approximations

♦ let $y = f(x)$. Let Δx denote a small increment in x. Recall that the increment in y corresponding to the increment in x, denoted by Δy, is given by $\Delta y = f(x + \Delta x) - f(x)$.

❖ The differential of x, denoted by dx, is defined by $dx = \Delta x$.

❖ The differential of y, denoted by dy, is defined by $dy = f'(x)\, dx$

or $dy = \left(\dfrac{dy}{dx}\right)\Delta x$.

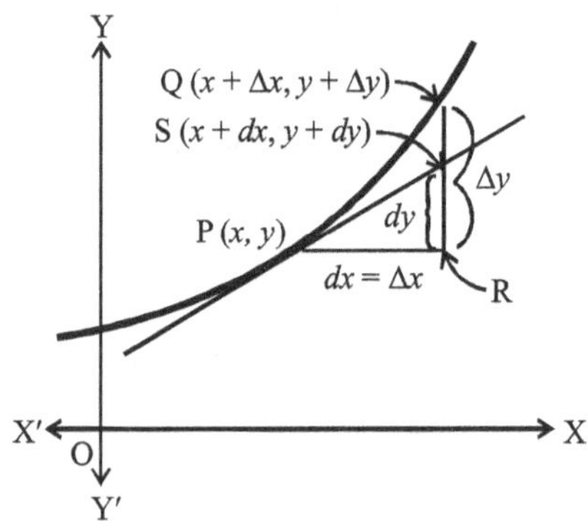

Maxima and Minima

♦ Let f be a function defined on an interval I.

❖ f is said to have a *maximum value* in I, if there exists a point c in I such that $f(c) > f(x)$, for all $x \in$ I.

❖ The number $f(c)$ is called the maximum value of f in I and the point c is called a *point of maximum value* of f in I.

❖ f is said to have a minimum value in I, if there exists a point c in I such that $f(c) < f(x)$, for all $x \in$ I.

❖ The number $f(c)$, in this case, is called the minimum value of f in I and the point c, in this case, is called a *point of minimum value* of f in I.

❖ f is said to have an extreme value in I if there exists a point c in I such that $f(c)$ is either a maximum value or a minimum value of f in I.

❖ The number $f(c)$, in this case, is called an extreme value of f in I and the point c is called an extreme point.

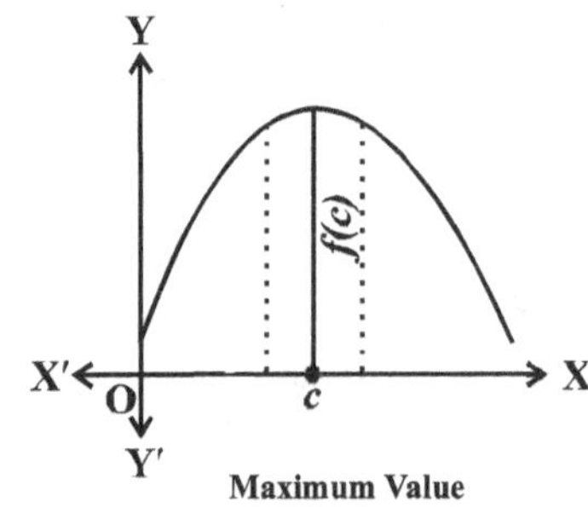

Maximum Value

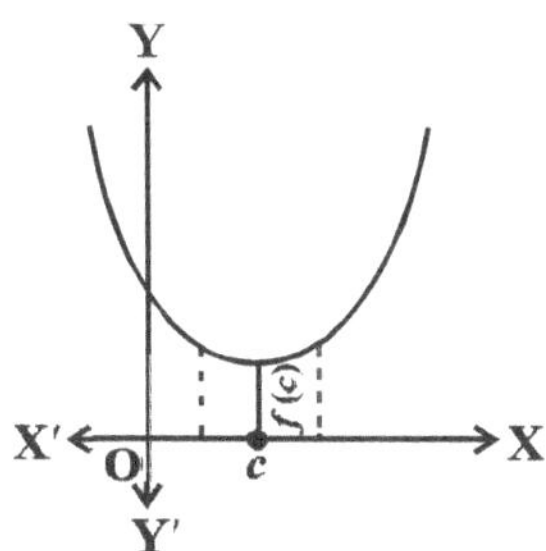

Minimum Value

♦ Every monotonic function assumes its maximum/minimum value at the end points of the domain of definition of the function.

♦ Every continuous function on a closed interval has a maximum and a minimum value.

♦ By a monotonic function f in an interval I, we mean that f is either increasing in I or decreasing in I.

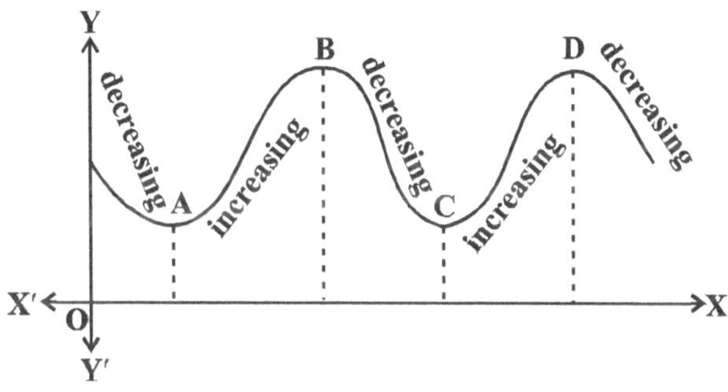

♦ The *local maximum value* and *local minimum value* of the function are referred to as *local maxima* and *local minima*, respectively, of the function.

♦ Let f be a real valued function and let c be an interior point in the domain of f. Then
   ❖ c is called a point of *local maxima* if there is an $h > 0$ such that $f(c) \geq f(x)$, for all x in $(c - h, c + h)$, $x \neq c$
   ❖ The value $f(c)$ is called the *local maximum value* of f.
   ❖ c is called a point of *local minima* if there is an $h > 0$ such that $f(c) \leq f(x)$, for all x in $(c - h, c + h)$
   ❖ The value $f(c)$ is called the *local minimum value* of f.

♦ Let f be a function defined on an open interval I. Suppose $c \in$ I be any point. If f has a local maxima or a local minima at $x = c$, then either $f'(c) = 0$ or f is not differentiable at c.

♦ A working rule for finding points of local maxima or points of local minima using only the first order derivatives.

First Derivative Test:

♦ Let f be a function defined on an open interval I.

    ❖ If $f'(x)$ changes sign from positive to negative as x increases through c, or $f'(x) > 0$ at every point sufficiently close to and to the left of c, and $f'(x) < 0$ at every point sufficiently close to and to the right of c, then c is a point of *local maxima*.

    ❖ If $f'(x)$ changes sign from negative to positive as x increases through c, i.e., if $f'(x) < 0$ at every point sufficiently close to and to the left of c, and $f'(x) > 0$ at every point sufficiently close to and to the right of c, then c is a point of *local minima*.

    ❖ If $f'(x)$ does not change sign as x increases through c, then c is neither a point of local maxima nor a point of local minima. Infact, such a point is called *point of inflection*.

Second Derivative Test:

♦ Let f be a function defined on an interval I and $c \in$ I. Let f be twice differentiable at c. Then

    ❖ $x = c$ is a point of local maxima if $f'(c) = 0$ and $f''(c) < 0$
    The value $f(c)$ is local maximum value of f.

    ❖ $x = c$ is a point of local minima if $f'(c) = 0$ and $f''(c) > 0$
    In this case, $f(c)$ is local minimum value of f.

    ❖ The test fails if $f'(c) = 0$ and $f''(c) = 0$.

Maximum and Minimum Values of a Function in a Closed Interval:

♦ Let f be a continuous function on an interval I $= [a, b]$. Then f has the absolute maximum value and f attains it at least once in I.

♦ Also, f has the absolute minimum value and attains it at least once in I.

♦ Let f be a differentiable function on a closed interval I and let c be any interior point of I. Then

    ❖ $f'(c) = 0$ if f attains its absolute maximum value at c.

    ❖ $f'(c) = 0$ if f attains its absolute minimum value at c.

Working Rule:

♦ **Step 1:** Find all critical points of f in the interval, i.e., find points x where either $f'(x) = 0$ or f is not differentiable.

♦ **Step 2:** Take the end points of the interval.

♦ **Step 3:** At all these points (listed in Step 1 and 2), calculate the values of f.

♦ **Step 4:** Identify the maximum and minimum values of f out of the values calculated in Step 3. This maximum value will be the absolute maximum (greatest) value of f and the minimum value will be the absolute minimum (least) value of f.

Past Years ONE-LINERS
JEE Main/Board

- The appropriate intervals for which the given function is increasing or decreasing. Comparing each factor equal to 0.
  E.g., $\sin x.\cos x\,(2\sin x + 1) = 0$ then, take $\sin x = 0$, $\cos x = 0$, $2\sin x + 1 = 0$ then find x.

- Taking Y' and putting $\dfrac{dy}{dx} = 0$ then optain critical points and using sign scheme for maxima and minima.

- Let slopes of two curves are m_1 and m_2 respectively they intersect orthogonaly if $\boxed{m_1.m_2 = -1}$.

- Let $P(x_1, y_1)$ as point of intersection on both the curves, then find slope of both the curves.

  where $m_1 = \left(\dfrac{df_1}{dx}\right)_{(x_1,y_1)}$ and $m_2 = \left(\dfrac{df_2}{dx}\right)_{(x_1,y_1)}$

  Hence, $\tan\theta = \pm\dfrac{m_1 - m_2}{1 + m_1.m_2}$.

- Using concept

  $$\tan^{-1}\left(\sqrt{\dfrac{1+\sin x}{1-\sin x}}\right) = \tan^{-1}\left(\tan\left(\dfrac{\pi}{4}+\dfrac{x}{2}\right)\right) \quad\Rightarrow\quad y = \dfrac{\pi}{4}+\dfrac{x}{2} \text{ or } \dfrac{dy}{dx} = \dfrac{1}{2}$$

  $$\text{Slope of Normal} = \dfrac{-1}{\left(\dfrac{dy}{dx}\right)} = -2$$

Tips/Tricks/Techniques ONE-LINERS
(Exam Special)

- **The length of perpendicular from origin (0,0) to the tangent drawn at the point (x_1, y_1) of the curve $y = f(x)$ is**

  $$\left|\dfrac{y_1 - x_1\left(\dfrac{dy}{dx}\right)_P}{\sqrt{1+\left(\dfrac{dy}{dx}\right)^2_P}}\right|$$

The length of perpendicular from origin to normal is

$$\left| \frac{x_1 + y_1 \left(\dfrac{dy}{dx}\right)_p}{\sqrt{1 + \left(\dfrac{dy}{dx}\right)_p^2}} \right|$$

- **Angle of interesection of two curves:**

 Let $y = f_1(x)$ and $y = f_2(x)$ be the two curves, meeting at some point $P(x_1, y_1)$
 $\therefore$ The angle of intersection of two curves θ is given by

$$\tan\theta = \pm\frac{m_1 - m_2}{1 + m_1 m_2},$$

 where $m_1 = \left(\dfrac{df_1}{dx}\right)_{(x_1, y_1)}$ and $m_2 = \left(\dfrac{df_2}{dx}\right)_{(x_1, y_1)}$

  ❖ If $\theta = \pm\dfrac{\pi}{2}$, $m_1 m_2 + 1 = 0 \Rightarrow \left(\dfrac{df_1}{dx}\right)_{(x_1, y_1)} \left(\dfrac{df_2}{dx}\right)_{(x_1, y_1)} = -1,$

 Such curves are called **ORTHOGONAL CURVES.**

  ❖ If $\theta = 0$, $m_1 = m_2 \Rightarrow \left(\dfrac{df_1}{dx}\right)_{(x_1, y_1)} = \left(\dfrac{df_2}{dx}\right)_{(x_1, y_1)}$.

 Then the curves are tangential at (x_1, y_1).

- **Consider a curve $y = f(x)$, then for the curve:**

  ❖ Length of tangent $= y\dfrac{\sqrt{1 + (dy/dx)^2}}{(dy/dx)}$

  ❖ Length of normal $= y\sqrt{1 + \left(\dfrac{dy}{dx}\right)^2}$

  ❖ Length of sub tangent $= y / \left(\dfrac{dy}{dx}\right)$

  ❖ Length of sub normal $= y\left(\dfrac{dy}{dx}\right)$

- **Properties of monotonic functions:**

  ❖ If $f(x)$ is strictly increasing function on an interval [a, b], then f^{-1} exists and it is also a strictly increasing function.

  ❖ If $f(x)$ is strictly increasing function on an interval [a, b] such that it is continuous, then f^{-1} is continuous on [f(a), f(b)].

- **Some standard geometrical results related to maxima & minima:**

  The following results can easily be established.
  - ❖ Area of rectangle with given perimeter is greatest when it is a square.
  - ❖ Perimeter of a rectangle with given area is least when it is a square.
  - ❖ Area of a rectangle inscribed in a given circle is greatest, if it is a square.
  - ❖ Area of a triangle inscribed in a given circle is greatest, of it is equilateral.
  - ❖ Semi vertical angle of a cone with given slant height and maximum volume is $\tan^{-1}\sqrt{2}$.
  - ❖ Height of a cylinder of maximum volume inscribed in a sphere of radius a is $2a/\sqrt{3}$.

- If normal makes an angle of θ with positive direction of x-axis, then

$$-\frac{dx}{dy} = \tan\theta \quad \text{or} \quad \frac{dy}{dx} = -\cot\theta$$

- If $\left(\frac{dy}{dx}\right)_P = \infty$, then the tangent at $P(x_1, y_1)$ to the given curve is parallel to y-axis and its equation is $x = x_1$.

- If $\left(\frac{dy}{dx}\right)_P = 0$, then the tangent at $P(x_1, y_1)$ to the given curve is parallel to x-axis and its equation is $y = y_1$

- If $\left(\frac{dy}{dx}\right)_P = 0$, then the normal at $P(x_1, y_1)$ is parallel to y-axis and its equation is $x = x_1$.

- If $\left(\frac{dy}{dx}\right)_P = \infty$, then the normal at $P(x_1, y_1)$ is parallel to x-axis and its equation is $y = y_1$.

- If $\frac{dy}{dx} > 0$, the tangent makes an acute angle with the x-axis.

- If $\frac{dy}{dx} < 0$, the tangent makes an obtuse angle with the x-axis

- If $\frac{dy}{dx} = 0$, the tangent to the curve is parallel to x-axis.

23

Integrals

Integration as an Inverse Process of Differentiation

- Integration is the inverse process of differentiation. We are given the derivative of a function and asked to find its primitive, i.e., the original function. Such a process is called **integration or anti differentiation.**
- Anti derivatives (or integrals) of the above cited functions are not unique. Actually, there exist infinitely many anti derivatives of each of these functions which can be obtained by choosing C arbitrarily from the set of real numbers. C is the **parameter** by varying which one gets different anti derivatives (or integrals) of the given function.
- Any arbitrary real number C, (also called **constant of integration**)
- $\int f(x)dx$ which will represent the entire class of anti derivatives read as the indefinite integral of **f** with respect to **x**. Symbolically, we write $\int f(x)dx = F(x) + C$.
- Some symbols/terms/phrases are given below.

Symbols/Terms/Phrases	Meaning
$\int f(x)dx$	Integral of f with respect to x
$f(x)$ in $\int f(x)\,dx$	Integrand
x in $\int f(x)\,dx$	Variable of integration
Integrate	Find the integral
An integral of f	A function F such that $F'(x) = f(x)$
Integration	The process of finding the integral
Constant of Integration	Any real number C, considered as constant function

- The formulae for the derivatives of many important functions are:

Derivatives	**Integrals (Anti derivatives)**

(i) $\dfrac{d}{dx}\left(\dfrac{x^{n+1}}{n+1}\right) = x^{n}$; $\displaystyle\int x^{n}\,dx = \dfrac{x^{n-1}}{n+1} + C,\ n \neq -1$

Particularly, we note that

$\dfrac{d}{dx}(x) = 1$; $\displaystyle\int dx = x + C$

(ii) $\dfrac{d}{dx}(\sin x) = \cos x$; $\displaystyle\int \cos x\,dx = \sin x + C$

(iii) $\dfrac{d}{dx}(-\cos x) = \sin x$; $\displaystyle\int \sin x\,dx = -\cos x + C$

(iv) $\dfrac{d}{dx}(\tan x) = \sec^{2}x$; $\displaystyle\int \sec^{2} x\,dx = \tan x + C$

(v) $\dfrac{d}{dx}(-\cot x) = \operatorname{cosec}^{2}x$; $\displaystyle\int \operatorname{cosec}^{2} x\,dx = -\cot x + C$

(vi) $\dfrac{d}{dx}(\sec x) = \sec x \tan x$; $\displaystyle\int \sec x \tan x\,dx = \sec x + C$

(vii) $\dfrac{d}{dx}(-\operatorname{cosec} x)$ $\displaystyle\int \operatorname{cosec} x \cot x\,dx$

$= \operatorname{cosec} x \cot x$; $= -\operatorname{cosec} x + C$

(viii) $\dfrac{d}{dx}(\sin^{-1} x) = \dfrac{1}{\sqrt{1-x^{2}}}$; $\displaystyle\int \dfrac{dx}{\sqrt{1-x^{2}}} = \sin^{-1} x + C$

(ix) $\dfrac{d}{dx}(-\cos^{-1} x) = \dfrac{1}{\sqrt{1-x^{2}}}$; $\displaystyle\int \dfrac{dx}{\sqrt{1-x^{2}}} = -\cos^{-1} x + C$

(x) $\dfrac{d}{dx}(\tan^{-1} x) = \dfrac{1}{1+x^{2}}$; $\displaystyle\int \dfrac{dx}{1-x^{2}} = \tan^{-1} x + C$

(xi) $\dfrac{d}{dx}(-\cot^{-1} x) = \dfrac{1}{1+x^{2}}$; $\displaystyle\int \dfrac{dx}{1+x^{2}} = -\cot^{-1} x + C$

(xii) $\dfrac{d}{dx}(\sec^{-1}x) = \dfrac{1}{x\sqrt{x^2-1}}$; $\displaystyle\int \dfrac{dx}{x\sqrt{x^2-1}} = \sec^{-1}x + C$

(xiii) $\dfrac{d}{dx}(-\operatorname{cosec}^{-1}x)$ $\qquad\displaystyle\int \dfrac{dx}{x\sqrt{x^2-1}} = -\operatorname{cosec}^{-1}x + C$

$\qquad = \dfrac{1}{x\sqrt{x^2-1}}$;

(xiv) $\dfrac{d}{dx}(e^x) = e^x$; $\qquad\displaystyle\int e^x\,dx = e^x + C$

(xv) $\dfrac{d}{dx}(\log 1\,x\,1) = \dfrac{1}{x}$; $\qquad\displaystyle\int \dfrac{1}{x}\,dx = \log|x| + C$

(xvi) $\dfrac{d}{dx}\left(\dfrac{a^x}{\log a}\right) = a^x$; $\qquad\displaystyle\int a^x\,dx = \dfrac{a^x}{\log a} + C$

♦ In practice, we normally do not mention the interval over which the various functions are defined. However, in any specific problem one has to keep it in mind.

Geometrical interpretation of indefinite integral:

♦ $\int 2x\,dx = x^2 + C = F_C(x)$ (say), implies that

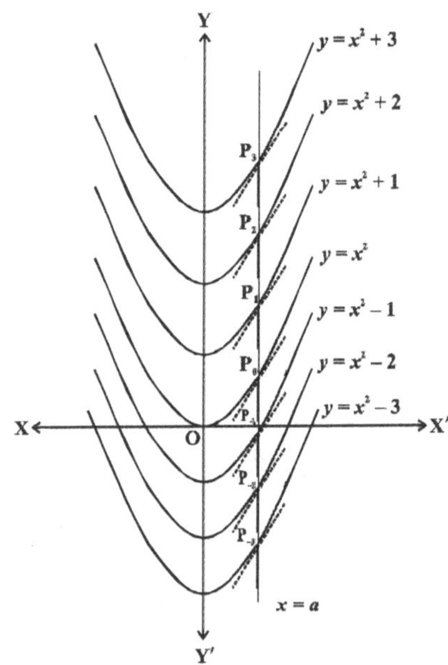

- The tangents to all the curves $y = F_C(x)$, $C \in \mathbf{R}$, at the points of intersection of the curves by the line $x = a$, $(a \in \mathbf{R})$, are parallel.
- The different values of C will correspond to different members of this family and these members can be obtained by shifting any one of the curves parallel to itself.

Some properties of indefinite integral:

- The process of differentiation and integration are inverses of each other in the sense of the following results:

$$\frac{d}{dx}\int f(x)\,dx = f(x) \text{ and } \int f'(x)\,dx = f(x) + C, \text{ where C is any arbitrary constant.}$$

- Two indefinite integrals with the same derivative lead to the same family of curves and so they are equivalent.
  $\int f(x)dx$ and $\int g(x)dx$ are equivalent.
  $\int f(x)dx = \int g(x)dx$

- $\int [f(x) + g(x)]\,dx = \int f(x)\,dx + \int g(x)\,dx$

- For any real number $k, \int k\, f(x)\,dx = k \int f(x)\,dx$

- A finite number of functions $f_1, f_2, ..., f_n$ and the real numbers, $k_1, k_2, ..., k_n$ giving

$$\int [k_1 f_1(x) + k_2 f_2(x) + ... + k_n f_n(x)]\,dx$$

$$= k_1 \int f_1(x)\,dx + k_2 \int f_2(x)\,dx + ... + k_n \int f_n(x)\,dx.$$

- To find an anti derivative of a given function, we search intuitively for a function whose derivative is the given function. The search for the requisite function for finding an anti derivative is known as integration by the method of inspection.
- We shall write only one constant of integration in the final answer.
- Determines a specific value of C giving unique anti derivative of the given function.
- Sometimes, F is not expressible in terms of elementary functions viz., polynomial, logarithmic, exponential, trigonometric functions and their inverses etc. We are therefore blocked for finding $\int f(x)dx$. For example, it is not possible to find $\int e^{-x^2}$ by inspection since we can not find a function whose derivative is e^{-x^2}.
- When the variable of integration is denoted by a variable other than x, the integral formulae are modified accordingly.

Comparison between differentiation and integration:

- Both are operations on functions.
- Both satisfy the property of linearity.
- We have already seen that all functions are not differentiable. Similarly, all functions are not integrable.
- The derivative of a function, when it exists, is a unique function. The integral of a function is not so. However, they are unique upto an additive constant.

- When a polynomial function P is differentiated, the result is a polynomial whose degree is 1 less than the degree of P. When a polynomial function P is integrated, the result is a polynomial whose degree is 1 more than that of P.

- We can speak of the derivative at a point. We never speak of the integral at a point, we speak of the integral of a function over an interval on which the integral is defined.

- The derivative of a function has a geometrical meaning, namely, the slope of the tangent to the corresponding curve at a point. Similarly, the indefinite integral of a function represents geometrically, a family of curves placed parallel to each other having parallel tangents at the points of intersection of the curves of the family with the lines orthogonal (perpendicular) to the axis representing the variable of integration.

- The derivative is used for finding some physical quantities like the velocity of a moving particle, when the distance traversed at any time t is known. Similarly, the integral is used in calculating the distance traversed when the velocity at time t is known.

Methods of Integration

Integration by substitution:

- Integral $\int f(x)dx$ can be transformed into another form by changing the independent variable x to t by substituting $x = g\,(t)$ then $dx \equiv g'(t)dt$

$$I = \int f(x)dx = \int f(g(t))g'(t)dt$$

- We make a substitution for a function whose derivative also occurs in the integrand as illustrated in the following examples.

- Some important integrals involving trigonometric functions.

    (i) $\int \tan x\, dx = \log |\sec x| + C$

    (ii) $\int \cot x\, dx = \log |\sin x| + C$

    (iii) $\int \sec x\, dx = \log |\sec x + \tan x| + C$

    (iv) $\int \operatorname{cosec} x\, dx = \log |\operatorname{cosec} x - \cot x| + C$

Integration using trigonometric identities:

- When the integrand involves some trigonometric functions, we use some known identities to find the integral.

    (i) $\sin^2 x = \dfrac{1 - \cos 2x}{2}$

    (ii) $\cos^2 x = \dfrac{1 + \cos 2x}{2}$

    (iii) $\sin^3 x = \dfrac{3\sin x + \sin 3x}{4}$

(iv) $\cos^3 x = \dfrac{3\cos x + \cos 3x}{4}$

(v) $\sin x \cdot \sin y = \dfrac{1}{2}[\cos(x-y) + \cos(x+y)]$

(vi) $\cos x \cdot \cos y = \dfrac{1}{2}[\cos(x+y) + \cos(x-y)]$

(vii) $\sin x \cdot \cos y = \dfrac{1}{2}[\sin(x+y) + \sin(x-y)]$

Integrals of Some Particular Functions

(i) $\displaystyle\int \dfrac{dx}{x^2 - a^2} = \dfrac{1}{2a}\log\left|\dfrac{x-a}{x+a}\right| + C$

(ii) $\displaystyle\int \dfrac{dx}{a^2 - x^2} = \dfrac{1}{2a}\log\left|\dfrac{a+x}{a-x}\right| + C$

(iii) $\displaystyle\int \dfrac{dx}{x^2 + a^2} = \dfrac{1}{a}\tan^{-1}\dfrac{x}{a} + C$

(iv) $\displaystyle\int \dfrac{dx}{\sqrt{x^2 - a^2}} = \log\left|x + \sqrt{x^2 - a^2}\right| + C$

(v) $\displaystyle\int \dfrac{dx}{\sqrt{a^2 - x^2}} = \sin^{-1}\dfrac{x}{a} + C$

(vi) $\displaystyle\int \dfrac{dx}{\sqrt{x^2 + a^2}} = \log\left|x + \sqrt{x^2 - a^2}\right| + C$

(vii) To find the integral $\displaystyle\int \dfrac{dx}{ax^2 + bx + c}$, we write

$$ax^2 + bx + c = a\left[x^2 + \dfrac{b}{a}x + \dfrac{c}{a}\right] = a\left[\left(x + \dfrac{b}{2a}\right)^2 + \left(\dfrac{c}{a} - \dfrac{b^2}{4a^2}\right)\right]$$

Put $x + \dfrac{b}{2a} = t$ so that $dx = dt$ and writing

$\dfrac{c}{a} - \dfrac{b^2}{4a^2} = \pm k^2$. The integral reduced to the form $\dfrac{1}{a}\displaystyle\int \dfrac{dt}{t^2 \pm k^2}$.

(viii) To find the integral of the type $\displaystyle\int \frac{dx}{\sqrt{ax^2+bx+c}}$, proceeding as in (7).

(ix) To find the integral of the type $\displaystyle\int \frac{px+q}{ax^2+bx+c}\,dx$, where p, q, a, b, c are constants, we are to find real numbers A, B such that

$$px+q = \text{A}\frac{d}{dx}(ax^2+bx+c)+\text{B} = \text{A}\,(2ax+b)+\text{B}$$

To determine A and B, we equate from both sides the coefficients of x and the constant terms. A and B are thus obtained and hence the integral is reduced to one of the known forms.

(x) For the evaluation of the integral of the type $\displaystyle\int \frac{(px+q)\,dx}{\sqrt{ax^2+bx+c}}$, we proceed as in (9).

Integration by Partial Fractions

♦ A rational function is defined as the ratio of two polynomials in the form $\dfrac{\text{P}(x)}{\text{Q}(x)}$, where P (x) and Q(x) are polynomials in x and Q$(x) \neq 0$.

♦ If the degree of P(x) is less than the degree of Q(x), then the rational function is called proper, otherwise, it is called improper.

♦ The improper rational functions can be reduced to the proper rational functions by long division process. Thus, if $\dfrac{\text{P}(x)}{\text{Q}(x)}$ is improper, then

$$\frac{\text{P}(x)}{\text{Q}(x)} = \text{T}(x) + \frac{\text{P}_1(x)}{\text{Q}(x)},$$ where T(x) is a polynomial in x and $\dfrac{\text{P}_1(x)}{\text{Q}(x)}$ is a proper rational function.

♦ A proper rational function which we shall consider here for integration purposes will be those whose denominators can be factorised into linear and quadratic factors.

♦ It is always possible to write the integrand as a sum of simpler rational functions by a method called partial fraction decomposition.

S. No.	Form of the rational function	Form of the partial fraction
1.	$\dfrac{px+q}{(x-a)(x=b)}, a \neq b$	$\dfrac{A}{x-a} + \dfrac{B}{x-b}$
2.	$\dfrac{px+q}{(x-a)^2}$	$\dfrac{A}{x-a} + \dfrac{B}{(x-a)^2}$
3.	$\dfrac{px^2+qx+r}{(x-a)(x-b)(x-c)}$	$\dfrac{A}{x-a} + \dfrac{B}{x-b} + \dfrac{C}{x-c}$
4.	$\dfrac{px^2+qx+r}{(x-a)^2(x-b)}$	$\dfrac{A}{x-a} + \dfrac{B}{(x-a)^2} + \dfrac{C}{x-b}$
5.	$\dfrac{px^2+qx+r}{(x-a)(x^2+bx+c)}$	$\dfrac{A}{x-a} + \dfrac{Bx+C}{x^2+bx+c}$

where $x^2 + bx + c$ cannot be factorised further.

Integration by Parts

- For given function $f(x)$ and $g(x)$, we have

$$\int f(x) \cdot g(x)dx = f(x) \int g(x)\,dx - \int (f'(x)\int g(x)dx)\,dx$$

If we take $f(x)$ as the first function and $g(x)$ as the second function.
- Then this preference in this order can be decided by the word ILATE, where
  I → stands for Inverse function.
  L → stands for Logarithmic function.
  A → stands for Algebraic function.
  T → stands for Trigonometric function.
  E → stands for Exponential function.
  The formula may be stated as follows:
- "The integral of the product of two functions = (first function) × (integral of the second function) – Integral of [(differential coefficient of the first function) × (integral of the second function)]"
- It is worth mentioning that integration by parts is not applicable to product of functions in all cases.
- Observe that while finding the integral of the second function, we did not add any constant of integration.
- Usually, if any function is a power of x or a polynomial in x, then we take it as the first function. However, in cases where other function is inverse trigonometric function or logarithmic function, then we take them as first

function.

Integral of the type $\int e^x[f(x)+f'(x)]dx$:

- $\int e^x[f(x)+f'(x)]\,dx = e^x f(x) + C$

Integrals of some more types:

- $I = \int \sqrt{x^2-a^2}\,dx = \dfrac{x}{2}\sqrt{x^2-a^2} - \dfrac{a^2}{2}\log\left|x+\sqrt{x^2-a^2}\right| + C$

- $\int \sqrt{x^2+a^2}\,dx = \dfrac{1}{2}x\sqrt{x^2+a^2} + \dfrac{a^2}{2}\log\left|x+\sqrt{x^2+a^2}\right| + C$

- $\int \sqrt{a^2-x^2}\,dx = \dfrac{1}{2}x\sqrt{a^2-x^2} + \dfrac{a^2}{2}\sin^{-1}\dfrac{x}{a} + C$

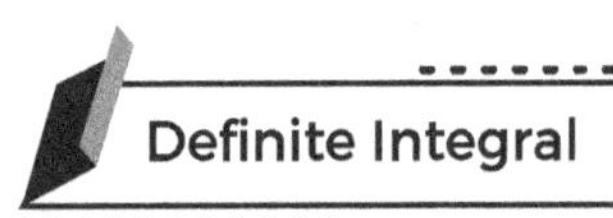
Definite Integral

- The definite integral has a unique value.

- A definite integral is denoted by $\int_a^b f(x)\,dx$, where a is called the lower limit of the integral and b is called the upper limit of the integral.

- The definite integral is introduced either as the limit of a sum or if it has an anti derivative F in the interval $[a, b]$, then its value is the difference between the values of F at the end points, i.e., $F(b) - F(a)$.

Definite integral as the limit of a sum:

- The definite integral $\int_a^b f(x)\,dx$ is the area bounded by the curve $y = f(x)$, the ordinates $x = a$, $x = b$ and the x-axis.

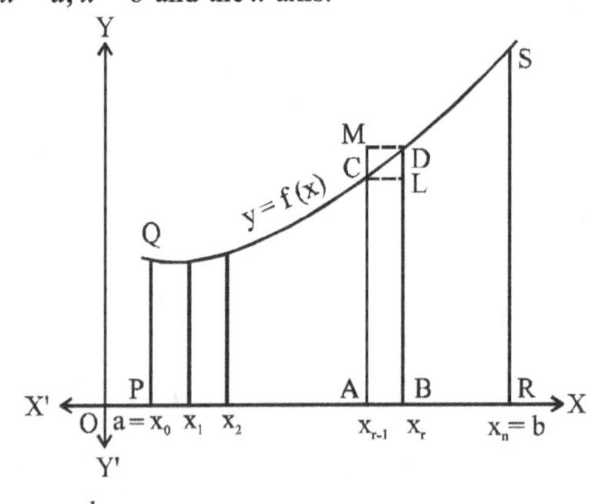

$$\int_a^b f(x)\,dx = \lim_{h\to 0} h\,[f(a)+f(a+h)+\ldots+f(a+(n-1)h]$$

$$\text{or } \int_a^b f(x)\,dx = (b-a)\lim_{x\to\infty}\frac{1}{n}[f(a)+f(a+h)+\ldots+f(a+(n-1)h]$$

Where $h = \dfrac{b-a}{n} \to 0$ as $n \to \infty$

♦ The value of the definite integral of a function over any particular interval depends on the function and the interval, but not on the variable of integration that we choose to represent the independent variable.

♦ The variable of integration is called a *dummy variable*.

Fundamental Theorem of Calculus

Area function:

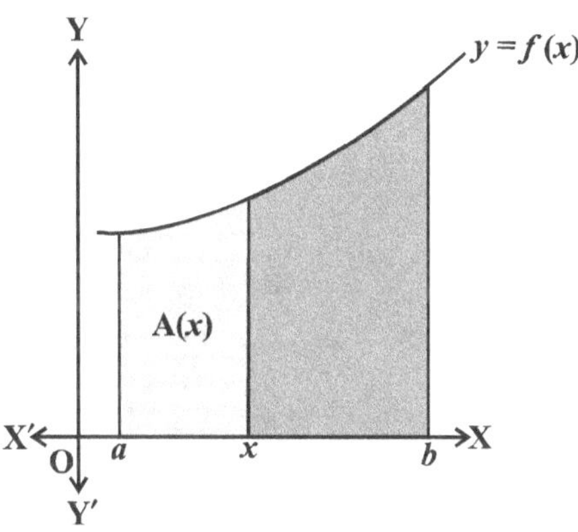

♦ The area of this shaded region is a function of x. We denote this function of x by A(x). We call the function A(x) as Area function and is given by

$$A(x) = \int_a^x f(x)\,dx$$

First fundamental theorem of integral calculus:

♦ **Theorem 1** Let f be a continuous function on the closed interval $[a, b]$ and let A (x) be the area function. Then $A'(x) = f(x)$, for all $x \in [a, b]$.

Second fundamental theorem of integral calculus:

♦ **Theorem 2** Let f be continuous function defined on the closed interval $[a, b]$ and F be an anti derivative of f. Then

$$\int_a^b f(x)\,dx = [F(x)]_a^b = F(b) - F(a).$$

♦ This theorem is very useful, because it gives us a method of calculating the definite integral more easily.

♦ The crucial operation in evaluating a definite integral is that of finding a function whose derivative is equal to the integrand. This strengthens the relationship between differentiation and integration.

- In $\int_a^b f(x)\, dx$, the function f needs to be well defined and continuous in $[a, b]$. Steps for calculating $\int_a^b f(x)\, dx$.
- Find the indefinite integral $\int f(x)dx$. Let this be $F(x)$. There is no need to keep integration constant C
- Evaluate $F(b) - F(a) = [F(x)]_a^b$, which is the value of $\int_a^b f(x)\, dx$.

Evaluation of Definite Integrals by Substitution

- To evaluate $\int_a^b f(x)\, dx$, by substitution, the steps could be as follows:
- Consider the integral without limits and substitute, $y = f(x)$ or $x = g(y)$ to reduce the given integral to a known form.
- Integrate the new integrand with respect to the new variable without mentioning the constant of integration.
- Resubstitute for the new variable and write the answer in terms of the original variable.
- Find the values of answers obtained in (3) at the given limits of integral and find the difference of the values at the upper and lower limits.
- In order to quicken this method, we can proceed as follows: After performing steps 1, and 2, there is no need of step 3. Here, the integral will be kept in the new variable itself, and the limits of the integral will accordingly be changed, so that we can perform the last step.

Some Properties of Definite Integrals

- Some important properties of definite integrals. These will be useful in evaluating the definite integrals more easily.

$$P_0: \int_a^b f(x)\, dx = \int_a^b f(t)\, dt$$

$$P_1: \int_a^b f(x)\, dx = -\int_b^a f(x)\, dx. \text{ In particular, } \int_a^a f(x)\, dx = 0$$

$$P_2: \int_a^b f(x)\, dx = \int_a^c f(x)\, dx + \int_c^b f(x)\, dx$$

$$P_3: \int_a^b f(x)\, dx = \int_a^b f(a+b-x)\, dx$$

$$\mathbf{P_4}: \int_0^a f(x)\,dx = \int_0^a f(a-x)\,dx$$

(Note that P_4 is a particular case of P_3)

$$\mathbf{P_5}: \int_0^{2a} f(x)\,dx = \int_0^a f(x)\,dx + \int_0^a f(2a-x)\,dx$$

$$\mathbf{P_6}: \int_0^{2a} f(x)\,dx = 2\int_0^a f(x)\,dx,\ \text{if}\ (2a-x)=f(x)\ \text{and}\ =0\ \text{if}\ f(2a-x)=-f(x)$$

$\mathbf{P_7}:$ (i) $\displaystyle\int_{-a}^a f(x)\,dx = 2\int_0^a f(x)\,dx$, if f is an even function, i.e., if $f(-x)=f(x)$.

(ii) $\displaystyle\int_{-a}^a f(x)\,dx = 0$, if f is an odd function, i.e., if $f(-x)=-f(x)$.

Past Years ONE-LINERS
JEE Main/Board

- Write the integrand as a sum of simpler rational functions by a method partical fraction decomposition.

$$\frac{px^2+qx+r}{(x-a)(x^2+bx+c)} = \frac{A}{x-a}+\frac{Bx+c}{x^2+bx+c}\ \text{where}\ x^2+bx+c\ \text{cannot be}$$

factorised further

- If $f(x) = [x]$ = greatest integer fuction such that $f(x) \le x$ then

$$I= \int_0^n [x]dx = \int_0^1 0\,dx + \int_1^2 1\,dx + \int_2^3 2\,dx + \ldots\ldots + \int_{[n]}^n [n]\,dx.$$

- For integral of function $\dfrac{1}{x^P\left(1+x^2\right)^{\frac{m}{n}}}$, where q is multiple of n. We convert it

in the form of $\dfrac{1}{x^P + \dfrac{2m}{n}\left(\dfrac{1}{x^2}+1\right)^{\frac{m}{n}}}$ and substitute $1+\dfrac{1}{x^q}=u$.

- Use the property $\displaystyle\int_0^a f(x)dx = \int_0^a f(a-x)dx$ and after simplification additing to previous integral.

- Use the property $\displaystyle\int_a^b f(x)dx = \int_a^b f(a+b-x)dx$ and after simplification adding to previous integral

- $\displaystyle In = \int \tan^n x\,dx = \frac{\tan^{n-2} x}{n-1} - In-2$ where $n \in N$.

- For integral of $I = \int \dfrac{P(x)}{[f(x)]^n}\,dx$. we convert it in the form $I = \int \dfrac{P\left(\dfrac{1}{x}\right)}{f\left(\dfrac{1}{x}\right)^n}\,dx$

  and $P\left(\dfrac{1}{x}\right) = A\int^1\left(\dfrac{1}{x}\right) + B$ then integrate by Substitution Method.

- Leibniz integral rule: For a continuous real value function g of one real variable and real valued differentiable functions f_1 and f_2 of one real variable.

$$\frac{d}{dx}\int_{f_1(x)}^{f_2(x)} g(t)\,dt = g(f_2(x))f_2^1(x) - g(f_1(x))f_1^1(x).$$

Tips/Tricks/Techniques ONE-LINERS
(Exam Special)

- **Some Important Substitutions are:**

Function	Substitutions
$\sqrt{a^2 - x^2}$	$x = a\sin\theta$ or $x = a\cos\theta$
$\sqrt{a^2 + x^2}$	$x = a\tan\theta$
$\sqrt{x^2 - a^2}$	$x = a\sec\theta$

- $\displaystyle\int e^{ax}\sin bx\,dx = \dfrac{e^{ax}}{a^2 + b^2}(a\sin bx - b\cos bx) + c$

$$= \dfrac{e^{ax}}{\sqrt{a^2 + b^2}}\sin(bx - \tan^{-1} b/a) + c$$

- $\displaystyle\int e^{ax}\cos bx\,dx = \dfrac{e^{ax}}{a^2 + b^2}(a\cos bx + b\sin bx) + c$

$$= \dfrac{e^{ax}}{\sqrt{a^2 + b^2}}\cos(bx - \tan^{-1} b/a) + c$$

- **Differentiation of integration (leibnithz's rule) :**

$$\frac{d}{dt}\left[\int_{\phi(t)}^{\Psi(t)} f(x)\,dx\right] = f\{\psi(t)\}\,\psi'(t) - f\{\phi(t)\}\,\phi'(t)$$

- $\displaystyle\int_a^b f(x)\,dx = (b-a)\int_0^1 f((b-a)x + a)\,dx.$

♦   If f (x) is defined on [a, b], then

$$\left| \int_a^b f(x)dx \right| \le \int_a^b |f(x)|\, dx$$

♦   **Reduction formulae for definite integration:**

(i) $\int_0^\infty e^{-ax} \sin bx\, dx = \dfrac{b}{a^2 + b^2}$

(ii) $\int_0^\infty e^{-ax} \cos bx\, dx = \dfrac{a}{a^2 + b^2}$

(iii) $\int_0^\infty e^{-ax} x^n dx = \dfrac{n!}{a^n + 1}$

♦   If $\int f(x)dx = \phi(x)$, then $\int f(ax + b)dx = \dfrac{1}{a}\phi(ax + b)$

♦ $\int (ax + b)^n dx = \dfrac{1}{a} \cdot \dfrac{(ax + b)^{n+1}}{n+1} + c, \quad n \ne -1$

♦ $\int \dfrac{1}{ax + b} dx = \dfrac{1}{a}\log |ax + b| + c$

♦ $\int e^{ax+b} dx = \dfrac{1}{a} e^{ax+b} + c$

♦ $\int a^{bx+c} dx = \dfrac{1}{b} \cdot \dfrac{a^{bx+c}}{\log a} + c, \quad a > 0 \text{ and } a \ne 1$

♦ $\int \dfrac{f'(x)}{f(x)} dx = \log\{f(x)\} + c$

♦ $\int \{f(x)\}^n f'(x)\, dx = \dfrac{\{f(x)\}^{n+1}}{n+1}, \quad n \ne -1$

♦ $\int \dfrac{f'(x)}{\sqrt{f(x)}} dx = 2\sqrt{f(x)} + c$

♦ $\int [xf'(x) + f(x)]dx = x f(x) + c$

Area Under Simple Curves

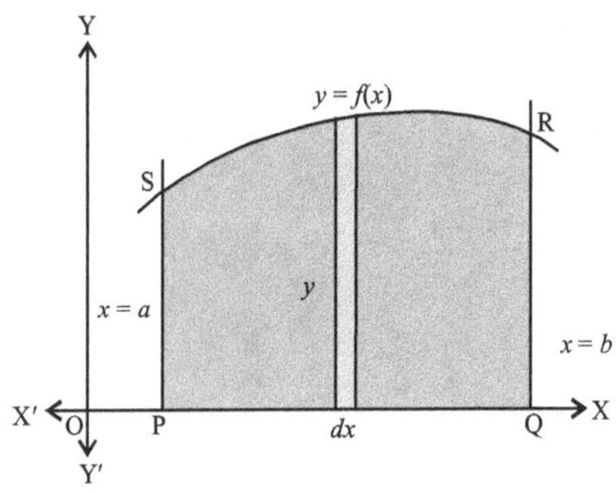

- The area A of the region bounded by the curve $y = f(x)$, x-axis and the lines $x = a$ and $x = b$ is given by

$$A = \int_a^b y\,dx = \int_a^b f(x)\,dx$$

- The area A of the region bounded by the curve $x = g(y)$, y-axis and the lines $y = c$, $y = d$ is given by

$$A = \int_c^d x\,dy = \int_c^d g(y)\,dy$$

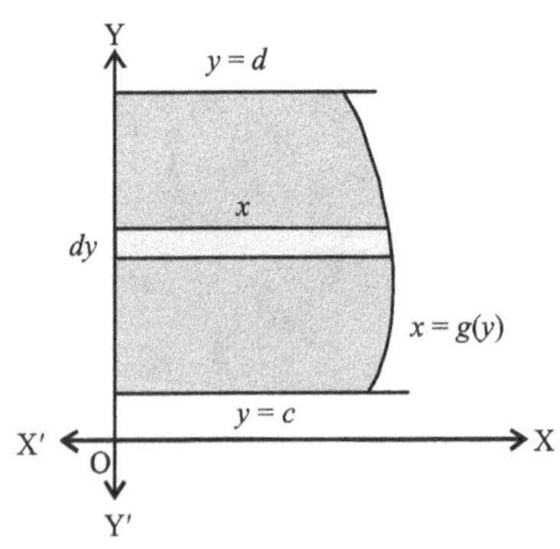

Note:

♦ If the position of the curve under consideration is below the x-axis, then since $f(x) < 0$ from $x = a$ to $x = b$, as shown in Fig., the area bounded by the curve, x-axis and the ordinates $x = a$, $x = b$ come out to be negative. But, it is only the numerical value of the area which is taken into consideration. Thus,

if the area is negative, we take its absolute value, i.e., $\left| \int_a^b f(x)\, dx \right|$.

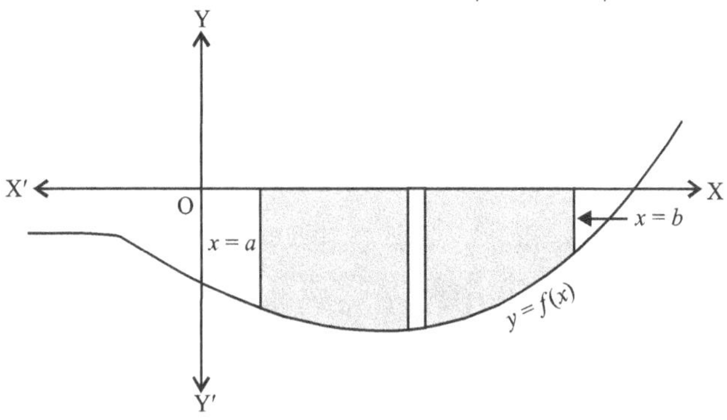

♦ Generally, it may happen that some portion of the curve is above x-axis and some is below the x-axis as shown in the Fig. Here, $A_1 < 0$ and $A_2 > 0$. Therefore, the area A bounded by the curve $y = f(x)$, x-axis and the ordinates $x = a$ and $x = b$ is given by $A = |A_1| + A_2$.

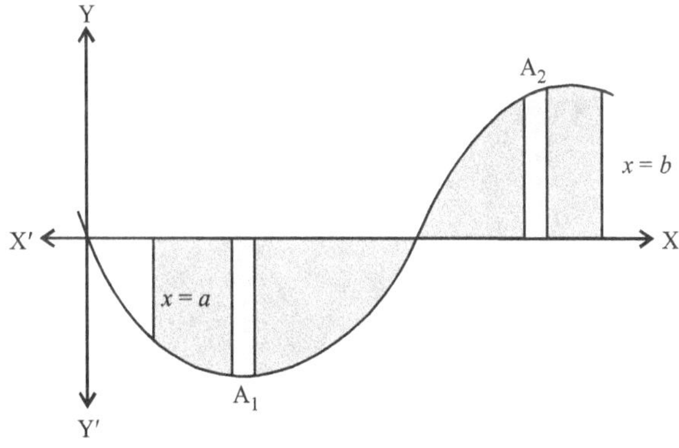

Area Between Two Curves

♦ Suppose we are given two curves represented by $y = f(x)$, $y = g(x)$, where $f(x) \geq g(x)$ in $[a, b]$ as shown in Fig. Here the points of intersection of these two curves are given by $x = a$ and $x = b$ obtained by taking common values of y from the given equation of two curves.

♦ As indicated in the Fig., elementary strip has height $f(x) - g(x)$ and width dx so that the elementary area

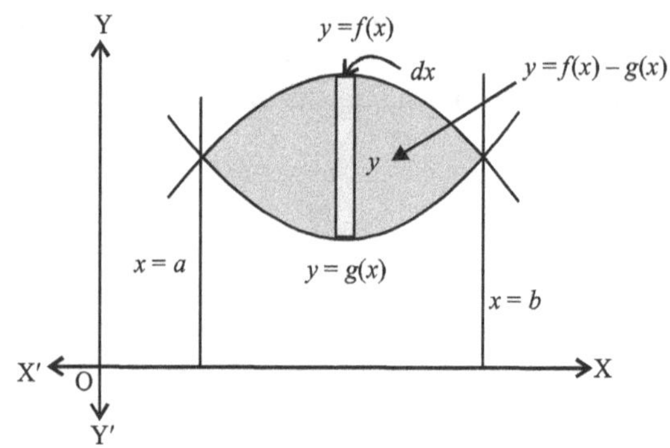

$dA = [f(x) - g(x)]\,dx$, and the total area A can be taken as

$$A = \int_a^b [f(x) - g(x)]dx$$

♦ **Alternatively,**

A = [area bounded by $y = f(x)$, x-axis and the lines $x = a$, $x = b$]

  – [area bounded by $y = g(x)$, x-axis and the lines $x = a$, $x = b$]

$$= \int_a^b f(x)\,dx - \int_a^b g(x)dx = \int_a^b [f(x) - g(x)]\,dx\,,$$

where $f(x) \geq g(x)$ in $[a, b]$

♦ If $f(x) \geq g(x)$ in $[a, c]$ and $f(x) \leq g(x)$ in $[c, b]$, where $a < c < b$ as shown in the Fig. then the area of the regions bounded by curves can be written as

♦ Total area = Area of the region ACBDA + Area of the region BPRQB

$$= \int_a^c [f(x) - g(x)]\,dx + \int_c^b [g(x) - f(x)]dx$$

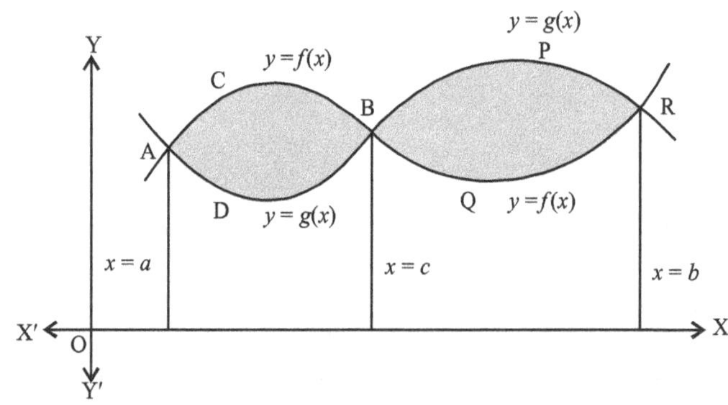

Past Years ONE-LINERS
NEET/JEE Main/Board

◆ Here, A = Area bounded by two curves

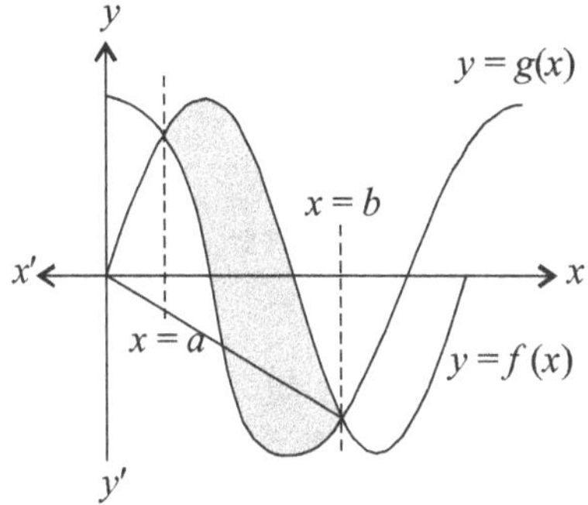

Area $A = \int\limits_{a}^{b} [f(x) - g(x)]\, dx$

◆ $f(x) = x^2 + 1,\ g(x) = x^3$

$\text{gof}(x) = g\,[f(x)] = [f(x)]^3 = (x^2 + 1)^3$

$$A = \int_{x=\alpha}^{x=\beta} \text{gof}(x)\, dx = \int\limits_{x=\alpha}^{x=\beta} (x^2 + 1)^3 dx$$

◆ Parabola 1: $x^2 = 4ay$

Parabola 2: $y = b + \sqrt{x}$

$\sqrt{x} = y - b$

$\therefore (y - b)^2 = x$

Line: $px + ay = r$

$$A = \int\limits_{0}^{\alpha} (b + \sqrt{x})\,dx + \int\limits_{\alpha}^{\beta} \frac{1}{q}(r - px)\,dx - \int\limits_{0}^{\beta} \frac{x^2}{4a}\,dx$$

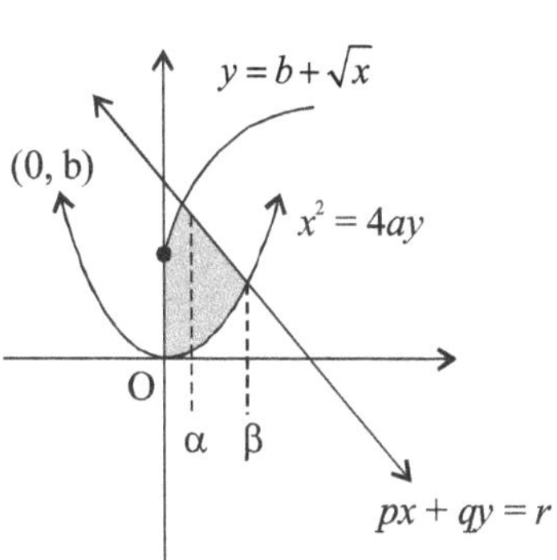

Tips/Tricks/Techniques ONE-LINERS
(Exam Special)

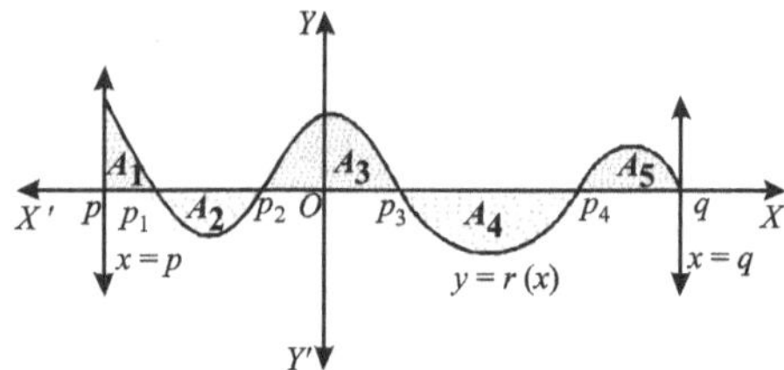

In this case, area of the whole plane region bounded by the function $y = r(x)$ and x-axis between the lines $x = p$ and $x = q$ is the sum of the areas A_1, A_2, A_3 A_4 and A_5 i.e. total area $= A_1 + A_2 + A_3 + A_4 + A_5$

$$= \int_{p}^{p_1} r(x)\,dx + \left|\int_{p_1}^{p_2} r(x)\,dx\right| + \left|\int_{p_2}^{p_3} r(x)\,dx\right| + \left|\int_{p_3}^{p_4} r(x)\,dx\right| + \int_{p_4}^{q} r(x)\,dx$$

Here p_1, p_2, p_3 and p_4 are the values of x at the points, where the curve $y = r(x)$, $x \in [p, q]$ intersects the x-axis and

$$p < p_1 < p_2 < p_3 < p_4 < q$$

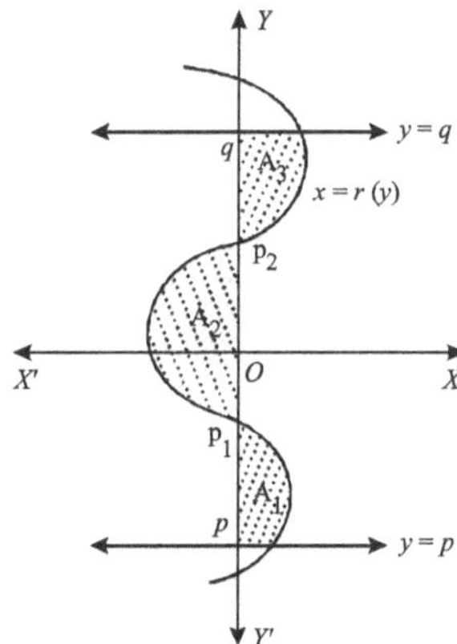

In the figure, parts A_1 and A_3 are right of the y-axis and part A_2 is left of the y-axis.

In this case, area of the whole plane region bounded by the function $x = r(y)$ and y-axis between abscissae p and q (i.e., between the lines $y = p$ and $y = q$) is the sum of the areas A_1, A_2 and A_3 i.e. Total area $= A_1 + A_2 + A_3$

$$= \int\limits_{p}^{p_1} r(y)\,dy + \left|\int\limits_{p_1}^{p_2} r(y)\,dy\right| + \int\limits_{p_2}^{q} r(y)\,dy$$

Here, p_1 and p_2 are the values of y at the points where the curve $x = r\,(y)$, $y \in [p, q]$ intersects the y-axis and $p < p_1 < p_2 < q$.

- Whole area of the ellipse, $\dfrac{x^2}{a^2} + \dfrac{y^2}{b^2} = 1$ is πab.

- Area enclosed between the parabolas $y^2 = 4ax$ and $x^2 = 4by$ is $16ab/\,3$
- Area included between the parabola $y^2 = 4ax$ and the line $y = mx$ is $8a^2/3m^3$.
- If the given curve is symmetric about any axis or about line, then the required area is obtained by finding the area of one symmetrical part and multiplying it by the number of such symmetrical parts.
- The area is always considered to be positive. Hence if a part of the area is above the axis of x (which is positive) and the remaining part is below the x-axis (which is negative), then the required area is obtained by finding the areas of the two parts separately and adding their numerical values.

25 Differential Equations

- In general, an equation involving derivative (derivatives) of the dependent variable with respect to independent variable (variables) is called a **differential equation.**

- A differential equation involving derivatives of the dependent variable with respect to only one independent variable is called an **ordinary differential equation,** e.g.,

$$2\frac{d^2y}{dx^2} + \left(\frac{dy}{dx}\right)^3 = 0 \text{ is an ordinary differential equation}$$

- We shall prefer to use the following notations for derivatives:

$$\frac{dy}{dx} = y', \frac{d^2y}{dx^2} = y'', \frac{d^3y}{dx^3} = y'''$$

Order of a differential equation:

- **Order** of a differential equation is defined as the order of the highest order derivative of the dependent variable with respect to the independent variable involved in the given differential equation.

$$\frac{dy}{dx} = e^x \text{ and } \frac{d^2y}{dx^2} + y = 0$$

The order of these equations are 1, 2.

Degree of a differential equation:

- To study the degree of a differential equation, the key point is that the differential equation must be a polynomial equation in derivatives, i.e., y', y'', y''' etc.

- The **degree** of a differential equation, when it is a polynomial equation in derivatives, the highest power (positive integral index) of the highest order derivative involved in the given differential equation.

- Order and degree (if defined) of a differential equation are always positive integers.

General and Particular Solutions of a Differential Equation

- The solution which contains arbitrary constants is called the **general solution (primitive)** of the differential equation.
- The solution free from arbitrary constants i.e., the solution obtained from the general solution by giving particular values to the arbitrary constants is called a **particular solution** of the differential equation.

Formation of a Differential Equation whose General Solution is given

- For this, we differentiate the given equation as many times as the number of arbitrary constants present in the equation.

Procedure to form a differential equation that will represent a given family of curves:

- If the given family F_1 of curves depends on only one parameter then it is represented by an equation of the form
$$F_1(x, y, a) = 0$$
- If the given family F_2 of curves depends on the parameters a, b (say) then it is represented by an equation of the from
$$F_2(x, y, a, b) = 0$$

Methods of Solving First Order, First Degree Differential Equations

Differential equations with variables separable:

- A first order-first degree differential equation is of the form $\dfrac{dy}{dx} = F(x, y)$
- Provides the solutions of given differential equation in the form
$$H(y) = G(x) + C$$
- Here, H(y) and G(x) are the anti derivatives of $\dfrac{1}{h(y)}$ and g(x) respectively and C is the arbitrary constant.

Homogeneous differential equations:

- A function F(x, y) is said to be **homogeneous function of degree n** if $F(\lambda x, \lambda y) = \lambda^n F(x, y)$ for any nonzero constant λ.

- A differential equation of the form $\dfrac{dy}{dx} = F(x, y)$ is said to be **homogeneous** if $F(x, y)$ is a homogenous function of degree zero.

  To solve a homogeneous differential equation of the type
  $$\dfrac{dy}{dx} = F(x, y) = g\left(\dfrac{y}{x}\right).$$

- The homogeneous differential equation is in the form $\dfrac{dx}{dy} = F(x, y)$ where, F (x, y) is homogenous function of degree zero, then we make substitution $\dfrac{x}{y} = v$ i.e., $x = vy$ and we proceed further to find the general solution as discussed above by writing $\dfrac{dx}{dy} = F(x, y) = h\left(\dfrac{x}{y}\right).$

Linear differential equations:

- A differential equation of the from
  $$\dfrac{dy}{dx} + Py = Q$$
  where, P and Q are constants or functions of x only, is known as a **first order linear differential equation.**

Steps involved to solve first order linear differential equation:

- Write the given differential equation in the form
  $$\dfrac{dy}{dx} + Py = Q \text{ where P, Q are constants or functions of x only.}$$

- Find the Integrating Factor (I.F) $= e^{\int P\,dx}$.
- Write the solution of the given differential equation as
  $$y(\text{I.F.}) = \int (Q \times \text{I.F.})dx + C$$

Past Years ONE-LINERS
JEE Main/Board

- Using integrating factors $e^{\int P\,dx}$ in $\dfrac{dy}{dx} + Py = Q$, where P and Q are constants or functions of x only.

- Let $e^y = t$ and $e^y \dfrac{dy}{dx} = \dfrac{dt}{dx}$

  Thus $e^y\left(\dfrac{dy}{dx} - 1\right) = e^x \Rightarrow \dfrac{dt}{dx} - t = e^x$

♦ By linear differential equation compare the expression with $\dfrac{dx}{dy} + Px = Q$

♦ By using variable separable method,

$$\dfrac{dy}{dx} = \dfrac{f(y)}{g(x)} \Rightarrow \dfrac{dy}{f(y)} = \dfrac{dx}{g(x)}$$

Now integrating both the sides,

$$\int \dfrac{dy}{f(y)} = \int \dfrac{dx}{g(x)}$$

♦ If the equation is of the form $\dfrac{dy}{dx} = f(x)g(y)$ then solution is given as $\int \dfrac{dy}{g(y)} = \int f(x)\, dx + C$

Tips/Tricks/Techniques ONE-LINERS
(Exam Special)

- -

♦ **Different equation reducible to variable separable form**

$$\dfrac{dy}{dx} = f(ax + by + c)$$

To solve this type of differential equations, we put

$$ax + by + c = v \text{ and } \dfrac{dy}{dx} = \dfrac{1}{b}\left(\dfrac{dv}{dx} - a\right)$$

$$\therefore \quad \dfrac{dv}{a + bf(v)} = dx$$

So solution is by integrating, $\displaystyle\int \dfrac{dv}{a + bf(v)} = \int dx$

♦ **Solution of differential equation of the form** $\dfrac{d^2y}{dx^2} = f(x)$

Its solution can be obtained by integrating it with respect to x twice.

♦ **Solution by inspection**

If we can write the differential equation in the form $f(f_1(x, y))\, d\,(f_1(x, y)) + f(f_2(x, y))d\,(f_2(x, y)) + ... = 0$, then each term can be easily integrated separately. For this the following results must be memorized.

❖ $d(x + y) = dx + dy$
❖ $d(xy) = xdy + ydx$

❖ $d\left(\dfrac{x}{y}\right) = \dfrac{ydx - xdy}{y^2}$

- ❖ $d\left(\dfrac{x^2}{y}\right) = \dfrac{2xydx - x^2dy}{y^2}$

- ❖ $d\left(\dfrac{x^2}{y^2}\right) = \dfrac{2xy^2dx - 2x^2ydy}{y^4}$

- ❖ $d\left(\tan^{-1}\dfrac{x}{y}\right) = \dfrac{ydx - xdy}{x^2 + y^2}$

- ❖ $d[\ln(xy)] = \dfrac{xdy + ydx}{xy}$

- ❖ $d\left(\ln\left(\dfrac{x}{y}\right)\right) = \dfrac{ydx - xdy}{xy}$

- ❖ $d\left(-\dfrac{1}{xy}\right) = \dfrac{xdy + ydx}{x^2y^2}$

- ❖ $d\left(\dfrac{e^x}{y}\right) = \dfrac{ye^xdx - e^xdy}{y^2}$

- ❖ $d(x^my^n) = x^{m-1}y^{n-1}(mydx + nxdy)$

- ❖ $d\left(\sqrt{x^2 + y^2}\right) = \dfrac{xdx + ydy}{\sqrt{x^2 + y^2}}$

- ◆ Arbitrary constants present in a given solution of a differential equation are said to be independent arbitrary constants, if it is impossible to get a solution equivalent to the given solution containing fewer number of arbitrary constants.

- ◆ A differential equation is a non-linear differential equation if
  - ❖ its degree is more than one
  - ❖ any of the differential co-efficient has exponent more than one
  - ❖ exponent of the dependent variable is more than one.
  - ❖ products containing dependent variable and its differential co-efficients are present.

  e.g. $\left(\dfrac{d^2y}{dx^2}\right)^3 + 2\left(\dfrac{dy}{dx}\right)^2 - 5y = x^4$ is a non-linear differential equation because

  its degree 3 is more than one.

- ◆ The degree of a linear differential equation is always one. But the converse is not always true.

  e.g. $\dfrac{dy}{dx} = \dfrac{x^2 + y^2}{2xy}$ is of degree 1 and order 1 but it is not linear, because it can

  be written as $xy\dfrac{dy}{dx} = \dfrac{x^2 + y^2}{2}$ in which y and $\dfrac{dy}{dx}$ are multiplied together

26   Vector Algebra

Some Basic Concepts

- **Vector :** A quantity that has magnitude as well as direction is called a **vector**. Notice that a directed line segment is a vector, denoted as $\overrightarrow{AB}$ or simply as $\vec{a}$, and read as 'vector $\overrightarrow{AB}$' or 'vector $\vec{a}$'.

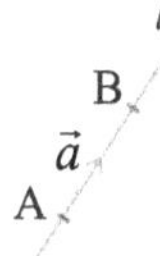

- **Initials & Terminal Point :** The point A from where the vector $\overrightarrow{AB}$ starts is called its **initial point,** and the point B where it ends is called its **terminal point**.

- **Magnitude :** The distance between initial and terminal points of a vector is called the **magnitude** (or length) of the vector, denoted as $|\overrightarrow{AB}|$, or $|\vec{a}|$, or a. The arrow indicates the direction of the vector.

- **Position vector :** The vector $\overrightarrow{OP}$ having O and P as its initial and terminal points, respectively, is called the **position vector** of the point P with respect to O. Using distance formula (from Class XI), the magnitude of $\overrightarrow{OP}$ (or $\vec{r}$) is given by

$$|\vec{r}| = |\overrightarrow{OP}| = \sqrt{x^2 + y^2 + z^2}$$

- **Direction Cosines :** Consider the position vector $\overrightarrow{OP}$ (or $\vec{r}$) of a point P(x, y, z) as in Fig. The angles α, β, γ made by the vector $\vec{r}$ with the positive directions of x, y and z-axes respectively, are called its **direction angles**. The cosine values of these angles, i.e., cos α, cos β and cos γ are called **direction cosines** of the vector $\vec{r}$, and usually denoted by l, m and n, respectively.

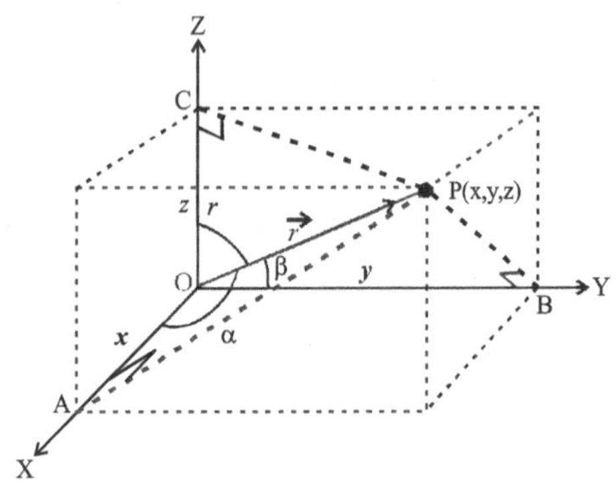

Here, we have $l = \cos\alpha = \dfrac{x}{r}$, $m = \cos\beta = \dfrac{y}{r}$, $n = \cos\gamma = \dfrac{z}{r}$

α, β, γ = Direction angles

cos α, cos β, cos γ = Direction of cosines

- One may note that $l^2 + m^2 + n^2 = 1$ but $a^2 + b^2 + c^2 \neq 1$, in general.

Types of Vectors

- **Zero Vector :** A vector whose initial and terminal points coincide, is called a **zero vector (or null vector),** and denoted as $\vec{O}$. Zero vector can not be assigned a definite direction as it has zero magnitude, alternatively, it may be regarded as having any direction.
- **Unit Vector :** A vector whose magnitude is unity (i.e., 1 unit) is called a **unit vector.** The unit vector in the direction of a given vector $\vec{a}$ is denoted by $\hat{a}$.
- **Coinitial Vectors :** Two or more vectors having the same initial point are called **coinitial vectors.**
- **Collinear Vectors :** Two or more vectors are said to be **collinear** if they are parallel to the same line, irrespective of their magnitudes and directions.
- **Equal Vectors :** Two vectors $\vec{a}$ and $\vec{b}$ are said to be **equal,** if they have the same magnitude and direction regardless of the positions of their initial points, and written as $\vec{a} = \vec{b}$.
- **Negative of a Vector :** A vector whose magnitude is the same as that of a given vector (say, $\overrightarrow{AB}$), but direction is opposite to that of it, is called **negative**

of the given vector. For example, $\overrightarrow{BA}$ vector is negative of the vector $\overrightarrow{AB}$, and written as $\overrightarrow{BA} = -\overrightarrow{AB}$.

Note : The vectors defined above are such that any of them may be subject to its parallel displacement without changing its magnitude and direction. Such vectors are called **free vectors**.

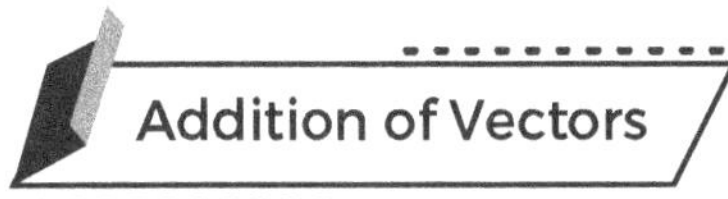

Addition of Vectors

Triangle Law of Vector Addition:

♦ A vector $\overrightarrow{AB}$ simply means the displacement from a point A to the point B. Now consider a situation that a girl moves from A to B and then from B to C.

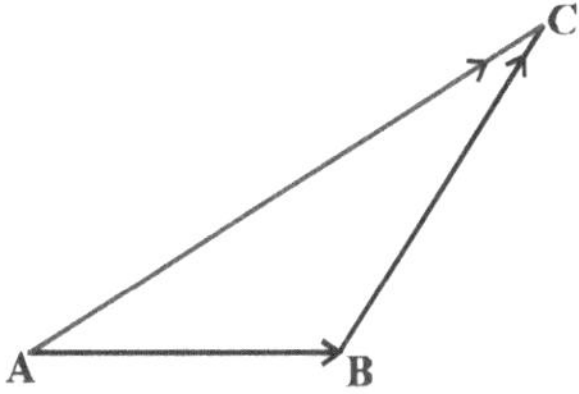

The net displacement made by the girl from point A to the point C, is given by the vector $\overrightarrow{AC}$ and expressed as

$$\overrightarrow{AC} = \overrightarrow{AB} + \overrightarrow{BC}$$

This is known as the **triangle law of vector addition**.

Parallelogram Law of Vector Addition:

♦ If we have two vectors $\vec{a}$ and $\vec{b}$ represented by the two adjacent sides of a parallelogram in magnitude and direction, then their sum $\vec{a} + \vec{b}$ is represented in magnitude and direction by the diagonal of the parallelogram through their common point. This is known as the **parallelogram law of vector addition**.

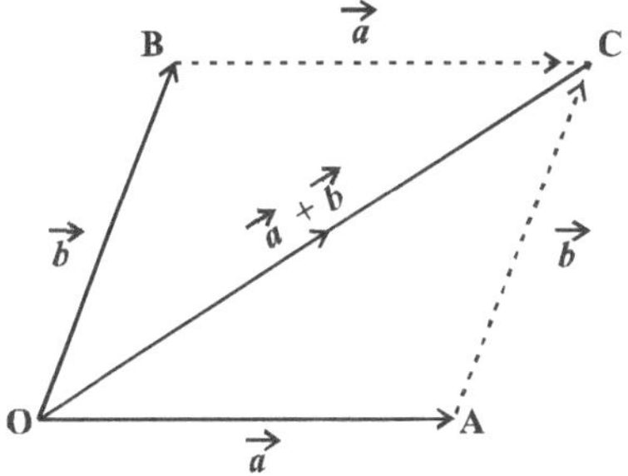

Properties of Vector Addition :

- **Property 1 :** For any two vectors $\vec{a}$ and $\vec{b}$,

  $$\vec{a} + \vec{b} = \vec{b} + \vec{a} \qquad \textbf{(Commutative } \text{property)}$$

- **Property 2 :** For any three vectors $\vec{a}$, $\vec{b}$ and $\vec{c}$

  $$(\vec{a} + \vec{b}) + \vec{c} = \vec{a}(\vec{b} + \vec{c}) \quad \textbf{(Associative } \text{property)}$$

- The associative property of vector addition enables us to write the sum of three vectors $\vec{a}, \vec{b}, \vec{c}$ as $\vec{a} + \vec{b} + \vec{c}$ without using brackets.

- Note that for any vector $\vec{a}$, we have

  $$\vec{a} + \vec{0} = \vec{0} + \vec{a} = \vec{a}$$

  Here, the zero vector is called the **additive identity** for the vector addition.

Multiplication of a Vector by a Scalar

- Let $\vec{a}$ be a given vector and λ a scalar. Then the product of the vector $\vec{a}$ by the scalar λ, denoted as $\lambda\vec{a}$, is called the **multiplication of vector $\vec{a}$ by the scalar λ.**

- Note that, $\lambda\vec{a}$ is also a vector, collinear to the vector $\vec{a}$. The vector $\lambda\vec{a}$ has the direction same (or opposite) to that of vector $\vec{a}$ according as the value of λ is positive (or negative).

- Also, the magnitude of vector $\lambda\vec{a}$ is $|\lambda|$ times the magnitude of the vector $\vec{a}$, i.e.,

  $$|\lambda\vec{a}| = |\lambda||\vec{a}|$$

Components of a Vector :

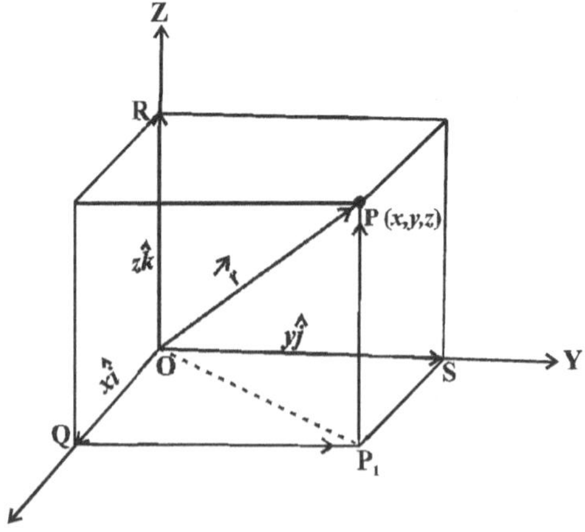

♦ The position vector of P with reference to O is given by

$$\overrightarrow{OP} \ (\text{or} \ \vec{r}) = x\hat{i} + y\hat{j} + z\hat{k}$$

This form of any vector is called its **component form**. Here, x, y and z are called as the **scalar components** of $\vec{r}$, and $x\hat{i}$, $y\hat{j}$ and $z\hat{k}$. are called the **vector components** of $\vec{r}$ along the respective axes. Sometimes x, y and z are also termed as **rectangular components**.

♦ The length of any vector $\vec{r} = x\hat{i} + y\hat{j} + z\hat{k}$ is given by

$$|\vec{r}| = \left| x\hat{i} + y\hat{j} + z\hat{k} \right| = \sqrt{x^2 + y^2 + z^2}$$

♦ If $\vec{a}$ and $\vec{b}$ are any two vectors given in the component form $a_1\hat{i} + a_2\hat{j} + a_3\hat{k}$ and $b_1\hat{i} + b_2\hat{j} + b_3\hat{k}$, respectively, then

❖ the sum (or resultant) of the vectors $\vec{a}$ and $\vec{b}$ is given by

$$\vec{a} + \vec{b} = (a_1 + b_1)\hat{i} + (a_2 + b_2)\hat{j} + (a_3 + b_3)\hat{k}$$

❖ the difference of the vector $\vec{a}$ and $\vec{b}$ is given by

$$\vec{a} - \vec{b} = (a_1 - b_1)\hat{i} + (a_2 - b_2)\hat{j} + (a_3 - b_3)\hat{k}$$

❖ the vectors $\vec{a}$ and $\vec{b}$ are equal if and only if
$a_1 = b_1, a_2 = b_2$ and $a_3 = b_3$

❖ the multiplication of vector $\vec{a}$ by any scalar λ is given by

$$\lambda\vec{a} = (\lambda a_1)\hat{i} + (\lambda a_2)\hat{j} + (\lambda a_3)\hat{k}$$

♦ **Note :**

❖ If the vectors $\vec{a}$ and $\vec{b}$ are given in the component form, i.e. $\vec{a} = a_1\hat{i} + a_2\hat{j} + a_3\hat{k}$ and $\vec{b} = b_1\hat{i} + b_2\hat{j} + b_3\hat{k}$, then the two vectors are collinear if and only if

$$b_1\hat{i} + b_2\hat{j} + b_3\hat{k} = \lambda(a_1\hat{i} + a_2\hat{j} + a_3\hat{k})$$

$$\Rightarrow b_1\hat{i} + b_2\hat{j} + b_3\hat{k} = (\lambda a_1)\hat{i} + (\lambda a_2)\hat{j} + (\lambda a_3)\hat{k}$$

$$\Rightarrow b_1 = \lambda a_1, b_2 = \lambda a_2, b_3 = \lambda a_3$$

$$\Rightarrow \frac{b_1}{a_1} = \frac{b_2}{a_2} = \frac{b_3}{a_3} = \lambda$$

❖ If $\vec{a} = a_1\hat{i} + a_2\hat{j} + a_3\hat{k}$, then a_1, a_2, a_3 are also called direction ratios of $\vec{a}$.

❖   In case if it is given that l, m, n are direction cosines of a vector, then

$l\hat{i} + m\hat{j} + n\hat{k} = (\cos\alpha)\hat{i} + (\cos\beta)\hat{j} + (\cos\gamma)\hat{k}$ is the unit vector in the direction of that vector, where α, β and γ are the angles which the vector makes with x, y and z axes respectively.

Vector Joining Two Points :

♦   If $P_1(x_1, y_1, z_1)$ and $P_2(x_2, y_2, z_2)$ are any two points, then the vector joining P_1 and P_2 is the vector $\overrightarrow{P_1P_2}$.

Using the properties of vector addition,

$$\overrightarrow{OP_1} + \overrightarrow{P_1P_2} = \overrightarrow{OP_2}$$
$$\overrightarrow{P_1P_2} = \overrightarrow{OP_2} - \overrightarrow{OP_1}$$

$i.e.,\ \overrightarrow{P_1P_2} = (x_2\hat{i} + y_2\hat{j} + z_2\hat{k}) - (x_1\hat{i} + y_1\hat{j} + z_1\hat{k})$
$$= (x_2 - x_1)\hat{i} + (y_2 - y_1)\hat{j} + (z_2 - z_1)\hat{k}$$

The magnitude of vector $\overrightarrow{P_1P_2}$ is given by

$$\left|\overrightarrow{P_1P_2}\right| = \sqrt{(x_2 - x_1)^2 + (y_2 - y_1)^2 + (z_2 - z_1)^2}$$

Section Formula :

♦   Let P and Q be two points represented by the position vectors $\overrightarrow{OP}$ and $\overrightarrow{OQ}$, respectively, with respect to the origin O.

♦   Then the line segment joining the points P and Q may be divided by a third point, say R, in two ways internally and externally.

♦   Here, we intend to find the position vector $\overrightarrow{OR}$ for the point R with respect to the origin O.

♦   **Case I :** When R divides PQ internally the position vector of the point R which divides P and Q internally in the ratio of $m : n$ is given by

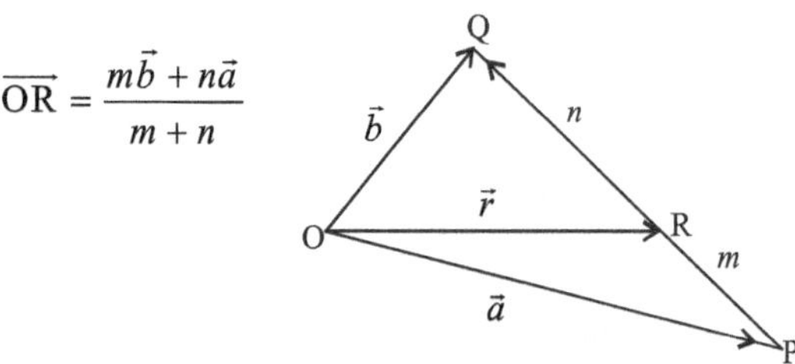

$$\overrightarrow{OR} = \frac{m\vec{b} + n\vec{a}}{m + n}$$

♦   **Case II :** When R divides PQ **externally** position vector of the point R which divides the line segment PQ externally in the ratio $m : n$ is given by

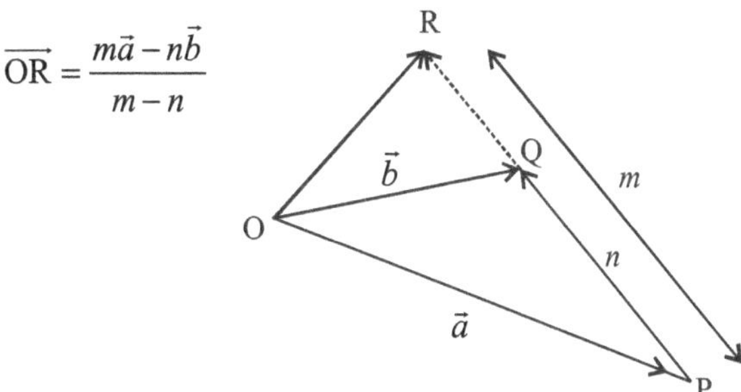

$$\overrightarrow{OR} = \frac{m\vec{a} - n\vec{b}}{m - n}$$

♦ **Note :** If R is the midpoint of PQ , then $m = n$. And therefore, from Case I, the midpoint R of $\overrightarrow{PQ}$, will have its position vector as

$$\overrightarrow{OR} = \frac{\vec{a} + \vec{b}}{2}$$

Product of Two Vectors

Scalar (or dot) product of two vectors

♦ The **scalar product** of two nonzero vectors $\vec{a}$ and $\vec{b}$, denoted by $\vec{a}.\vec{b}$, is defined as $\vec{a}.\vec{b} = |\vec{a}|.|\vec{b}| \cos\theta$, where, θ is the angle between $\vec{a}$ and $\vec{b}, 0 \leq \theta \leq \pi$.

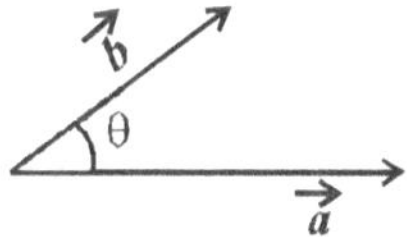

♦ **Properties of Scalar (or dot) product :**

❖ $\vec{a}.\vec{b}$ is a real number.

❖ Let $\vec{a}, \vec{b}$ and $\vec{c}$ be $\vec{a}.(\vec{b} + \vec{c}) = \vec{a}.\vec{b} + \vec{a}.\vec{c}$

❖ Let $\vec{a}$ and $\vec{b}$ be any two vectors, and λ be any scalar, Then $(\lambda\vec{a}).\vec{b} = \lambda(\vec{a}.\vec{b}) = \vec{a}.(\lambda\vec{b})$

❖ Let $\vec{a}$ and $\vec{b}$ be two nonzero vectors, then $\vec{a}.\vec{b} = 0$ if and only if $\vec{a}$ and $\vec{b}$ are **perpendicular** to each other. i.e. $\vec{a}.\vec{b} = 0 \Leftrightarrow \vec{a} \perp \vec{b}$

❖ If $\theta = 0$, then $\vec{a}.\vec{b} = |\vec{a}|.|\vec{b}|$

❖ If $\theta = \pi$, then $\vec{a}.\vec{b} = -|\vec{a}||\vec{b}|$

❖ In view, for mutually perpendicular unit vectors $\hat{i}, \hat{j}$ and $\hat{k}$, we have

$$\hat{i}.\hat{i} = \hat{j}.\hat{j} = \hat{k}.\hat{k} = 1,$$

$$\hat{i}.\hat{j} = \hat{j}.\hat{k} = \hat{k}.\hat{i} = 0$$

❖ The angle between two nonzero vectors $\vec{a}$ and $\vec{b}$ is given by

$$\cos\theta = \frac{\vec{a}.\vec{b}}{|\vec{a}||\vec{b}|}, \text{ or } \theta = \cos^{-1} = \left(\frac{\vec{a}.\vec{b}}{|\vec{a}||\vec{b}|}\right)$$

❖ The scalar product is **commutative.** i.e. $\vec{a}.\vec{b} = \vec{b}.\vec{a}$

❖ If two vectors $\vec{a}$ and $\vec{b}$ are given in component form as $a_1\hat{i} + a_2\hat{j} + a_3\hat{k}$ and $b_1\hat{i} + b_2\hat{j} + b_3\hat{k}$, then their scalar product is given as

$$\vec{a}.\vec{b} = (a_1\hat{i} + a_2\hat{j} + a_3\hat{k}).(b_1\hat{i} + b_2\hat{j} + b_3\hat{k})$$

$$\vec{a}.\vec{b} = a_1b_1 + a_2b_2 + a_3b_3$$

Projection of a vector on a line :

♦ Suppose a vector $\overrightarrow{AB}$ makes an angle θ with a given directed line l (say), in the **anticlockwise direction**. Then the projection of $\overrightarrow{AB}$ on l is a vector $\vec{p}$ (say) with magnitude $|\overrightarrow{AB}||\cos\theta|$, and the direction of $\vec{p}$ being the same (or opposite) to that of the line l, depending upon whether $\cos\theta$ is positive (or negative). The vector $\vec{p}$ is called the **projection vector**, and its magnitude $|\vec{p}|$ is simply called as the **projection** of the vector $\overrightarrow{AB}$ on the directed line l.

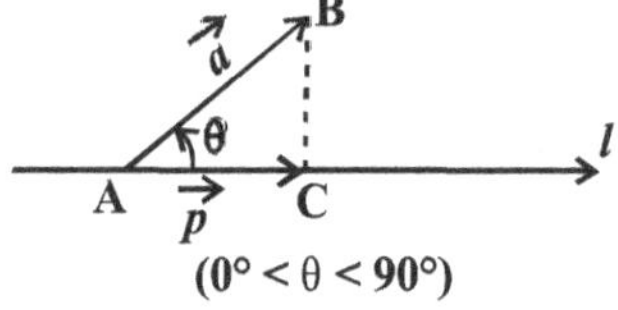

$$(0° < \theta < 90°)$$

♦ **Properties of Projection of Vector :**

❖ If $\vec{p}$ is the unit vector along a line l, then the projection of a vector $\vec{a}$ on the line l is given by $\vec{a}.\vec{p}$.

❖ Projection of a vector $\vec{a}$ on other vector $\vec{b}$, is given by

$$\vec{a}.\vec{b}, \text{ or } \vec{a}.\left(\frac{\vec{b}}{|\vec{b}|}\right), \text{ or } \frac{1}{|\vec{b}|}(\vec{a}.\vec{b})$$

❖ If $\theta = 0$, then the projection vector of $\overrightarrow{AB}$ will be $\overrightarrow{AB}$ itself and if $\theta = \pi$, then the projection vector of $\overrightarrow{AB}$ will be $\overrightarrow{BA}$.

❖ If $\theta = \dfrac{\pi}{2}$ or $\theta = \dfrac{3\pi}{2}$, then the projection vector of $\overrightarrow{AB}$ will be zero vector.

◆ **Note :** If α, β and γ are the direction angles of vector $\vec{a} = a_1\hat{i} + a_2\hat{j} + a_3\hat{k}$,

then its direction cosines may be given as $\cos\alpha = \dfrac{\vec{a}.\hat{i}}{|\vec{a}||\hat{i}|} = \dfrac{a_1}{|\vec{a}|}$, $\cos\beta = \dfrac{a_2}{|\vec{a}|}$,

$\cos\gamma = \dfrac{a_2}{|\vec{a}|}$

Also, note that $|\vec{a}|\cos\alpha, |\vec{a}|\cos\beta$ and $|\vec{a}|\cos y$ are respectively the projections

of $\vec{a}$ along OX, OY and OZ. i.e., the scalar components a_1, a_2 and a_3 of the

vector $\vec{a}$, are precisely the projections of $\vec{a}$ along x-axis, y-axis and z-axis,

respectively.

Vector (or cross) product of two vectors :

◆ The **vector product** of two nonzero vectors $\vec{a}$ and $\vec{b}$, is denoted by $\vec{a} \times \vec{b}$ and
defined as

$$\vec{a} \times \vec{b} = |\vec{a}||\vec{b}|\sin\theta\,\hat{n}$$

where, θ is the angle between $\vec{a}$ and $\vec{b}$, $0 \leq \theta \leq r$ and $\hat{n}$ is a unit vector
perpendicular to both $\vec{a}$ and $\vec{b}$.

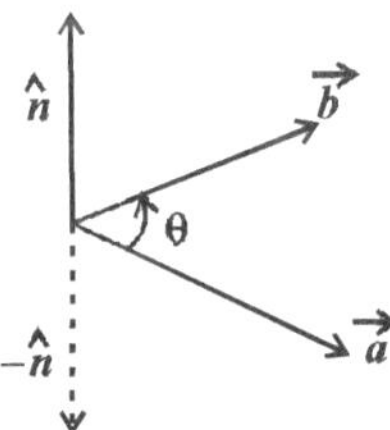

Properties of vector (or cross) product of two vectors :

❖ $\vec{a} \times \vec{b}$ is a vector.

❖ If $\vec{a}$, $\vec{b}$ and $\vec{c}$ are any three vectors and λ be a scalar, then $\vec{a} \times (\vec{b} + \vec{c}) =$

$\vec{a} \times \vec{b} + \vec{a} \times \vec{c}$

❖ Let $\vec{a}$ and $\vec{b}$ be any two vectors and λ be any scalar. Then $\lambda(\vec{a} \times \vec{b}) =$

$(\lambda\vec{a}) \times \vec{b} = \vec{a} \times (\lambda\vec{b})$

❖ Let $\vec{a}$ and $\vec{b}$ be two nonzero vectors. Then $\vec{a} \times \vec{b} = \vec{0}$ if and only if $\vec{a}$ and

$\vec{b}$ are **parallel (or collinear)** to each other, i.e., $\vec{a} \times \vec{b} = \vec{0} \Leftrightarrow \vec{a} \| \vec{b}$

❖ If $\theta = \dfrac{\pi}{2}$ then $\vec{a} \times \vec{b} = |\vec{a}||\vec{b}|$

❖ In view of for mutually perpendicular unit vectors $\hat{i}$, $\hat{j}$ and $\hat{k}$, we have

$$\hat{i} \times \hat{i} = \hat{j} \times \hat{j} = \hat{k} \times \hat{k} = 0$$

$$\hat{i} \times \hat{j} = \hat{k}, \ \hat{j} \times \hat{k} = \hat{i}, \ \hat{k} \times \hat{i} = \hat{j}$$

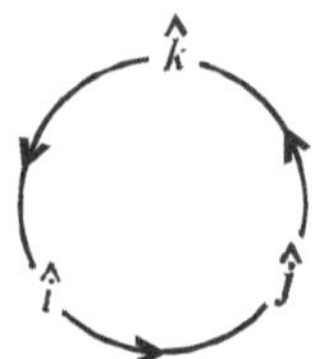

❖ In terms of vector product, the angle between two vectors $\vec{a}$ and $\vec{b}$ may be given as

$$\sin \theta = \frac{|\vec{a} \times \vec{b}|}{|\vec{a}| \cdot |\vec{b}|}$$

❖ It is always true that the vector product is **not commutative,** as $\vec{a} \times \vec{b} = -\vec{b} \times \vec{a}$.

Indeed, $\vec{a} \times \vec{b} = |\vec{a}||\vec{b}| \sin \theta \, \hat{n}$.

❖ In view of the property (iv) and (vii), we have

$$\hat{j} \times \hat{i} = -\hat{k}, \hat{k} \times \hat{j} = -\hat{i} \text{ and } \hat{i} \times \hat{k} = -\hat{j}$$

❖ If $\vec{a}$ and $\vec{b}$ represent the adjacent sides of a triangle then its area is given as $\dfrac{1}{2}|\vec{a} \times \vec{b}|$.

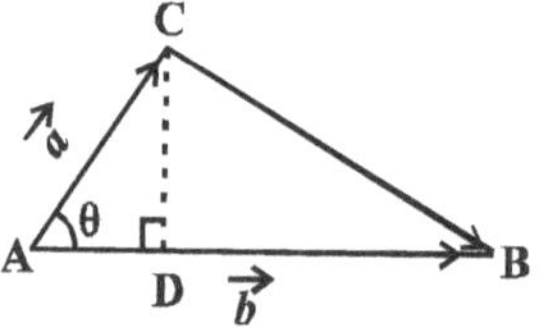

❖ If $\vec{a}$ and $\vec{b}$ represent the adjacent sides of a parallelogram, then its area is given by $|\vec{a} \times \vec{b}|$.

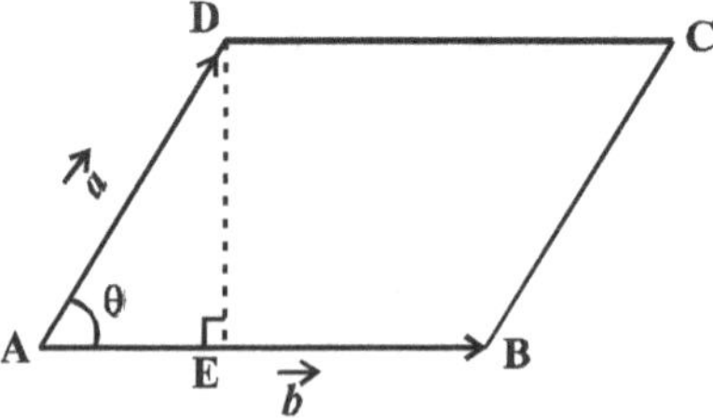

Area of parallelogram ABCD $= |\vec{b}||\vec{a}| \sin \theta = |\vec{a} \times \vec{b}|$

❖ Let $\vec{a}$ and $\vec{b}$ be two vectors given in component form as $a_1\hat{i} + a_2\hat{j} + a_3\hat{k}$ and $b_1\hat{i} + b_2\hat{j} + b_3\hat{k}$, respectively. Then their cross product may be given by

$$\vec{a} \times \vec{b} = \begin{vmatrix} \hat{i} & \hat{j} & \hat{k} \\ a_1 & a_2 & a_3 \\ b_1 & b_2 & b_3 \end{vmatrix}$$

Scalar Triple Product

♦ Let $\vec{a}$, $\vec{b}$ and $\vec{c}$ be any three vectors. The scalar product of $\vec{a}$ and $(\vec{b} \times \vec{c})$, i.e., $\vec{a}.(\vec{b} \times \vec{c})$ is called the **scalar triple product** $\vec{a}$, $\vec{b}$ and $\vec{c}$ in this order and is denoted by $[\vec{a}, \vec{b}, \vec{c}]$ or $(\vec{a}.\vec{b}.\vec{c})$. We thus have

$$[\vec{a}, \vec{b}, \vec{c}] = \vec{a}.(\vec{b} \times \vec{c}).$$

Properties of Scalar Triple Product :

❖ Since $(\vec{b} \times \vec{c})$ is a vector, $\vec{a}.(\vec{b} \times \vec{c})$ is a scalar quantity, i.e., $[\vec{a}, \vec{b}, \vec{c}]$ is a scalar quantity.

❖ Geometrically, the magnitude of the scalar triple product is the volume of a parallelopiped formed by adjacent sides given by the three vectors $\vec{a}$, $\vec{b}$ and $\vec{c}$. So the volume of the parallelopiped is $= |\vec{a}.(\vec{b} \times \vec{c})|$.

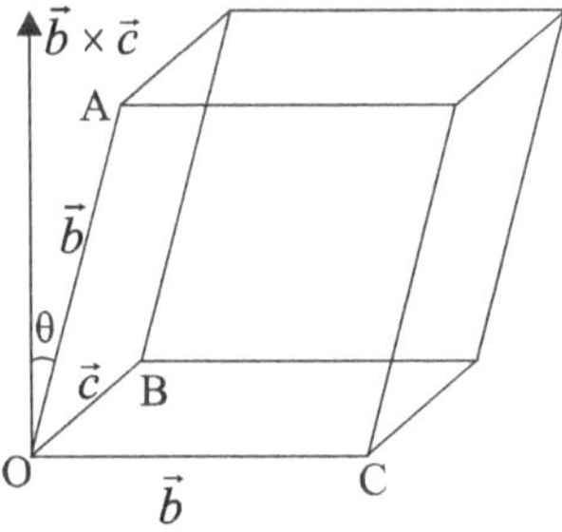

❖ If $\vec{a} = a_1\hat{i} + a_2\hat{j} + a_3\hat{k}$, $\vec{b} = b_1\hat{i} + b_2\hat{j} + b_3\hat{k}$ and $\vec{c} = c_1\hat{i} + c_2\hat{j} + c_3\hat{k}$ then

$$\vec{a}.(\vec{b} \times \vec{c}) = \begin{vmatrix} a_1 & a_2 & a_3 \\ b_1 & b_2 & b_3 \\ c_1 & c_2 & c_3 \end{vmatrix}$$

❖ If $\vec{a}, \vec{b}$ and $\vec{c}$ be any three vecotrs, then

$$[\vec{a}, \vec{b}, \vec{c}] = [\vec{b}, \vec{c}, \vec{a}] = [\vec{c}, \vec{a}, \vec{b}]$$

(cyclic permutation of three vectors does not change the value of the scalar triple product).

❖ In scalar triple product $\vec{a} \cdot (\vec{b} \times \vec{c})$, the dot and cross can be interchanged indeed.

$$\vec{a} \cdot (\vec{b} \times \vec{c}) = [\vec{a}, \vec{b}, \vec{c}] = [\vec{b}, \vec{c}, \vec{a}] = [\vec{c}, \vec{a}, \vec{b}] = \vec{c} \cdot (\vec{a} \times \vec{b}) = (\vec{a} \times \vec{b}) \cdot \vec{c}$$

❖ If the position of any two vectors are interchanged, then sign of scalar triple product changes.

$$[\vec{a}, \vec{b}, \vec{c}] = -[\vec{a}, \vec{c}, \vec{b}]$$

❖ If any two vectors are same, then scalar triple product becomes zero & it is true irrespective of the position of two equal vectors. $[\vec{a}, \vec{a}, \vec{b}] = 0$

Coplanarity of Three Vectors :

♦ **Theorem :** Three vectors $\vec{a}, \vec{b}$ and $\vec{c}$ are coplanar if and only if $\vec{a} \cdot (\vec{b} \times \vec{c}) = 0$

♦ **Note :** Coplanarity of four points can be discussed using coplanarity of three vectors. Indeed, the four points A, B, C and D are coplanar if the vectors $\overrightarrow{AB}$, $\overrightarrow{AC}$ and $\overrightarrow{AD}$ are coplanar.

Past Years ONE-LINERS
JEE Main/Board

♦ Angle between two vectors $\vec{a}$ and $\vec{b}$,

$$\cos\theta = \frac{\vec{a}.\vec{b}}{|\vec{a}||\vec{b}|} \quad \& \quad \cos\theta = \frac{\vec{a}^2 + \vec{b}^2 - \vec{c}^2}{2\vec{a}.\vec{b}}$$

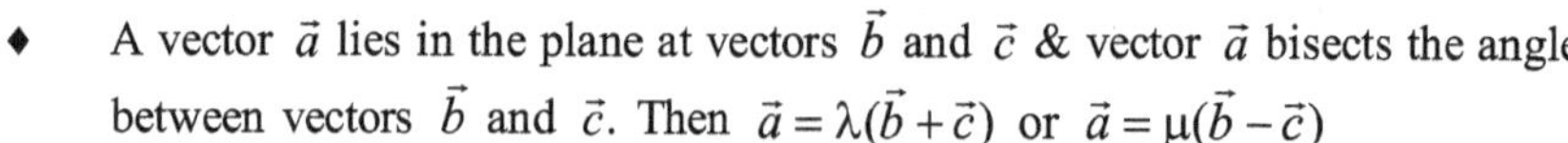

Projection of vector $\vec{a}$ on $\vec{b}$,

$$\text{Proj}_{\vec{b}}\, \vec{a} = \frac{\vec{a}.\vec{b}}{|\vec{b}|}$$

♦ A vector $\vec{a}$ lies in the plane at vectors $\vec{b}$ and $\vec{c}$ & vector $\vec{a}$ bisects the angle between vectors $\vec{b}$ and $\vec{c}$. Then $\vec{a} = \lambda(\vec{b} + \vec{c})$ or $\vec{a} = \mu(\vec{b} - \vec{c})$

♦ Let two vectors $\vec{a} = a_1\hat{i} + a_2\hat{j} + a_3\hat{k}$,

$$\vec{b} = b_1\hat{i} + b_2\hat{j} + b_3\hat{k}$$

vectors $\vec{a}$ and $\vec{b}$ are perpendicular $\Rightarrow \vec{a}.\vec{b} = 0$

vectors $\vec{a}$ and $\vec{b}$ are parallel $\Rightarrow \vec{a} = \lambda\vec{b}$

$$\vec{a} \times \vec{b} = \begin{vmatrix} \hat{i} & \hat{j} & \hat{k} \\ a_1 & a_2 & a_3 \\ b_1 & b_2 & b_3 \end{vmatrix}$$

- If three vectors $\vec{a}, \vec{b}$ and $\vec{c}$ are coplanar,

$$\vec{a} = \lambda[(\vec{b} \times \vec{c}) \times \vec{b}]$$

& $\quad |\vec{a} \times \vec{b}| \times \vec{c} = (\vec{a}.\vec{c})\vec{b} - (\vec{b}.\vec{c})\vec{a}$

- Let two vectors $\vec{a} = a_1\hat{i} + a_2\hat{j} + a_3\hat{k}$

$$\vec{b} = b_1\hat{i} + b_2\hat{j} + b_3\hat{k}$$

$$\vec{a} \times \vec{b} = \begin{vmatrix} \hat{i} & \hat{j} & \hat{k} \\ a_1 & a_2 & a_3 \\ b_1 & b_2 & b_3 \end{vmatrix}, \quad \sin\theta = \frac{|\vec{a} \times \vec{b}|}{|\vec{a}||\vec{b}|}$$

- Vectors $\vec{a}$ & $\vec{b}$ are unit vectors, $\therefore \ |\vec{a}| = |\vec{b}|$

$$\vec{a} \times (\vec{b} \times \vec{c}) = (\vec{a}.\vec{c})\vec{b} - (\vec{a}.\vec{b})\vec{c}$$

and $\cos\theta = \dfrac{\vec{a}.\vec{b}}{|\vec{a}||\vec{b}|}$

- Two vectors are collinear $\Rightarrow \vec{a} \times \vec{b} = \vec{0}$

Two vectors are non-collinear. Then $\vec{a} \times \vec{b} \neq \vec{0}$

But $\vec{a}.\vec{b}$ may or may not be zero.

Tips/Tricks/Techniques ONE-LINERS
(Exam Special)

- **Reciprocal vector :** A vector whose direction is same as that of a given vector $\vec{a}$ but its magnitude is the reciprocal of the magnitude of the given vector $\vec{a}$ is called the reciprocal of $\vec{a}$ and is denoted by $\vec{a}^{-1}$

Thus if $\vec{a} = a.\hat{a}$ then $\vec{a}^{-1} = \dfrac{1}{a}\hat{a}$

- **Localised vector and free vector :** A vector drawn parallel to a given vector through a specified point as the initial point, is known as a localised vector. If the initial point of a vector is not specified it is said to be a free vector.

- **Centroid of a triangle :**

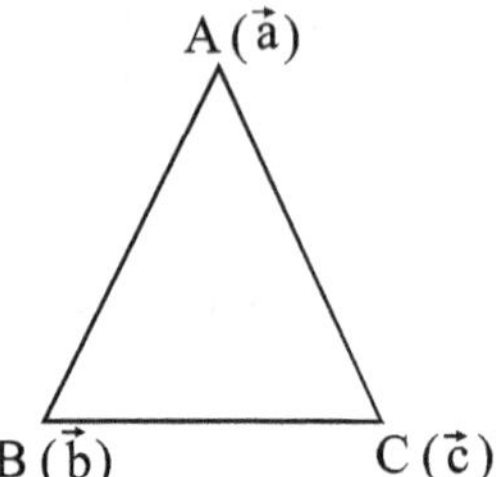

If $\vec{a}$, $\vec{b}$, $\vec{c}$ be P.V.'s of the vertices A, B, C of a triangle ABC respectively, then the P.V. of the centroid G of the triangle is $\dfrac{\vec{a} + \vec{b} + \vec{c}}{3}$.

Also, the P.V. of incentre I of $\triangle$ABC is

$$\dfrac{(BC)\,\vec{a} + (CA)\,\vec{b} + (AB)\,\vec{c}}{BC + CA + AB}$$

and the P.V. of orthocentre of $\triangle$ABC is

$$\dfrac{\vec{a}\,(\tan A) + \vec{b}\,(\tan B) + \vec{c}\,(\tan C)}{\tan A + \tan B + \tan C}.$$

- **Collinearity of three points :**   The necessary and sufficient condition that three points with P.V.'s $\vec{a}$, $\vec{b}$, $\vec{c}$ are collinear is that there exist three scalars x, y, z not all zero such that $x\,\vec{a} + y\,\vec{b} + z\,\vec{c} = 0 \Rightarrow x + y + z = 0$

- **Linear combination of vectors :** A vector $\vec{r}$ is said to be a linear combination of vectors $\vec{a}, \vec{b}, \vec{c}$ ...., etc, if there exist scalars x, y, z,..., etc., such that $\vec{r} = x\vec{a} + y\vec{b} + z\vec{c} + ...$

- **Linearly independent vectors :** A set of non-zero vectors $\vec{a}_1$, $\vec{a}_2$, ... $\vec{a}_n$ is said to be linearly independent, if $x_1\,\vec{a}_1 + x_2\,\vec{a}_2 + ... + x_n\,\vec{a}_n = 0$ $\Rightarrow x_1 = x_2 = ... = x_n = 0.$

- **Linearly dependent vectors :** A set of vectors $\vec{a}_1$, $\vec{a}_2$, ... $\vec{a}_n$ is said to be linearly dependent if there exist scalars x_1, x_2, ..., x_n not all zero such that $x_1\,\vec{a}_1 + x_2\,\vec{a}_2 + ... + x_n\,\vec{a}_n = 0.$

  Three vectors $\vec{a} = a_1\hat{i} + a_2\hat{j} + a_3\hat{k}$, $\vec{b} = b_1\hat{i} + b_2\hat{j} + b_3\hat{k}$ and $\vec{c} = c_1\hat{i} + c_2\hat{j} + c_3\hat{k}$ will be linearly dependent vectors iff

$$\begin{vmatrix} a_1 & a_2 & a_3 \\ b_1 & b_2 & b_3 \\ c_1 & c_2 & c_3 \end{vmatrix} = 0.$$

♦ **Vector triple product :** If $\vec{a}, \vec{b}, \vec{c}$ be any three vectors, then $(\vec{a} \times \vec{b}) \times \vec{c}$ and $\vec{a} \times (\vec{b} \times \vec{c})$ are known as vector triple product. Vector triple product of three vectors is a vector quantity.

❖ $\quad \vec{a} \times (\vec{b} \times \vec{c}) = (\vec{a}.\vec{c})\vec{b} - (\vec{a}.\vec{b})\,\vec{c}$

$\quad (\vec{a} \times \vec{b}) \times \vec{c} = (\vec{a}.\vec{c})\vec{b} - (\vec{b}.\vec{c})\vec{a}$

❖ $\quad$ The vector triple product is not commutative i.e.

$\quad \vec{a} \times (\vec{b} \times \vec{c}) \neq (\vec{a} \times \vec{b}) \times \vec{c}$

♦ $\vec{a}$ and $\vec{b}$ are parallel if and only if $\vec{a} = m\ \vec{b}$ for some non-zero scalar m.

♦ $\vec{a} = |\vec{a}|\hat{a}$

♦ $\vec{r}, \vec{a}, \vec{b}$ are coplanar if and only if $\vec{r} = \alpha\vec{a} + \beta\vec{b}$ for some scalars α and β.

♦ $|\vec{a}+\vec{b}| \leq |\vec{a}| + |\vec{b}|$

$|\vec{a}+\vec{b}| \geq |\vec{a}| - |\vec{b}|$

$|\vec{a}-\vec{b}| \leq |\vec{a}| + |\vec{b}|$

$|\vec{a}-\vec{b}| \geq |\vec{a}| - |\vec{b}|$

♦ Component of a vector $\vec{r}$ in the direction of $\vec{a}$ and perpendicular to $\vec{a}$ are

$$\left(\frac{\vec{r}.\vec{a}}{|\vec{a}|^2}\right)\vec{a} \quad \text{and} \quad \vec{r} - \left\{\frac{(\vec{r}.\vec{a})}{|\vec{a}|^2}\right\}\vec{a} \quad \text{respectively.}$$

♦ The unit vector $\hat{n}$ perpendicular to both $\vec{a}$ and $\vec{b}$ is given by $\hat{n} = \dfrac{(\vec{a} \times \vec{b})}{|\vec{a} \times \vec{b}|}$

♦ Volume of a tetrahedron with three coterminous edges

$$\vec{a}, \vec{b}, \vec{c} = \frac{1}{6}\left|[\vec{a}\ \ \vec{b}\ \ \vec{c}]\right|$$

♦ Volume of prism on a triangular base with three coterminous edges

$$\vec{a}, \vec{b}, \vec{c} = \frac{1}{2}\left|[\vec{a}\ \ \vec{b}\ \ \vec{c}]\right|$$

Direction Cosines and Direction Ratios of a Line

- Recall that if a directed line L passing through the origin makes angles α, β and γ with x, y and z-axes, respectively, called **direction angles**, then cosine of these angles, namely, $\cos \alpha$, $\cos \beta$ and $\cos \gamma$ are called **direction cosines** of the directed line L.

- If we reverse the direction of L, then the direction angles are replaced by their supplements, i.e., $\pi - \alpha, \pi - \beta$ and $\pi - \gamma$. Thus, the signs of the direction cosines are reversed.

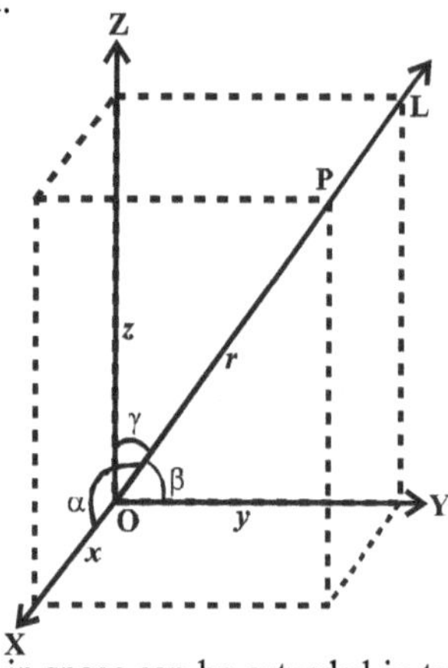

- Note that a given line in space can be extended in two opposite directions and so it has two sets of direction cosines.

- In order to have a unique set of direction cosines for a given line in space, we must take the given line as a directed line.

- These unique direction cosines are denoted by l, m and n.

- Any three numbers which are proportional to the direction cosines of a line are called the **direction ratios** of the line.

- If l, m, n are direction cosines and a, b, c are direction ratios of a line, then $a = \lambda l$, $b = \lambda m$ and $c = \lambda n$, for any non-zero $\lambda \in \mathbf{R}$.

- Let a, b, c be direction ratios of a line and let l, m and n be the direction cosines ($d.c's$) of the line. Then

$$l = \pm \frac{a}{\sqrt{a^2 + b^2 + c^2}}, m = \pm \frac{b}{\sqrt{a^2 + b^2 + c^2}}, n = \pm \frac{c}{\sqrt{a^2 + b^2 + c^2}}$$

Relation between the direction cosines of a line :

◆ Let l, m, n are direction cosines then, $l^2 + m^2 + n^2 = 1$

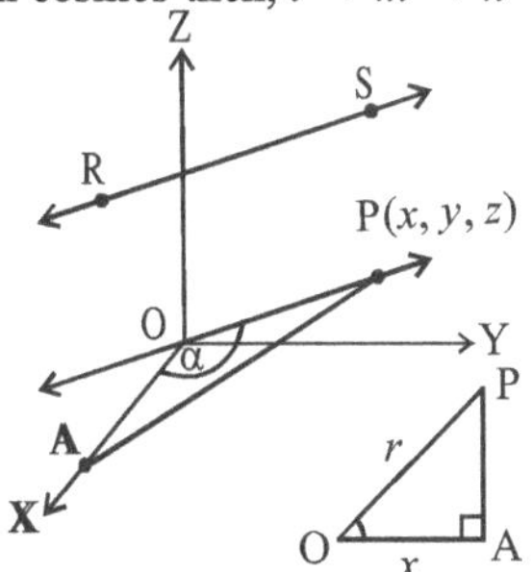

Direction cosines of a line passing through two points :

◆ The direction cosines of the line segment joining the points $P(x_1, y_1, z_1)$ and (x_2, y_2, z_2) are

$$\frac{x_2 - x_1}{PQ}, \frac{y_2 - y_1}{PQ}, \frac{z_2 - z_1}{PQ}$$

$$PQ = \sqrt{(x_2 - x_1)^2 + (y_2 - y_1)^2 + (z_2 - z_1)^2}$$

◆ The direction ratios of the line segment joining $P(x_1, y_1, z_1)$ and $Q(x_2, y_2, z_2)$ may be taken as

$$x_2 - x_1, y_2 - y_1, z_2 - z_1 \text{ or } x_1 - x_2, y_1 - y_2, z_1 - z_2$$

Equation of a Line in Space

◆ A **line** is uniquely determined if
  ❖ It passes through a given point and has given direction,
  ❖ It passes through two given points.

Equation of a line through a given point and parallel to a given vector :

◆ Let l be the line which passes through the point A and is parallel to a given vector $\vec{b}$.

◆ Let $\vec{r}$ be the position vector of an arbitrary point P on the line.

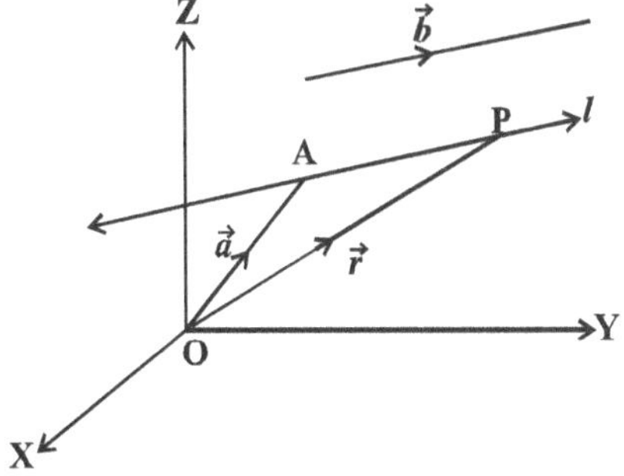

Hence, $\overrightarrow{AP} = \overrightarrow{OP} - \overrightarrow{OA}$

$$\lambda\vec{b} = \vec{r} - \vec{a}$$

$$\vec{r} = \vec{a} + \lambda\vec{b}$$

Cartesian form from vector form :

♦ Let the coordinates of the given point A be (x_1, y_1, z_1) and the direction ratios of the line be a, b, c. Consider the coordinates of any point P be (x, y, z). Then

$$\vec{r} = x\hat{i} + y\hat{j} + z\hat{k} \;;\; \vec{a} + x_1\hat{i} + y\hat{j} + z_1\hat{k}$$

$$\vec{b} = a\hat{i} + b\hat{j} + c\hat{k}$$

$$\frac{x - x_1}{a} = \frac{y - y_1}{b} = \frac{z - z_1}{c}$$

♦ If l, m, n are the direction cosines of the line, the equation of the line is

$$\frac{x - x_1}{l} = \frac{y - y_1}{m} = \frac{z - z_1}{n}$$

Equation of a line passing through two given points :

♦ Let $\vec{a}$ and $\vec{b}$ be the position vectors of two points $A(x_1, y_1, z_1)$ and $B(x_2, y_2, z_2)$, respectively that are lying on a line.

♦ Let $\vec{r}$ be the position vector of an arbitrary point $P(x, y, z)$, then P is a point on the line if and only if $\overrightarrow{AP} = \vec{r} - \vec{a}$ and $\overrightarrow{AP} = \vec{b} - \vec{a}$ are collinear vectors.

♦ Therefore, P is on the line if and only if

$$\vec{r} - \vec{a} = \lambda(\vec{b} - \vec{a})$$

$$\vec{r} = \vec{a} + \lambda(\vec{b} - \vec{a}), \lambda \in R$$

Cartesian form from vector form :

♦ We have $\vec{r} = x\hat{i} + y\hat{j} + z\hat{k}, \vec{a} = x_1\hat{i} + y_1\hat{j} + z_1\hat{k}$ and

$$\vec{b} = x_2\hat{i} + y_2\hat{j} + z_2\hat{k},$$

♦
$$\frac{x - x_1}{x_2 - x_1} = \frac{y - y_1}{y_2 - y_1} = \frac{z - z_1}{z_2 - z_1}$$

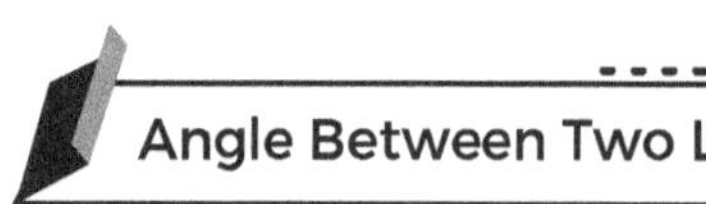

♦ Let L_1 and L_2 be two lines passing through the origin and with direction ratios a_1, b_1, c_1 and a_2, b_2, c_2, respectively.

♦ Let θ be the acute angle between L_1 and L_2.

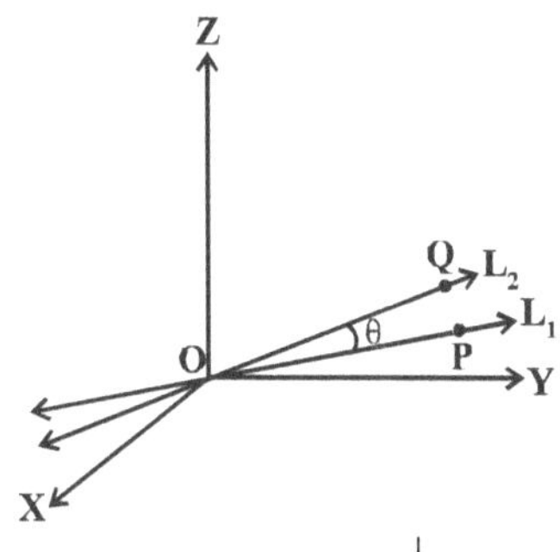

then, $\cos\theta = \left|\dfrac{a_1 a_2 + b_1 b_2 + c_1 c_2}{\sqrt{a_1^2 + b_1^2 + c_1^2}\,\sqrt{a_2^2 + b_2^2 + c_2^2}}\right|$

♦ If direction cosines, l_1, m_1, n_1 for L_1 and l_2, m_2, n_2 for L_2 are given, then
$\cos\theta = |\, l_1 l_2 + m_1 m_2 + n_1 n_2|$

♦ We find the angle between two lines when their equations are given. If θ is acute the angle between the lines

$$\vec{r} = \vec{a_1} + \lambda\, \vec{b_1} \text{ and } \vec{r} = \vec{a_2} + \mu\vec{b_2}$$

then, $\cos\theta = \left|\dfrac{\vec{b_1}\cdot\vec{b_2}}{|\vec{b_1}||\vec{b_2}|}\right|$

Condition of Perpendicularity and Parallelism for Two Lines :

♦ Perpendicular i.e. if $\theta = 90°$

$a_1 a_2 + b_1 b_2 + c_1 c_2 = 0$

♦ Parallel i.e. if $\theta = 0$

$$\dfrac{a_1}{a_2} = \dfrac{b_1}{b_2} = \dfrac{c_1}{c_2}$$

Shortest Distance Between Two Lines

♦ In a space, there are lines which are neither intersecting nor parallel. Such pair of lines are non coplanar and are called **skew lines**.

♦ For skew lines, the line of the shortest distance will be perpendicular to both the lines.

Distance between two skew lines :

♦ We now determine the shortest distance between two skew lines in the following way: Let l_1 and l_2 be two skew lines with equations

$$\vec{r} = \vec{a_1} + \lambda\vec{b_1}$$

$$\vec{r} = \vec{a_2} + \mu\vec{b_2}$$

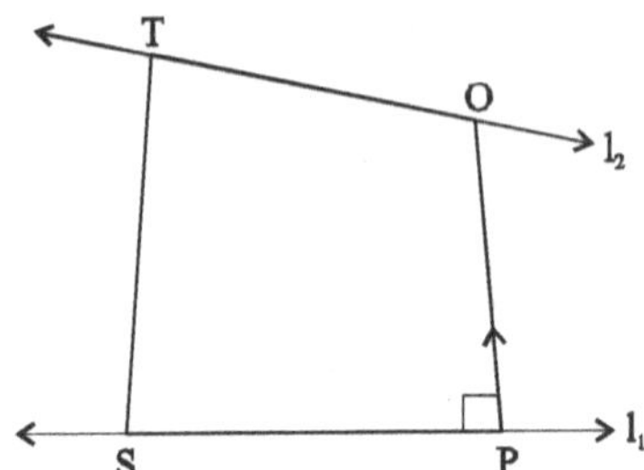

- The required shortest distance is

$$d = \left| \frac{\left(\vec{b_1} \times \vec{b_2}\right) \cdot \left(\vec{a_2} - \vec{a_1}\right)}{\left|\vec{b_1} \times \vec{b_2}\right|} \right|$$

- **Cartesian form :** The shortest distance between the lines

$$\left| \frac{\begin{vmatrix} x_2 - x_1 & y_2 - y_1 & z_2 - z_1 \\ a_1 & b_1 & c_1 \\ a_2 & b_2 & c_2 \end{vmatrix}}{\sqrt{(b_1 c_2 - b_2 c_1)^2 + (c_1 a_2 - c_2 a_1)^2 + (a_1 b_2 - a_2 b_1)^2}} \right|$$

Distance between parallel lines :

- If two lines l_1 and l_2 are parallel, then they are coplanar. Let the lines be given by

$$\vec{r} = \vec{a_1} + \lambda \vec{b}$$
$$\vec{r} = \vec{a_2} + \mu \vec{b}$$

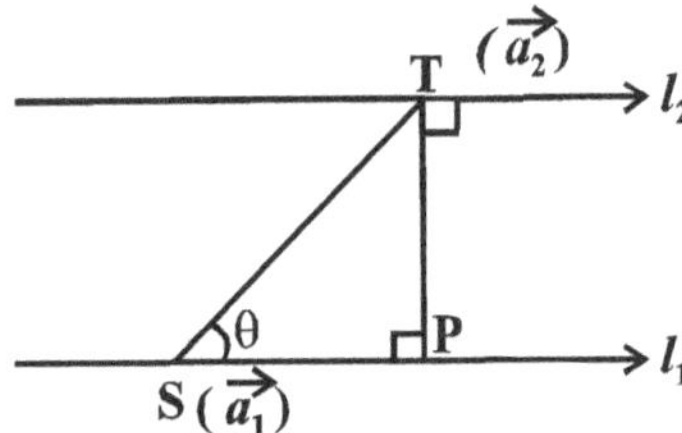

$$d = \left|\vec{PT}\right| = \left| \frac{\vec{b} \times \left(\vec{a_2} - \vec{a_1}\right)}{\vec{b}} \right|$$

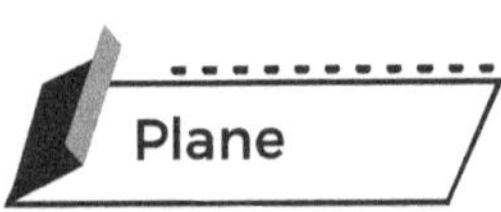

- A **plane** is determined uniquely if any one of the following is known:
    - ❖ The normal to the plane and its distance from the origin is given, i.e., equation of a plane in normal form.

❖   It passes through a point and is perpendicular to a given direction.
❖   It passes through three given non collinear points.

Equation of a plane in normal form :

◆   Let $\vec{r}$ be the position vector of the point P, then

$$\overrightarrow{NP} = \vec{r} - d\hat{n} \ \left(\text{as } \overrightarrow{ON} + \overrightarrow{NP} = \overrightarrow{OP} \right) \text{ Therefore,}$$

$$\left(\vec{r} - d\hat{n} \right) \cdot d\hat{n} = 0 \ \text{ or } \ \vec{r} \cdot \hat{n} = d$$

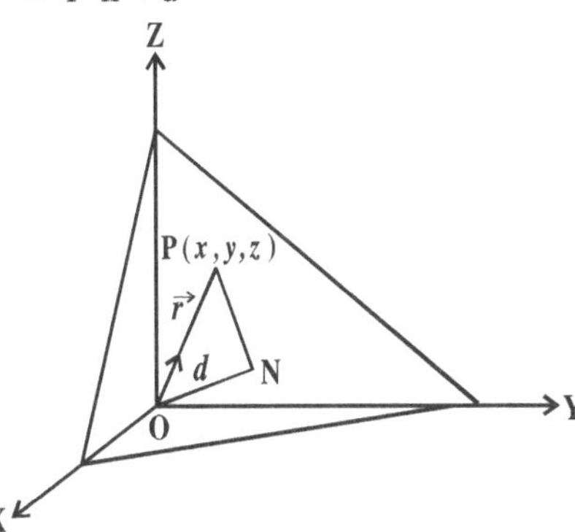

This is the **vector form** of the equation of the plane.

❖   **Cartesian form :** Let P(x, y, z) be any point on the plane. Then

$$\overrightarrow{OP} = \vec{r} = x\vec{i} + y\vec{j} + z\vec{k}$$

Let l, m, n be the direction cosines of $\hat{n}$. Then

$$\hat{n} = l\hat{i} + m\hat{j} + n\hat{k}$$

$$\left(x\hat{i} + y\hat{j} + z\hat{k} \right) \cdot \left(l\hat{i} + m\hat{j} + n\hat{k} \right) = d$$

$$lx + my + nz = d$$

This is the **cartesian** equation of the plane in the **normal form**.

Equation of a plane perpendicular to a given vector and passing through a given point :

◆   Let $\vec{r}$ be the position vector of any point P(x, y, z) in the plane. Then the point

P lies in the plane if and only if $\overrightarrow{AP}$ is perpendicular to $\vec{N}$. i.e., $\overrightarrow{AP} \cdot \vec{N} = 0$

This is the **vector** equation of the plane.

❖   **Cartesian form :** Let the given point A be (x_1, y_1, z_1), P be (x, y, z) and

direction ratios of $\vec{N}$ are A, B and C. Then,

$$\vec{a} = x_1 \hat{i} + y_1 \hat{j} + z_1 \hat{k}, \vec{r} = x \hat{i} + y \hat{j} + z \hat{k}$$

and $\vec{N} = A\hat{i} + B\hat{j} + C\hat{k}$

$$\left(\vec{r} - \vec{a} \right) \cdot \vec{N} = 0$$

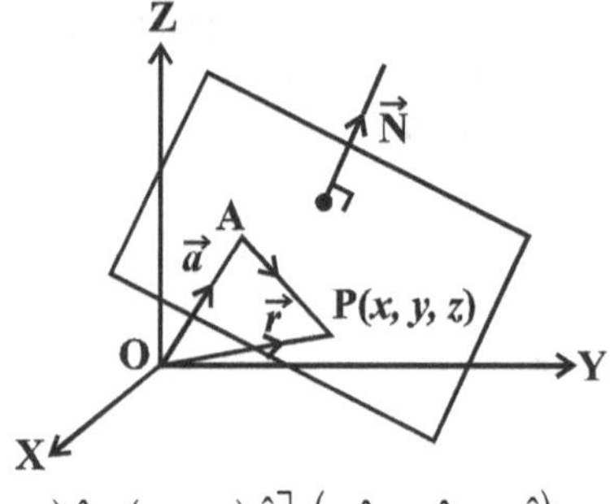

$$\left[(x-x_1)\hat{i}+(y-y_1)\hat{j}+(z-z_1)\hat{k}\right]\cdot\left(A\hat{i}+B\hat{j}+C\hat{k}\right)=0$$

$$A(x-x_1)+B(y-y_1)+C(z-z_1)=0$$

Equation of a plane passing through three non collinear points :

♦   Let R, S and T be three non collinear points on the plane with position vectors

$\vec{a},\vec{b}$ and $\vec{c}$ respectively.

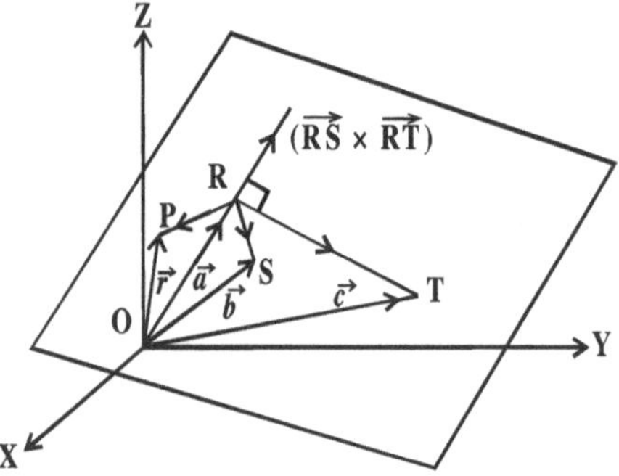

♦   Let $\vec{r}$ be the position vector of any point P in the plane.

♦   The equation of the plane passing through R and perpendicular to the vector

$\overrightarrow{RS}\times\overrightarrow{RT}$ is

$$(\vec{r}-\vec{a})\cdot\left[(\vec{b}-\vec{a})\times(\vec{c}-\vec{a})\right]=0$$

❖   **Cartesian form :** Let $(x_1,\ y_1,\ z_1)$, $(x_2,\ y_2,\ z_2)$ and (x_3,y_3,z_3) be the coordinates of the points R, S and T respectively. Let $(x,$ $y, z)$ be the coordinates of any point P on the plane with position vector $\vec{r}$. Then

$$\begin{vmatrix} x-x_1 & y-y_1 & z-z_1 \\ x_2-x_1 & y_2-y_1 & z_2-z_1 \\ x_3-x_1 & y_3-y_1 & z_3-z_1 \end{vmatrix}=0$$

Intercept form of the equation of a plane :

◆ Let the plane make intercepts a, b, c on x, y and z axes, respectively. Hence, the plane meets x, y and z-axes at (a, 0, 0), (0, 0, c), respectively. Therefore,

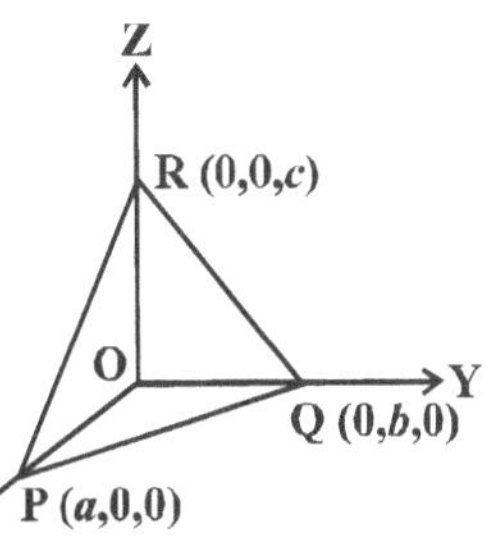

$$\frac{x}{a}+\frac{y}{b}+\frac{z}{c}=1$$

Plane passing through the intersection of two given planes L:

◆ Let P_1 and P_2 be two planes with equations $\vec{r}\cdot\hat{n}_1 = d_1$ and $\vec{r}\cdot\hat{n}_2 = d_2$ respectively.

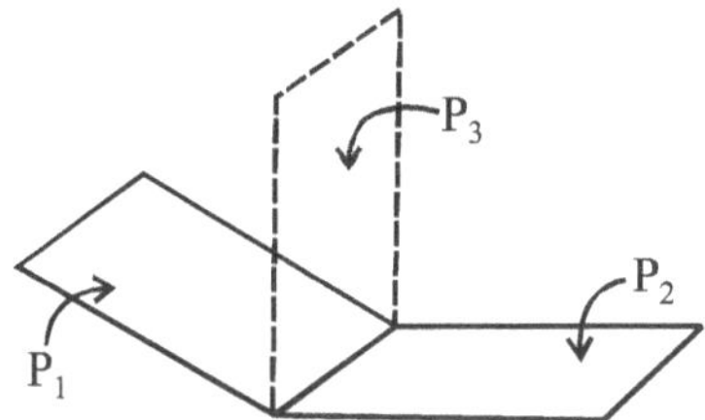

Then, any plane passing through the intersection of the planes

$$\vec{r}\cdot\hat{n}_1 = d_1 \text{ and } \vec{r}\cdot\hat{n}_2 = d_2$$

has the equation $\vec{r}\cdot(\vec{n}_1 +\lambda\vec{n}_2) = d_1 +\lambda d_2$

❖ **Cartesian form :** In Cartesian system,

$$\left(A_1 x+ B_1 y+ C_1 z - d_1\right)+\lambda\left(A_2 x+ B_2 y+ C_2 z - d_2\right)= 0$$

Coplanarity of Two Lines

◆ Let the given lines be

$$\vec{r} = \vec{a}_1 +\lambda\vec{b}_1 \text{ and } \vec{r} = \vec{a}_2 +\mu\vec{b}_2$$

Hence, $\left(\vec{a}_2 -\vec{a}_1\right)\cdot\left(\vec{b}_1 \times\vec{b}_2\right)=0$

❖ **Cartesian form :**

- Let (x_1, y_1, z_1) and (x_2, y_2, z_2) be the coordinates of the points A and B respectively.

- Let a_1, b_1, c_1 and a_2, b_2, c_2 be the direction ratios of $\vec{b}_1$ and $\vec{b}_2$, respectively. Then

$$\begin{vmatrix} x_2 - x_1 & y_2 - y_1 & z_2 - z_1 \\ a_1 & b_1 & c_1 \\ a_2 & b_2 & c_2 \end{vmatrix} = 0$$

Angle Between Two Planes

- The **angle between two planes** is defined as the angle between their normals.
- If $\vec{n}_1$ and $\vec{n}_2$ are normals to the planes and be the angle between the planes $\vec{r} \cdot \vec{n}_1 = d_1$ and $\vec{r} \cdot \vec{n}_2 = d_2$.

We have, $\cos\theta = \left| \dfrac{\vec{n}_1 \cdot \vec{n}_2}{\|\vec{n}_1\|\|\vec{n}_2\|} \right|$

- The planes are perpendicular to each other if $\vec{n}_1 . \vec{n}_2 = 0$ and parallel if $\vec{n}_1$ is parallel to $\vec{n}_2$.

  ❖ **Cartesian form :** Let θ be the angle between the planes,

  $$A_1 x + B_1 y \, C_1 z + D_1 = 0$$

  and $A_2 x + B_2 y + C_2 z + D_2 = 0$

  Therefore, $\cos\theta = \left| \dfrac{A_1 A_2 + B_1 B_2 + C_1 C_2}{\sqrt{A_1^2 + B_1^2 + C_1^2}\sqrt{A_2^2 + B_2^2 + C_2^2}} \right|$

- If the planes are at right angles, then $\theta = 90°$ and so $\cos\theta = 0$. Hence, $\cos\theta = A_1 A_2 + B_1 B_2 + C_1 C_2 = 0$.

- If the planes are parallel, then $\dfrac{A_1}{A_2} = \dfrac{B_1}{B_2} = \dfrac{C_1}{C_2}$.

Distance of a Point from a Plane

Vector form :

- Let the equation of the plane P, is in the form $\vec{r} \cdot \vec{N} = d$, where $\vec{N}$ is normal to the plane, then the perpendicular distance is $\dfrac{|\vec{a} . \vec{N} - d|}{|\vec{N}|}$

- The length of the perpendicular from origin O to the plane $\vec{r} \cdot \vec{N} = d$ is $\dfrac{|d|}{|\vec{N}|}$

  (since $\vec{a} = 0$)

❖ **Certesian form :**

Let $P(x_1, y_1, z_1)$ be the given point with position vector $\vec{a}$ and
$$Ax + By + Cz = D$$
be the Cartesian equation of the given plane. Then

$$= \left| \frac{Ax_1 + By_1 + Cz_1 - D}{\sqrt{A^2 + B^2 + C^2}} \right|$$

Angle Between a Line and a Plane

♦ The angle between a line and a plane is the complement of the angle between
the line and normal to the plane.

♦ Vector form $\vec{r} = \vec{a} + \lambda\vec{b}$ and the equation of the plane is $\vec{r} \cdot \vec{n} = d$. Then the

angle between the line and the normal to the plane is $\cos\theta = \left| \dfrac{\vec{b} \cdot \vec{n}}{|\vec{b}| \cdot |\vec{n}|} \right|$

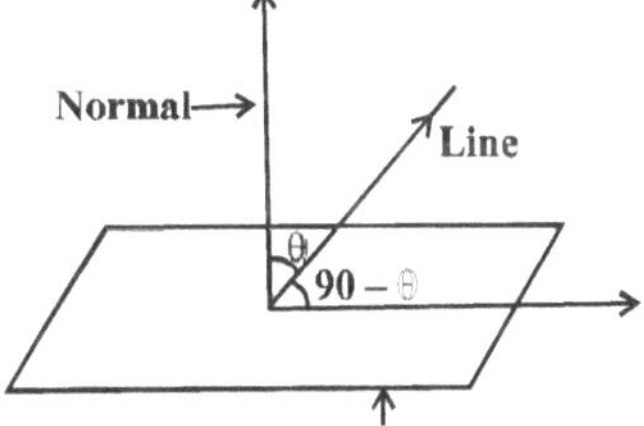

and so the angle ϕ between the line and the plane is given by $90 - \theta$, i.e., $\sin(90 - \theta) = \cos\theta$

$$\sin\phi = \left| \frac{\vec{b} \cdot \vec{n}}{|\vec{b}||\vec{n}|} \right| \text{ or } \phi = \sin^{-1} \left| \frac{\vec{b} \cdot \vec{n}}{|\vec{b}||\vec{n}|} \right|$$

Past Years ONE-LINERS
JEE Main/Board

♦ For coplanarity of two lines $\dfrac{x - x_1}{a_1} = \dfrac{y - y_1}{b_1} = \dfrac{z - z_1}{c_1}$ and

$\dfrac{x - x_2}{a_2} = \dfrac{y - y_2}{b_2} = \dfrac{z - z_2}{c_2}$. Use concept $\begin{vmatrix} x_2 - x_1 & y_2 - y_1 & z_2 - z_1 \\ a_1 & b_1 & c_1 \\ a_2 & b_2 & c_2 \end{vmatrix} = 0$

♦ To find image of a point (x_1, y_1, z_1) in a plane is given as

$$\frac{x - x_1}{a} = \frac{y - y_1}{b} = \frac{z - z_1}{c}$$

$$= \frac{-2(ax_1 + by_1 + cz_1 + d)}{a^2 + b^2 + c^2}$$

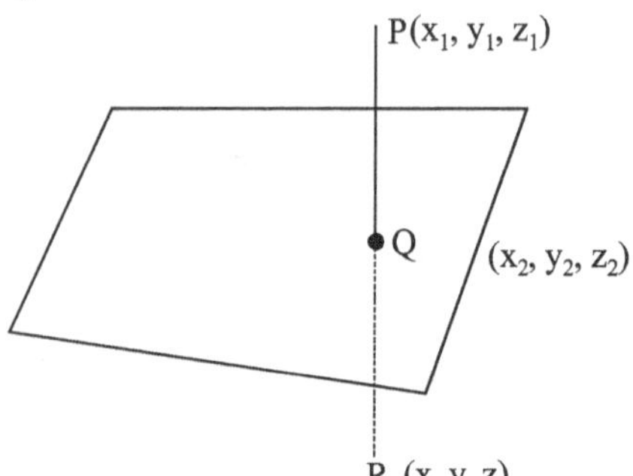

♦ To find the plane passing through the intersections of two plane P_1 and P_2, we use concept $P_1 + \lambda P_2 = 0$

♦ To get projection of a line segment joining two points on a line

Let $P = (x_1, y_1, z_1)$ and

$Q = (x_2, y_2, z_2)$

Let Direction cosines as

l, m, n then

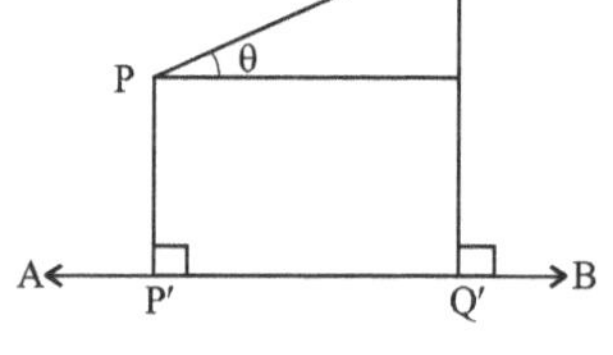

$$P'Q' = (x_2 - x_1)l + (y_2 - y_1)m + (z_2 - z_1)n$$

♦ Distance of a point from the plane is given in cartesian form as, let a point p

(x_1, y_1, z_1) and let a plane $ax + by + cz + d = 0$ then distance is $\left| \dfrac{ax_1 + by_1 + cz_1 + d}{\sqrt{a^2 + b^2 + c^2}} \right|$

Tips/Tricks/Techniques ONE-LINERS
(Exam Special)

♦ **Projection of a line segment joining two points on a line :**

Let PQ be a line segment where $P \equiv (x_1, y_1, z_1)$ and
$Q \equiv (x_2, y_2, z_2)$; and AB be a given line with dc's as ℓ, m, n.
If P' and Q' are the foot of perpendicular from P and Q to the line AB, then P'Q' is the projection of PQ on the line AB.

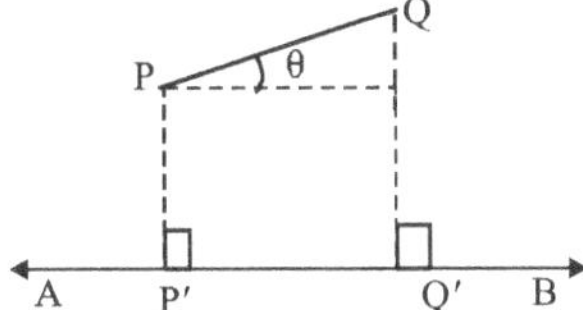

If the line segment PQ makes angle θ with the line AB, then projection of PQ on line AB is P'Q' = PQ cos θ. On replacing the value of cos θ in this, we shall get the following value of P'Q'.

P'Q' = $\ell(x_2 - x_1) + m(y_2 - y_1) + n(z_2 - z_1)$, where l, m, n are direction cosines of line AB.

♦ **Bisectors of the angles between two lines :**

The equation of the bisectors of the angle between the straight lines $\vec{r} = \vec{a} + \lambda\vec{b}$ and $\vec{r} = \vec{a} + r\vec{c}$ are given by

$$\vec{r} = \vec{a} + t\left\{\frac{\vec{b}}{|\vec{b}|} \pm \frac{\vec{c}}{|\vec{c}|}\right\}, \text{ where } t \in R.$$

♦ **Equation of the planes bisecting angles between two lanes :**
   ❖ **Vector form :** Equation of the planes bisecting the angle between planes
      $\vec{r} \cdot \vec{n}_1 = d_1$ and $\vec{r} \cdot \vec{n}_2 = d_2$ is

$$\left|\frac{\vec{r} \cdot \vec{n}_1 - d_1}{\vec{n}_1}\right| = \left|\frac{\vec{r} \cdot \vec{n}_2 - d_2}{\vec{n}_2}\right|$$

   ❖ **Cartesian form :** Equation of the planes bisecting the angles between the planes $a_1x + b_1y + c_1y + d_1 = 0$ and $a_2x + b_2y + c_2y + d_2 = 0$ is

$$\frac{a_1x + b_1y + c_1z + d_1}{\sqrt{a_1^2 + b_1^2 + c_1^2}} = \pm\frac{a_2x + b_2y + c_2z + d_2}{\sqrt{a_2^2 + b_2^2 + c_2^2}}$$

♦ **Bisector of the angle between the two planes containing the origin :** Let the equation of the two planes be
   $a_1x + b_1y + c_1z + d_1 = 0$ ...(i)
   and $a_2x + b_2y + c_2z + d_2 = 0$ ...(ii)
   Here d_1 and d_2 are positive.
   The equation of the bisector of the angle between the planes (i) and (ii) containing the origin is

$$\frac{a_1x + b_1y + c_1z + d_1}{\sqrt{a_1^2 + b_1^2 + c_1^2}} = \frac{a_2x + b_2y + c_2z + d_2}{\sqrt{a_2^2 + b_2^2 + c_2^2}}$$

♦ **Distance between two parallel planes :** Distance between two parallel planes $ax + by + cz + d_1 = 0$ and $ax + by + cz + d_2 = 0$ is given by

$$d = \left|\frac{d_2 - d_1}{\sqrt{a^2 + b^2 + c^2}}\right|$$

♦ **Ratio of division of a line segment by a plane :** The ratio in which the line segment PQ, joining $P(x_1, y_1, z_1)$ and $Q(x_2, y_2, z_2)$, is divided by plane ax + by + cz + d = 0 is $-\left(\dfrac{ax_1 + by_1 + cz_1 + d}{ax_2 + by_2 + cz_2 + d}\right)$.

♦ For x-axis, $\ell = 1$, m = 0, n = 0, hence
Projection of PQ on x-axis $= 1.(x_2 - x_1) + 0 + 0 = x_2 - x_1$
Projection of PQ on y-axis $= y_2 - y_1$
Projection of PQ on z-axis $= z_2 - z_1$

♦ $\because PQ^2 = (x_2 - x_1)^2 + (y_2 - y_1)^2 + (z_2 - z_1)^2$
= the sum of the squares of the projection of PQ on coordinate axes
$\therefore$ If a, b, c are the projections of a line segment on coordinate axes, then length of the segment $= \sqrt{a^2 + b^2 + c^2}$

♦ If a, b, c are projections of a line segment on coordinate axes then its dc's are
$$\pm\frac{a}{\sqrt{a^2 + b^2 + c^2}}, \pm\frac{b}{\sqrt{a^2 + b^2 + c^2}}, \pm\frac{c}{\sqrt{a^2 + b^2 + c^2}}$$

♦ The x-axis makes angles of $0, \dfrac{\pi}{2}, \dfrac{\pi}{2}$ with the axes of x, y, z respectively. So, the direction cosines of the x-axis are 1, 0, 0. Similarly the direction cosines of the y-axis and z-axis are respectively 0, 1, 0 and 0, 0, 1.

♦ If l, m, n are direction cosines of a line OP and (x, y, z) are the coordinates of P, then x = lr, y = mr and z = nr, where r = OP.

♦ Direction cosines of a line are unique but the direction ratios of a line are not unique. If a, b, c are the direction ratios of a line, then ka, kb, kc are also direction ratios of that line where k is any non-zero real number.

♦ The equation of plane contains only three independent constants, because, the equation may be reduced to
px + qy + rz + 1 = 0 by dividing by d, and $\dfrac{a}{d} = p$ etc.
If the plane passes through origin, d = 0. Hence, the equation reduces to ax + by + cz = 0.

28. Linear Programming

Linear Programming Problem and Its Mathematical Formulation

- The term **linear** implies that all the mathematical relations used in the problem are linear relations while the term **programming** refers to the method of determining a particular programme or plan of action.
- **Linear Programming Problem** is one that is concerned with finding the optimal value (maximum or minimum value) of a linear function (called objective function) of several variables (say x and y), subject to the conditions that the variables are non-negative and satisfy a set of linear inequalities (called linear constraints).

Terms Used in Linear Programming Problem:

- **Objective function** Linear function $Z = ax + by$, where a, b are constants, which has to be maximised or minimized is called a **linear objective function**.
- **Constraints:** The linear inequalities or equations or restrictions on the variables of a linear programming problem are called **constraints**.
- **Non-negative Constraints:** The conditions $x \geq 0, y \geq 0$ are called **non-negative** restrictions **(constraints)**.
- Variables are sometimes called decision variables.
- **Optimisation problem:** A problem which seeks to maximise or minimise a linear function (say of two variables x and y) subject to certain constraints as determined by a set of linear inequalities is called an **optimisation problem**.

Mathematical formulation of the problem :

- Formulation of LPP refers to translating the real-world problem into the form of mathematical equations which could be solved.

Steps towards formulating a Linear Programming problem:

- **Step 1:** Identify the decision variables which govern the behaviour of the objective function (which needs to be optimized).
- **Step 2 :** Write the objective function.
  Maximize (or minimize) $Z = ax + by$
- **Step 3 :** Writing the constraints.
  Subject to

$$a_1x + b_1y \,(\le, =, \ge)\, c_1$$
$$a_2x + b_2y \,(\le, =, \ge)\, c_2$$
$$a_3x + b_3y \,(\le, =, \ge)\, c_3$$

- ♦ **Step 4 :** The non-negativity restriction.
  $$x, y \ge 0$$

Graphical method of solving linear programming problems

The following Theorems are fundamental in solving linear programming problems:

- ♦ **Theorem 1:** Let R be the feasible region (convex polygon) for a linear programming problem and let $Z = ax + by$ be the objective function. When Z has an optimal value (maximum or minimum), where the variables x and y are subject to constraints described by linear inequalities, this optimal value must occur at a corner point (vertex) of the feasible region.

- ♦ **Theorem 2:** Let R be the feasible region for a linear programming problem, and let $Z = ax + by$ be the objective function. If R is **bounded,** then the objective function Z has both a **maximum** and a **minimum** value on R and each of these occurs at a corner point (vertex) of R.

- ♦ If the feasible region is unbounded, then a maximum or a minimum may not exist. However, if it exists, it must occur at a corner point of R.

- ♦ A **corner point** of a feasible region is a point in the region which is the intersection of two boundary lines.

- ♦ A feasible region of a system of linear inequalities is said to be **bounded** if it can be enclosed within a circle. Otherwise, it is called **unbounded**. Unbounded means that the feasible region does extend indefinitely in any direction.

Corner Point Method for solving linear programming problem.

The method comprises of the following steps:

- ♦ **Step 1:** Plot the graph of the inequalities describing the various constraints on the graph paper.

- ♦ **Step 2:** Find the feasible region of the linear programming problem and determine its corner points (vertices).

- ♦ **Step 3:** Evaluate the objective function $Z = ax + by$ at each corner point. Let M and m respectively be the largest and smallest values at these points.

- ♦ **Step 4:** If the feasible region is bounded, M and m respectively are the maximum and minimum values of the objective function. If the feasible region is unbounded, then

  - ❖ M is the maximum value of the objective function, if the open half plane determined by $ax + by > M$ has no point in common with the feasible region. Otherwise, the objective function has no maximum value.

  - ❖ m is the minimum value of the objective function, if the open half plane determined by $ax + by < m$ has no point in common with the feasible region. Otherwise, the objective function has no minimum value.

- ♦ The common region determined by all the constraints including non-negative constraints $x \ge 0$, $y \ge 0$ of a linear programming problem is called the **feasible region** (or **solution region**) for the problem.

- Points within and on the boundary of the feasible region represent **feasible solutions** of the constraints. Any point outside the feasible region is called **an infeasible solution**.
- Any point in the feasible region that gives the optimal value (maximum or minimum) of the objective function is called an **optimal solution**.
- If two corner points of the feasible region are both optimal solutions of the same type, i.e., both produce the same maximum or minimum, then any point on the line segment joining these two points is also an optimal solution of the same type.

Different Types of Linear Programming Problems

A few important linear programming problems are listed below:
- **Manufacturing problems:** In these problems, we determine the number of units of different products which should be produced and sold by a firm when each product requires a fixed manpower, machine hours, labour hour per unit of product, warehouse space per unit of the output etc., in order to make maximum profit.
- **Diet problems:** In these problems, we determine the amount of different kinds of constituents/nutrients which should be included in a diet so as to minimise the cost of the desired diet such that it contains a certain minimum amount of each constituent/nutrients.
- **Transportation problems:** In these problems, we determine a transportation schedule in order to find the cheapest way of transporting a product from plants/factories situated at different locations to different markets.

Past Years ONE-LINERS
JEE Main/Board

- If feasible region is bounded by $ax + by + c = 0$. x-axis and y-axis and maximum value of objective function $Z = Ax + By$ is K then for solution with feasible region, $ax + by + c = 0$ and $Ax + By = k$ must have atleast one positive solution.

Tips/Tricks/Techniques ONE-LINERS
(Exam Special)

- The term linear implies that all the mathematical relations used in the problem are linear relations.
- The term programming refers to the method of determining a particular programme or plan of action.
- A corner point of a feasible region is the point of intersection of two boundary lines, which form the region.
- A feasible region of a given system of linear inequalities is said to be bounded if it can be enclosed. Otherwise, it is unbounded. Unbounded means that the feasible region may extend indefinitely in any direction.
- The feasible region is always a convex region.
- Basic Feasible Solution A BFS is a basic solution which also satisfies the non-negativity restrictions.
- Optimum Basis Feasible Solution A BFS is said to be optimum, if it also optimizes (Max or min) the objective function.
- The maximum (or minimum) solution of the objective function occurs at the vertex (corner) of the feasible region.
- If two corner points produce the same maximum (or minimum) value of the objective function, then every point on the line segemnt joining these points will also give the same maximum (or minimum) value.

29 — Probability-2

Conditional Probability

- The probability of the event E is called the conditional probability of E given that F has already occurred, and is denoted by P (E|F).
  i.e. P (E|F) is given by

$$P(E|F)=\frac{P(E \cap F)}{P(F)} \text{ provided } P(F) \neq 0$$

Properties of conditional probability

- **Property 1:** Let E and F be events of a sample space S of an experiment, then we have $P(S|F) = P(F|F) = 1$.
- **Property 2:** If A and B are any two events of a sample space S and F is an event of S such that $P(F) \neq 0$, then
  $$P((A \cup B)|F) = P(A|F) + P(B|F) - P((A \cap B)|F)$$
- In particular, if A and B are disjoint events, then
  $$P((A \cup B)|F) = P(A|F) + P(B|F) \qquad (\because P(A \cap B|F) = 0)$$
- **Property 3:** Let E and F be the events of sample spaces of an experiment, then we have $P(E'|F) = 1 - P(E|F)$

Multiplication Theorem on Probability

Multiplication rule of probability for two events:

- Let E and F be two events associated with a sample space S. Clearly, the set $E \cap F$ denotes the event that both E and F have occurred. The event $E \cap F$ is also written as EF.
- The probability of event EF is obtained by using the conditional probability as obtained below :
  $$P(EF) = P(E \cap F) = P(E)\, P(F|E) \text{ provided } P(E) \neq 0$$
  $$= P(F)\, P(E|F) \text{ provided } P(F) \neq 0.$$
  The above result is known as the **multiplication rule of probability.**

Multiplication rule of probability for more than two events:

- If E, F and G are three events of sample space, we have

  $P(E \cap F \cap G) = P(E)\,P(F|E)\,P(G|(E \cap F)) = P(E)\,P(F|E)\,P(G|EF)$

Independent Events

- **Independent Events:** E and F are two events such that the probability of occurrence of one of them is not affected by occurrence of the other. Such events are called **independent events**

- Two events E and F are said to be independent, if

  $P(F|E) = P(F)$ provided $P(E) \neq 0$

  $P(E|F) = P(E)$ provided $P(F) \neq 0$

- Thus, by the multiplication rule of probability, we have

  $P(E \cap F) = P(E) \cdot P(F)$

  ❖ Two events E and F are said to be **dependent** if they are not independent, i.e. if

  $P(E \cap F) \neq P(E) \cdot P(F)$

  ❖ Sometimes there is a confusion between independent events and mutually exclusive events. Term 'independent' is defined in terms of 'probability of events' whereas mutually exclusive is defined in term of events (subset of sample space). Moreover, mutually exclusive events never have an outcome common, but independent events, may have common outcome. Clearly, 'independent' and 'mutually exclusive' do not have the same meaning.

  ❖ Three events A, B and C are said to be mutually independent, if

  $$P(A \cap B) = P(A)\,P(B)$$
  $$P(A \cap C) = P(A)\,P(C)$$
  $$P(B \cap C) = P(B)\,P(C)$$

  and $\quad P(A \cap B \cap C) = P(A)\,P(B)\,P(C)$

  If at least one of the above is not true for three given events, we say that the events are not independent.

Bayes' Theorem

Partition of a sample space:

- A set of events $E_1, E_2, ..., E_n$ is said to represent a partition of the sample space S if

  (a) $E_i \cap E_j = \phi,\, i \neq j,\, i, j = 1, 2, 3, ..., n$

  (b) $E_1 \cup E_2 \cup .... \cup E_n = S$ and

  (c) $P(E_i) > 0$ for all $i = 1, 2, ..., n.$

- In other words, the events E_1, E_2, ..., E_n represent a partition of the sample space S if they are pairwise disjoint, exhaustive and have nonzero probabilities.

Theorem of total probability:

- Let $\{E_1, E_2, ..., E_n\}$ be a partition of the sample space S, and suppose that each of the events E_1, E_2, ..., E_n has nonzero probability of occurrence. Let A be any event associated with S, then

$$P(A) = P(E_1) P(A|E_1) + P(E_2) P(A|E_2) + ... + P(E_n) P(A|E_n)$$

$$= \sum_{j=1}^{n} P(E_j) P(A|E_j)$$

Bayes' Theorem

- If E_1, E_2, ..., E_n are n non empty events which constitute a partition of sample space S, i.e. E_1, E_2, ..., E_n are pairwise disjoint and $E_1 \cup E_2 \cup ... \cup E_n = S$ and A is any event of nonzero probability, then

$$P(E_i|A) = \frac{P(E_i)P(A|E_i)}{\sum_{j=i}^{n} P(E_j)P(A|E_j)} \quad \text{for any } i = 1, 2, 3, ... n$$

- **Note:** The following terminology is generally used when Bayes' theorem is applied.
  - The events E_1, E_2, ..., E_n are called **hypotheses**.
  - The probability $P(E_i)$ is called the **priori probability** of the hypothesis E_i.
  - The conditional probability $P(E_i|A)$ is called a **posteriori probability** of the hypothesis E_i.
  - **Bayes' theorem** is also called the formula for the probability of "causes".

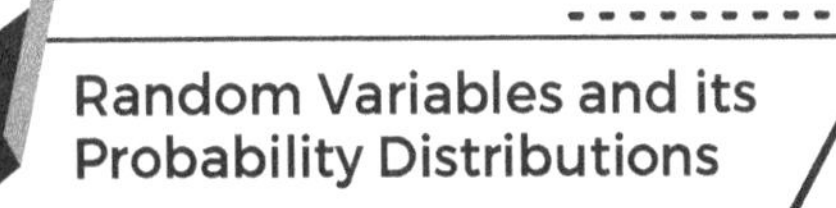

- A rule which assigns to each outcome of the experiment a single real number. This single real number may vary with different outcomes of the experiment. Hence, it is a variable. Also its value depends upon the outcome of a random experiment and, hence, is called **random variable**. A random variable is usually denoted by **X**.

- **Random variable:** A random variable is a real valued function whose domain is the sample space of a random experiment.

Probability distribution of a random variable:

- In general, the probability distribution of a random variable X is defined as follows:

X	x_1	x_2	....	x_n
P(X)	p_1	p_2	....	p_n

where, $\quad p_i > 0, \; \sum\limits_{i=1}^{n} p_i = 1, i = 1, 2....n$

♦ The real numbers $x_1, x_2,..., x_n$ are the possible values of the random variable X and p_i $(i = 1, 2,..., n)$ is the probability of the random variable X taking the value x_i i.e., $P(X = x_i) = p_i$

♦ **Note:** If x_i is one of the possible values of a random variable X, the statement $X = x_i$ is true only at some point(s) of the sample space. Hence, the probability that X takes value x_i is always nonzero, i.e. $P(X = x_i) \neq 0$.

♦ Also for all possible values of the random variable X, all elements of the sample space are covered. Hence, the sum of all the probabilities in a probability distribution must be one.

Mean of a random variable:

♦ Let X be a random variable whose possible values $x_1, x_2, x_3, ..., x_n$ occur with probabilities $p_1, p_2, p_3,..., p_n$, respectively. The mean of X, denoted by μ, is the number

$$\sum_{i=1}^{n} x_i p_i$$

♦ The mean of a random variable X is also called the **expectation** of X, denoted by **E(X).**

Thus, $E(X) = \mu = \sum\limits_{i=1}^{n} x_i p_i = x_1 p_1 + x_2 p_2 + ... + x_n p_n$.

♦ In other words, the mean or expectation of a random variable X is the sum of the products of all possible values of X by their respective probabilities.

Variance of a random variable:

♦ Let X be a random variable whose possible values $x_1, x_2,..., x_n$ occur with probabilities $p(x_1), p(x_2),..., p(x_n)$ respectively.

Let $\mu = E(X)$ be the mean of X. The **variance** of X, denoted by **Var (X)** or σ_x^2 is defined as,

$$\sigma_x^2 = \text{Var}(X) = \sum_{i=1}^{n} (x_i - \mu)^2 \, p(x_i)$$

or equivalently $\sigma_x^2 = E(X - \mu)^2$

♦ The non-negative number

$$\sigma_x = \sqrt{\text{Var}(X)} = \sqrt{\sum_{i-1}^{n} (x_i - \mu)^2 \, p(x_i)}$$

is called the **standard deviation** of the random variable X.

♦ Another formula to find the variance of a random variable,

$$\text{Var}(X) = E(X^2) - [E(X)]^2, \text{ where } E(X^2) = \sum_{i-1}^{n} x_i^2\, p(x_i)$$

Bernoulli Trials and Binomial Distribution

Bernoulli trials:

♦ Trials of a random experiment are called **Bernoulli trials**, if they satisfy the following conditions :
  ❖ There should be a finite number of trials.
  ❖ The trials should be independent.
  ❖ Each trial has exactly two outcomes : success or failure.
  ❖ The probability of success remains the same in each trial.

♦ The outcome of any trial is independent of the outcome of any other trial. In each of such trials, the probability of success or failure remains constant.

♦ **Probability of success** is denoted by p while probability of Failure is denoted by q where q = 1 − p.

Binomial distribution:

♦ The probability of x successes in n-Bernoulli trials is

$$\frac{n!}{x!(n-x)!}p^x q^{n-x} \text{ or } {}^nC_x p^x q^{n-x}$$

Thus $P(x \text{ successes}) = {}^nC_x p^x q^{n-x}, x = 0, 1, 2,..., n. \ (q = 1 - p)$

♦ The probability distribution of number of successes in an experiment consisting of n Bernoulli trials may be obtained by the binomial expansion of $(q + p)^n$. Hence, this distribution of number of successes X can be written as

X	0	1	2	...	x	...	n
$P(X)$	${}^nC_0 q^n$	${}^nC_1 q^{n-1}p^1$	${}^nC_2 q^{n-2}p^2$		${}^nC_x q^{n-x}p^x$		${}^nC_n p^n$

The above probability distribution is known as **binomial distribution** with parameters n and p, because for given values of n and p, we can find the complete probability distribution.

♦ The probability of x successes $P(X = x)$ is also denoted by $P(x)$ and is given by $P(x) = {}^nC_x q^{n-x}p^x, x = 0, 1,..., n. \ (q = 1 - p)$. This $P(x)$ is called the **probability function** of the binomial distribution.

♦ A **binomial distribution** with n-Bernoulli trials and probability of success in each trial as p, is denoted by **B(n, p).**

Past Years ONE-LINERS
JEE Main/Board

- Conditional property $\Rightarrow P(E/F) = \dfrac{P(E \cap F)}{P(F)}$

  Probability of success, $P(x \text{ successes}) = {}^nC_x p^x q^{n-x}$ where $q = 1 - p$

- Expected value of X,

$$E(X) = \sum_{i=1}^{n} x_i P_i = x_1 P_1 + x_2 P_2 + \ldots + x_n P_n$$

- Probability of happening at least one of them,

$$P = P(A_1 \cup A_2 \cup A_3 \ldots A_n) = 1 - P\, P(A_1 U A_2 U A_3 \ldots A_n)$$
$$= 1 - P(\overline{A_1})P(\overline{A_2})P(\overline{A_3})\ldots P(\overline{A_n})$$
$$P = 1 - (1 - P_1)(1 - P_2)(1 - P_3) \ldots (1 - P_n)$$

- Multiplication Theorem on probability,

  $P(EF) = P(E \cap F) = P(E)P(F/E)$

  OR

  $P(EF) = P(E \cap F) = P(F)P(E/F)$

- Bayes' Theorem,

$$P(A) = \sum_{j=1}^{n} P(E_j)P(A/E_j) = P(E_1)\, P(A/E_1) + P(E_2)\, P(A/E_2) + \ldots$$
$$+ P(E_n)P(A/E_n)$$

- Let total numbers are n and 3 different numbers are selected. Then total ways of their selection $= {}^nC_3$

  $\therefore$ Total number of possible outcomes $= {}^nC_3$

  Pobability of an event, $P(E) = \dfrac{\text{Total No. of favourable outcomes}}{\text{Total No. of possible outcomes}}$

- The conditions for three events E, F and G to be independent,

$$P(E \cap F) = P(E)\, P(F),\ P(F \cap G) = P(F)\, P(G),$$
$$P(E \cap G) = P(E)\, P(G),\ P(E \cap F \cap G) = P(E)\, P(F)\, P(G),$$

Tips/Tricks/Techniques ONE-LINERS
(Exam Special)

- -

♦ **Extension of multiplication theorem for independent events**:

If $A_1, A_2...,A_n$ are independent events associated with a random experiment, then

$$P(A_1 \cap A_2 \cap A_3 \cap ... \cap A_n) = P(A_1)P(A_2)... P(A_n).$$

♦ **Probability of occurence of at least one of the *n* independent events:**

If $p_1, p_2, p_3, ...,$ pn be the probabilities of happening of n independent events $A_1, A_2, A_3, ..., A_n$ respectively, then

❖ Probability of happening none of them

$$= P(\bar{A}_1 \cap \bar{A}_2 \cap \bar{A}_3 .... \cap \bar{A}_n)$$

$$= P(\bar{A}_1).P(\bar{A}_2).P(\bar{A}_3)....P(\bar{A}_n)$$

$$= (1 - p_1)(1 - p_2)(1 - p_3)....(1 - p_n)$$

❖ Probability of happening at least one of them

$$= P(A_1 \cup A_2 \cup A_3 .... \cup An)$$

$$= 1 - P(\overline{A_1 \cup A_2 \cup ...... \cup A_n})$$

$$= 1 - P(\bar{A}_1)P(\bar{A}_2)P(\bar{A}_3)....P(\bar{A}_n)$$

$$= 1 - (1 - p_1)(1 - p_2)(1 - p_3)...(1 - p_n)$$

♦ **Probability regarding n letters and their envelopes:**

If n letters corresponding to n envelopes are placed in the envelopes at random, then

❖ Probability that all letters are in right envelopes $= \dfrac{1}{n!}$

❖ Probability that all letters are not in right envelopes
$$= 1 - \dfrac{1}{n!}$$

❖ Probability that no letters is in right envelopes
$$= \dfrac{1}{2!} - \dfrac{1}{3!} + \dfrac{1}{4!} - ....+ (-1)^n \dfrac{1}{n!}$$

❖ Probability that exactly r letters are in right envelopes

$$= \left[\frac{1}{2!} - \frac{1}{3!} + \frac{1}{4!} - \ldots + (-1)^{n-r}\frac{1}{(n-r)!}\right]$$

♦ **Expected frequency of successes in binomial distribution:**

Let X be the binomial variate and n, p be the parameters. Then the frequency of $X = r$ successes is given by $f(r) = N \times p(r) = N \times {}^{n}C_{r}p^{r}q^{n-r}$; $r = 0,\ 1,\ 2, \ldots, n$

Where N is the number the times the trial is repeated.

♦ Let X and Y be random variables on the sample space S and 'k' are real number. Then

    ❖ $E(kX) = kE(X)$

    ❖ $E(X+Y) = E(X) + E(Y)$

♦ Mean, variance and standard deviation of binomial distribution are np, npq, $\sqrt{npq}$ respectively.

♦ If np = integer, the binomial distribution will be unimodel and the mean = mode.

♦ If A & B are two independent events, then

    ❖ A & $\overline{B}$ are independent,

    ❖ $\overline{A}$ & B are independent

    ❖ $\overline{A}$ & $\overline{B}$ are independent.

♦ $P(A \cap B) \le P(A)P(B) \le P(A \cup B) \le P(A) + P(B)$.